The Arthurian Tradition

The Arthur

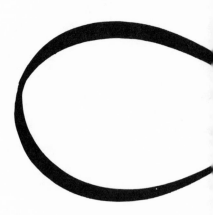

the university of alabam

ian Tradition

Essays in Convergence

Edited by

Mary Flowers Braswell

and

John Bugge

ress · tuscaloosa and london

Library of Congress Cataloging-in-Publication Data

The Arthurian tradition.

  Bibliography: p.
  Includes index.
  1. Arthurian romances—History and criticism.
I. Braswell, Mary Flowers, 1943–. II. Bugge,
John M., 1941–.
PN57.A6A78   1988   809′.93351   86-24945
ISBN 0-8173-0347-2

British Library Cataloguing-in-Publication Data is available.

To
David L. Boyd

Contents

CONTENTS

Illustrations

Acknowledgments

I am grateful to a number of people for making this book possible. My thanks to Malcolm MacDonald of The University of Alabama Press for his support of the project from its inception, and to Judith Knight for wisdom and guidance as the book emerged. A generous and timely collection development grant in the area of Arthurian Studies presented to The University of Alabama at Birmingham's Mervyn H. Sterne Library by the Network of Alabama Academic Libraries greatly facilitated work on this manuscript. And a stipened from the Graduate School of UAB made possible some important, last-minute additions to the galleys. I am indebted to my friend and colleague, Kieran Quinlan, for his assistance with the proofs; to Mildred Leake Day for invaluable advice, especially during the early stages of this project; and to my mother, Mary, and my husband, John, for sharing in both my periodic frustrations and my excitement along the way. And finally, to my friend and former graduate student, David Boyd, who, with intelligence and good humor, assisted in every phase of this production until the barge sailed at last to Avalon, I owe a very special debt of thanks.   MFB

The Arthurian Tradition

Introduction

The popularity of the Arthurian legend, now at least a millennium old and showing no signs of abating, has proved a mixed blessing to those who study it seriously. On the one hand, scholars benefit from a huge corpus of primary material, from better methodological tools and techniques available in a cumulative tradition of critical commentary, and certainly from an expanding catachumenate of increasingly avid pupils. Courses on King Arthur fill up with students eager to try an approach to Malory by way of Mary Stewart or to test Wace's *Roman de Brut* against an archaeological investigation of the Winchester Round Table. Outside classroom windows, contemporary "knights" joust in open fields or hurl papier-mâché rocks with half-scale model *ballistae*, while guest lecturers conversant with fifth-century naval warfare or Wagner's learned distortions of the Tristram legend suddenly are in ample supply. Novelists crowd the bestseller lists with works assessing Guinevere's incipient feminism or assigning neo-fascist motives to the treachery of Mordred—the Arthurian field being one of the few that can claim a steady increase in the supply of primary sources. All this suggests that Geoffrey Ashe is right when he argues that we are experiencing a "new matter of Britain" in all its splendid profusion.

Profusion has its problems, however. Perhaps overwhelmed by it, too many scholars seem to react by turning away, out-

1

ward toward their own academic preserves, to pursue one set of texts, one group of artifacts, or the achievements of a certain historical period, to the exclusion of other periods. Specialization may be the necessary evil it is often described as being, but in the field of Arthurian studies it is counterproductive to the obvious need for a broad and holistic interdisciplinary approach. Knowledge of ancient military strategy must be allowed to make sense of previously enigmatic statements in chronicle accounts; modern applications of medieval cartography should shed light on the geography of medieval romances; insight into medieval political theory must bring the portrait of Arthur into sharper focus. It is pointless even to speak of Arthurian studies if we are unwilling to cross and, if necessary, efface disciplinary boundaries. All such disparate scholarly areas must converge.

The problem of convergence was a central issue studied at the conference on Arthurian Studies—actually, the first of its kind—held in Birmingham, Alabama, in the fall of 1984, at which specialists in the medieval grail legend heard analyses of contemporary retellings and Tennysonians learned of previously unsuspected roots of Victorian medievalism. The mix of specialties—history, geography, art, archaeology, myth, and literature, to name the most prominent—caused more than a few fences of isolation to topple and gave rise to a resolve among some participants to keep them down. This book is partly a result of that resolve.

Generally speaking, previous collections of Arthurian essays have been concerned only with the Middle Ages,[1] concentrating on a single author or work,[2] a particular discipline (usually literature), or one geographical area.[3] This book aims to be broader in scope, to include both medieval and modern works of art, literature, and history, as well as authors and artists ranging from Geoffrey of Monmouth to William Dyce. Although the focus of the essays remains predominantly literary, most are interdisciplinary in method and bring history or aesthetics, theology or philosophy to bear on their conclusions. They are directed toward both the specialist and the informed generalist. We hope the variety of approaches to the tradition illustrated here will encourage the opening of similar new pathways of exploration by those who read these essays.

In his keynote essay for this volume, Geoffrey Ashe is far from jesting when he envisions the complete Arthurian scholar as something of a tour director who guides his followers across the downs and crags of the tradition in order to view the terrain from all possible perspectives. He stresses the need to "relate things to each other even when they appear very diverse," lest the tour turn out to be "chaos, a mere succession of dissimilar sights." A specialist himself in the historical background of the earliest Arthurian material, Ashe highlights the need for close archaeological and textual research while keeping an ear cocked to local myth for hints about where legend and history might converge. Posing several illustrative cases of such convergence, some of them highly significant in the world of Arthurian scholarship, he provides a kind of manifesto for the interdisciplinary spirit that informs the remaining essays in this volume.

Two studies follow, which approach Geoffrey of Monmouth's *Historia Regum Britanniae* from substantially different angles of attack. Maureen Fries finds a concept of medieval tragedy implicit in the Arthurian section of this twelfth-century chronicle, one that finds its way into subsequent retellings of the story, at least through Malory. In her view, Geoffrey's treatment of the rise and fall of a great man, and of his concept of kingship, are to be traced ultimately to Boethian philosophy and its view that unruled passion disturbs the rule of self and disqualifies one for the rule of others. Fries regards this ethical principle as the basis for almost all serious literary treatment of Arthur's fall throughout the Middle Ages.

Mary Thompson addresses the *Historia* through the descriptions of battles in Caesar's *Commentarius de bello Gallico*, which she regards as a possible indirect source for Arthur's war in Gaul. She finds striking similarities between the two works—geographical locations of skirmishes, size of armies, military tactics, and coincidence of names. Thompson also proposes that attitudes expressed in the *Historia,* notably un-complimentary sentiments directed at the Britons and laudatory statements about the Romans, might have been oc-casioned by Caesar's work. Although we can only guess whether Geoffrey knew Caesar's account firsthand, evidence here suggests that Arthur's continental campaign was not purely Geoffrey's invention.

Moving from a context of military history to one of twelfth-century political economy, Jean Blacker-Knight speculates on Wace's attitude toward the art of translation in his rendition of Geoffrey's work, the *Roman de Brut.* Suiting his poem to an Anglo-Norman courtly audience, Wace "depoliticized" the *Historia* by removing Geoffrey's plea for a strong, united rule in England; by disregarding the prophecies of Merlin, thus reducing Merlin from sage to magician; and by changing Arthur from a hero to a courtier, a king dispensing largesse. Blacker-Knight suggests that because Wace was eager to pla-cate Henry II, he molded Arthur in Henry's image and chose to omit administrative details from Geoffrey's version—those dealing with the disposition of ecclesiastical powers, for ex-ample—because of their political sensitivity at Henry's court. Placing the poem in the context of other contemporary rendi-tions of "historical" works, she deduces a theory of translation adjusted to the realities of twelfth-century court life.

In his discussion of "sexually ambiguous imagery" in *Erec et Enide,* Jan Nelson reveals a different side of the twelfth-century court—specifically, the mind-set of Chrétien de Troyes as he creates the two principal characters in his ro-mance. According to Nelson, four of the animal images in the poem—the sparrow hawk, the stag, the goat, and the leop-ard—are used in a complex manner to exemplify the emo-tional states of both Erec and Enide. The stag (male) and the sparrow hawk (female) become ambiguous when viewed more closely, and the goat (the hunted) and the leopard (the hunter) reverse roles as the romance progresses. Taken to-gether, these images form a whole, an ideal union of knight and lady. Nelson suggests that it is from this perspective, es-sentially that of Jungian psychology, that the characters are best understood: as representative of the male and female aspects—the *animus* and the *anima*—of an essentially androgynous individual. It is through this carefully chosen imagery that Chrétien educates his audience concerning this aspect of his romance.

For Stephen Atkinson, education of the reader is also a concern of Sir Thomas Malory's "The Tale of the 'Sankgreall'" in the *Morte Darthur*. He sees Malory's sixth book as a kind of problematic tutorial which, its lessons properly internalized, aids the reader in understanding the crucial last sections of the *Morte*. The reader's expectations are thwarted; the natural response to seemingly conventional symbols is overturned, while puzzles and incongruencies abound—all these test the reader's powers of interpretation, forcing him or her to develop higher heuristic skill both for the Grail material and for what follows.

Caroline Eckhardt's essay examines the uniquely double view of Arthur in fourteenth- and fifteenth-century English history. Because some people continued to expect his return to the British throne, Arthur was seen as a prophetic character, one whose reputation often was manipulated by monarchs for political gain. Arthur, however, is a nostalgic character as well, representing a lost utopian golden past. Thus, as Eckhardt sees it, the figure of Arthur simultaneously projects both forward and backward. In a careful analysis supported by texts not widely known, she notes that the matter actually is more complicated: each perspective embodies its own antithesis. Thus Arthur, "the once and future king," serves as a particularly complex symbol in political thought at the end of the English Middle Ages.

By the end of the sixteenth century, the name Arthur had become inextricably tied to political factionalism and the monarchist position. Perhaps it was this tie as much as the Enlightenment in succeeding centuries that caused the legend temporarily to lose its appeal. When—toward the end of the eighteenth century, as part of the beginning of the Romantic movement—all Europe embarked on a quest for national identity, for national heroes, for truths to embody each nation's past, the search inevitably led to a revival of interest in the medieval past. There was a new desire to know the period accurately, its architecture and painting, armor and weapons, dress and habits. Medievalism was embraced by authors, painters, and architects, all of whom, working almost as archaeologists examining and reconstructing man's past, created works they hoped would reflect absolute historical correctness. Simultaneously, a version of "chivalry" underwent a revival. It was spurred, in part, by the appearance of Arthurian tales in works edited by Thomas Percy and George Ellis and by two new editions of Malory published early in the nineteenth century.

In her essay on Victorian history painting, Debra Mancoff relates these trends to an important Arthurian fresco cycle created by the English painter William Dyce. Commissioned by Prince Albert for Queen Victoria's Robing Room in the New Palace of Westminster, the cycle consists of "seven frescoes illustrative of the cultural virtues drawn from the Arthurian legend." In this first major pictorial work of the Arthurian Revival, Dyce was faced with the task of using current notions of chivalry to restructure a shared literary past. Mancoff shows how Dyce accomplished this task by devoting each fresco to a single Arthurian hero who embodied some virtue characteristic of the Victorian gentleman. Thus, Galahad was made to represent Chastity and Simple Faith; King Arthur unhorsed and spared by Lancelot became Generosity. The work, left unfinished at Dyce's death, anticipates Tennyson's allegorical method in his *Idylls of the King*.

During the Victorian medieval revival, editors took their places beside writers and artists as creators and shapers of a renewed Arthurian tradition, particularly as the tradition was rendered by Malory. Although, in the fifteenth century, William Caxton had altered the arrangement of the *Morte Darthur* to make it more "coherent," it was not until about the 1860s that Malory's editors became expurgators seeking to "improve" the work. In her essay on the subject, Marylyn J. Parins has assembled samples from the major bowdlerized editions and examined the mind-set of the men who produced them, providing insight into the ways of nineteenth-century prudery. Concentrating on the episodes of Arthur's conception, Lancelot's tryst with Elaine, and Lancelot's night with Guinevere in Meleagaunt's castle, Parins shows how editors contorted Malory's events, sanitized his language, and deleted entire episodes—all in order to make the medieval work suitable for Victorian youth.

The most prominent shaper of the Arthurian story during the Victorian era was Tennyson, whose debt to Malory, the *Queste del Saint Graal*, and other medieval works is well known. Another influence on *Idylls of the King*, however, seems to have gone undetected until now: St. Augustine. In his essay, David L. Boyd argues that Augustine's writings, especially *The City of God* and the *Confessions*, contributed to the *Idylls* certain theological dimensions not found in Malory's work or in the *Queste*. For example, there are similarities between Augustine's description of the Celestial City and Tennyson's portrayals of Camelot in *The Coming of Arthur*, while the realms of the Earl of Doorm and the Red Knight are reminiscent of the City of Man. Certain features of Lancelot's character suggest that Tennyson based his struggling sinner on Augustine's self-portrait in his *Confessions*. Boyd finds further evidence that Augustine's theory of moral illumination informed Tennyson's imagery and that the self-centered will—the *animalis homo* of the *Confessions*—is instrumental in causing the fall of Camelot. The essay suggests that the presence of such a normative patristic doctrine in the *Idylls* adds an important theological dimension to Tennyson's work.

Whereas Boyd sees medieval Christian theology as reinforcing Tennyson's use of the Arthurian legend, providing a positive standard by which to judge Victorian society, John Bugge demonstrates that the twentieth-century characters who model themselves on the old heroic archetypes are denied access to reality and thus to their own true identity. Walker Percy's Arthurian saga is undercut by the modern-day "existential philosophy of cognition." To Percy, myth equals illusion, like the movies created by Bob Merlin—a "specious modern world of merely celluloid reality." Adherence to the concept of the old symbols prevents man from being aware of his own *individual* predicament, of his own *personal* search. Thus for *Lancelot* Lamar (ever guided by his namesake, "that old nonexistent Catholic brawler and adulterer, Lancelot du Lac"), the grail quest ends in nothingness and despair. For Harry Percival, however, who forsakes the world of cloistered contemplation in favor of the active life—for "a little church in Alabama"—and "impersonates" no one but himself, life can at last begin.

In the book's final essay, Charles Moorman considers a group of contemporary Arthurian novelists to determine why the legend remains so popular today, and why certain novelistic treatments among these succeed while others fail. He notes that "the central tragic universal concept" of the story makes it irresistible to modern writers. Recalling C. S. Lewis's pronouncement—the Arthurian story is like a cathedral to which succeeding centuries of builders have contributed their share—Moorman asserts that modern novelists must learn that one cannot merely smooth over the surface fabric of the edifice, thereby making the old story somewhat less "gothick"-seeming to contemporary tastes. Successful modern versions go much further. They thoroughly (sometimes violently) restructure the story, re-creating it according to modern expectations. Thus, Moorman argues, only the author who writes his or her own Arthuriad and endows it with contemporary relevance can be said to be a full participant in the ongoing tradition.

We feel that each essay makes a significant contribution to the particular academic discipline in which its author works, largely because of the material each writer brings to bear from outside that discipline. Beyond that, we believe this collection, when taken as a whole, says something about the direction in which Arthurian scholarship should be heading. The variety of interests illustrated here can only hint at the richness of the Arthurian "matter" that informs so many areas of our collective cultural experience; yet, with the exception of certain examples of critical commentary on *Sir*

Gawain and the Green Knight and the works of Chrétien de Troyes, too little Arthurian criticism shows a strong interdisciplinary thrust. For example, scant attention has been paid to the influence of pictorial art on nineteenth- and twentieth-century authors; the relationship between features of neo-gothic architecture and those of Arthurian poetry of the Victorian age needs investigating; minor, even unpopular writing needs to be examined for the social history it might yield; and late medieval Arthurian ballads and lyrics, in their contemporary musical settings, remain a much neglected subject. Certainly now is the time for a body of serious critical commentary to emerge on modern Arthurian literary works, one that would take into consideration such issues as the influence of the scientific and technological revolutions of the twentieth century on ancient myth. All this, however, will demand that Arthurian scholars who now expend their efforts at the periphery of this vast field of study turn their endeavors back toward a common center, allowing them to converge with those of others doing the same.

Mary Flowers Braswell
John Bugge

9

The Convergence of Arthurian Studies

GEOFFREY ASHE

In contrast to the other essays in this book, this offering, I can
assure the reader, will not be informative. What I want to do
is submit a few thoughts that have taken shape over the years.
"The Convergence of Arthurian Studies"—in what way am I
qualified to speak on such a theme? I am well aware that in
most of the specific fields are many who know far more than I
do. It has been my own case, almost by accident, to find myself in a special position—not as having an exceptional
knowledge of any one area of Arthurian studies (apart, perhaps, from that of historical origins, where there is little
knowledge to be had anyhow) but as being involved from several angles, as being acquainted with the subject from several
perspectives. My becoming in some degree an "all-rounder"
has given me the uncommon, maybe even unique, status of
"Arthurian consultant."

What this means in practice is that those planning novels
about the Arthurian Legend, or planning tours of places connected with it, tend to drift toward me, to ask my opinion or
advice. Consequently, I find a certain Ashe imprint on a
number of works of fiction that have been published over recent decades. The same sort of thing has happened with a
number of study tours.

The Arthurian tour is a welcome institution that has grown

up since the mid-1970s. Actually, the idea occurred to me a long time ago, partly because tourism was "in the family." My father once headed a travel agency, and in my youth I saw a good deal of the business. After becoming interested in the Arthurian legend, I went to my father's old travel agency and spoke to the man who had succeeded to his position. It was a Catch-22 situation. "Prove that there is a demand for an Arthurian tour," he said. "Set one up, and then perhaps we'll sponsor some more." So I dropped the idea. But eventually tours began to happen. The first, I believe, was conducted by the Smithsonian Institution in 1972. Then came a series sponsored by Temple University in Philadelphia. After those, university extension departments started taking an interest, notably the University of California at Berkeley. The Berkeley Arthurian tour is now an annual event. Recently, in a departure from the purely academic approach, another tour was arranged by the History Book Club. With all of these, I have had the pleasure of being associated for part of the tour at least, and once or twice for the whole of it.

Here, perhaps, I ought to make an admission. Anyone who has gone on such a tour knows that to a certain extent it is an exercise in bluff. I am reminded of a remark heard on a tour of another kind which I was once invited to guide. Organized by a California commune, it was called "A Tour of Mystical England." The party arrived, eighty-five of them, in Glastonbury where I live, and I took them up hills and around the abbey and so forth. A party of that size trails off and gets broken up. I was told later that at the tail end of the procession members had been heard saying angrily, "When are we going to see something mystical?" I'm sorry—I tried. Similarly, on an Arthurian tour, there are stretches where I wouldn't blame a participant for asking, "When are we going to see something Arthurian?"

True, there are well over a hundred places up and down Britain connected with the Arthurian legend. They include, incidentally, five places where Excalibur was thrown into the water and at least fifteen caves where King Arthur lies asleep. Among those places are a few truly spectacular sites, such as

11

Glastonbury and Tintagel. For the tour guide, however, much of the job consists of pointing out features of the landscape known in the local folklore as Arthur's Tump or Arthur's Bump or something like that and trying to spin yarns about them. I recall a cartoon in *Punch*. Here was an open field with a stone sticking up a foot or so from the ground, and some tourists and an old man pointing at the stone with his stick and saying, "No, there ain't no *official* guide to the old castle here, but I'll do my best." Nevertheless, although some Arthurian tourism is like that, some is considerably better. Many tour members do find something of authentic value to take away with them, an impression borne out by the many who have contacted me afterward to say so.

The experience of guiding will serve as an introduction to the theme I want to take up. If you are going to do it, you have to survey the Arthurian legend from a variety of angles, because you will be going to places that belong to widely different periods and widely different types of tradition. Furthermore, you must relate things to each other even when they appear extremely diverse, because, if you fail to do so, the tour will descend into chaos and become a mere succession of dissimilar sights.

To begin with, as a guide, you must consider what is most familiar to most people, the scenario of Arthurian romance as it developed in the Middle Ages. That involves going to Winchester, which Malory said was Camelot. In Winchester's castle hall is the famous Round Table, that massive disk hung on the wall and painted in segments which make it look like a gigantic dart board. We know roughly when it was made and, very probably, why. It is not the original Round Table, but it is related to the romances and the medieval vogue for them that inspired its making, and the tour guide's audience should understand this.

A knowledge of the themes of romance is not enough, however. One must, in addition, take into account the great tradition of Arthur in Wales, which is altogether another matter. One might, for example, be going to Carmarthen, the reputed birthplace of Merlin, or to Dinas Emrys, the ancient hill-fort in Snowdonia, where Merlin makes his first appearance in major literature—and if so, you will have to deal with a quite different body of legend.

Again, you must consider what might be called quasi-history. Unlike many heroes, Arthur has a sort of official biography, created in the twelfth century by Geoffrey of Monmouth in that extraordinary book, *The History of the Kings of Britain.* Geoffrey introduces places that surely will figure in your itinerary: Tintagel, for instance, which he presents as the scene of Arthur's begetting and presumably birth; and Caerleon in southeast Wales, a Roman city where Geoffrey portrays Arthur holding court with a splendor that makes this passage a forerunner of later romance accounts of Camelot.

You must consider places where history and myth overlap. Glastonbury is the supreme instance. It has a profound past as the site of what probably was the first British Christian community and of one of the greatest medieval abbeys. The city makes disputed claims that may or may not carry historical weight, such as the discovery of Arthur's grave in the twelfth century. Glastonbury has a strange ambience shading into myth—the Grail theme, the story of Joseph of Arimathea, mysteries even more exotic than those that have been speculated about in modern times.

You must consider real history, or what may be real history, as it relates directly to Arthur. There is the battle of Badon, for example, undoubtedly the authentic British success against invading Saxons with which his name is sometimes linked, and which has been located, conjecturally, at various places likely to be included on a tour. In the background is the broader question: What was going on in the British Isles and neighboring Europe in the fifth and sixth centuries, so far as we can piece it together? How much light may be thrown upon Arthurian stories by recorded realities?

You must consider topography and local lore, Arthur's Tumps and Bumps, some of them impressive sights with literary standing. In Scotland, for instance, Melrose Abbey has a cluster of hills beside it where, according to a Border tale immortalized by Sir Walter Scott, Arthur and his knights lie asleep.

You must consider the findings of archaeology. At Castle Dore, in Cornwall, is the reputed home of Mark, the king in the Tristan-Iseult story. Excavation here has supplied hints about the possible origins of the story (or some of it) in that part of the country. Cadbury Castle, in Somerset, the scene of the most famous Arthurian excavation, is thought to be the site of Camelot. Most tours include these places, as well as others where archaeology might shed light.

Then, again, there are issues raised by the modern literature, the new writing in this field. We have the novels of Mary Stewart, Marion Bradley, and others, plus new poetry and drama embodying the legend in new guises. It has been my experience that many Arthurian tourists, having read some of the new writing, wish to relate it to the visible landscape. If they have read Mary Stewart, for example, they want to see Merlin's cave or Merlin's hill. To a certain extent, their wishes can be met, and to that extent they should be.

Each of these fields, including that of modern literature, has its own experts; the tour guide must have some acquaintance with them all and must be able to synthesize. The need for synthesis takes us considerably beyond tourism. I urge the need for this kind of contact and overlap, this bringing together of special knowledge and specialized data, in a much wider sense. Experts in various fields should be encouraged to talk with each other rather than remain shut up in their specialties. This is the *convergence* I speak of, and I believe it to be important and valuable for mutual enlightenment and enrichment.

The reader should be aware that one of the major pioneering works of Arthurian scholarship adopted exactly the multiple approach I am suggesting: *Arthur of Britain*, by E. K. Chambers, which appeared in 1927 and has been reprinted.[1] Chambers, of course, is better known for his work on the Elizabethan theater; but he turned aside to do the book on Arthur. It might be easy to assume, without looking at the book, that it has been superseded by later scholarship; and in some ways, it has. Yet, re-reading the book recently, I was struck by Chambers's grasp of his subject and his penetration of it, by the number of things he already knew. Most of all, however, I was struck by the way in which Chambers related the things he knew to each other. He actually did try to make a survey of the entire subject under the various heads I spoke of, so far as could be done in the 1920s. He even reviewed the local folklore, the topography, such stories as the one about the ghosts of Arthur's knights riding over the Cadbury hill at mid-summer, all that precious trivia so liable to get lost in the shuffle. Chambers studied the historical background with care and thought the evidence for Arthur was slight, that one was bound to be skeptical; but he weighed the data as judiciously as he could with the knowledge then available. In one respect, his book still has not been superseded. As he did in his work on Shakespeare, he reproduces the early documentary matter, quoting all the relevant passages in an enormous appendix. I know of no other place, even today, where one can find the early materials (the Latin ones, at least) assembled verbatim as can be found in *Arthur of Britain.*

Nor has anything quite like it been produced since. I am not forgetting that great compilation edited by Roger Sherman Loomis, *Arthurian Literature in the Middle Ages,* in which thirty scholars say far more than Chambers could about individual aspects. I still find that, as a concise and concentrated, all-round appraisal, Chambers's one-man job stands by itself, even though we must read later authors to realize in what ways his ideas have been modified or replaced.

Today, as one can see by looking at the list of members of the International Arthurian Society or the papers read at its congresses, most Arthurian scholars are students and exponents of medieval literature. That is to say, they are concerned chiefly with that amazing literary growth, surging up from the twelfth century into the thirteenth and rising to another peak during the fifteenth in Malory, which created the Arthurian legend in its familiar form—the King and Queen, Sir Lancelot, the Round Table, the Grail, Camelot, and all the

15

rest. Medieval scholarship has made priceless contributions to the appreciation and understanding of that great body of romance literature. In recent years, however, as I have remarked, we have seen a growth of *modern* literature—the novels, plays, and poems Arthurian tourists are apt to know. Until recently, these modern works were not accepted as part of the canon; they were regarded as the province of newspaper reviewers, literary critics, and connoisseurs of contemporary fiction. Scholars generally did not see them as validly adding to the picture or as truly a part of the mythos, enlarging and enriching it. They saw them as subsisting in another, unimportant compartment and as not warranting serious discussion.

Today, however, the situation is undergoing a welcome change. Some of the credit is due to such students of the tradition as Professor Valerie Lagorio, who conducts seminars in modern Arthurian literature without in any way abandoning her distinguished position as a medievalist. Increasingly, we can observe an altered attitude, not just in teaching but in publications and, indeed, in some of the papers read at the conference from which the present book evolved. The new writing is being taken seriously. It is an encouraging conversion, this increase of awareness that the Matter of Britain was not closed and sealed off with Malory or Tennyson, that the thing can still happen again. Every manifestation is coming to be recognized as part of a single cycle. It is not a question of the authentic Arthurian Legend on one side and a jumble of irrelevant modern stuff on the other; more and more, it is realized that they belong together, that the two areas of interest converge and blend.

Let me turn, if somewhat abruptly, to a much more specific case, an instance of the academic approach demonstrably failing by not taking cognizance of another sort of perspective, when it could have gained by acknowledging it. Most readers are familiar with *Perlesvaus*, a Grail romance written early in the thirteenth century. It may be recalled that the author of the romance claims he got his material from a Latin document on the Isle of Avalon, by which he means Glastonbury, at a religious house where they are said to have had the entire story. Scholars disagree whether Glastonbury Abbey made a true contribution to Grail romance, but this author's claim to have been there and to have made a first-hand investigation usually has been rejected. Professor Loomis did not like *Perlesvaus* and thus dismissed the claim. His method of refuting it was to call the author a liar and insinuate that he was insane (a tactic that seems to fall below the proper standards of scholarship!). Loomis, however, briefly advances a solitary argument—that in the course of the story, Lancelot visits a religious community at Glastonbury—or Avalon, as the author calls it—but that the description of Lancelot's approach to the place (the location of the buildings and so forth) does not fit Glastonbury Abbey. Therefore, Loomis contends, the author never went there, and his statement about a Glastonbury source is worthless.

Well, it's quite true: the description does not fit the abbey. The trouble is, neither Loomis nor his informants ever bothered to go to Glastonbury and take a proper look. If one does go there, one discovers that, in approaching by the old road Lancelot would have used, and turning up toward the hills, the landscape unfolds exactly as *Perlesvaus* describes. Its author was using a tradition that speaks of early Christian settlement on the higher ground; that is where he imagines the community to have been in Arthur's time. In the light of archaeology, he may be right. In any case, the anonymous author's description is accurate; therefore, his assertion of having done first-hand study at Glastonbury is credible. To find the place, though, Professor Loomis would have had to walk from the abbey site for perhaps twenty minutes, turn down a side road, and come back up. My impression is that he never did so.

Here, we can see how plodding, on-the-spot exploration of local topography can provide fresh insight into a work. Indeed, the insight leads further afield, because it suggests as well what Malory's intention may have been at the close of his own narrative, where Lancelot and other survivors retire as hermits to a little valley between two hills near Glastonbury. I am fairly certain Malory had some notion of the same area in the neighborhood of a spring that *Perlesvaus* mentions. No amount of documentary analysis would ever have shown this, however; one must go and look.

May I venture a slight digression pursuant to the same point about direct knowledge on the spot? Another great Arthurian site is, of course, Tintagel, that towering Cornish headland with the ruins of a castle on it, jutting into the Atlantic. One approaches it through Tintagel village, unfortunately the one place where the Arthurian legend has created a tourist trap. (Here, direct knowledge may at least serve as a warning to the prospective visitor.) You will see such things as King Arthur's Car Park and Merlin's Gift Shoppe and Tristan's Crafts, or an edifice called "the Arthurian Hall of Chivalry," a building full of phony stained glass and phony armour and much else that is equally phony. It was built by a man who made a great deal of money from the manufacture and sale of custard; then, because he was interested in things having to do with King Arthur, he built the Hall of Chivalry and sold knighthoods of the Round Table. The Custard King is no longer there; the Hall of Chivalry, alas, is.

To come to the point: you leave the village behind and go down a ravine to a cove between two headlands. The headland on the left is the one with the castle ruins. It also has remains of a much earlier settlement that appears to date from the Arthur period. A tradition of this settlement very probably underlies Geoffrey of Monmouth's tale of the Duke of Cornwall's stronghold and of Uther and Ygerne and the begetting of Arthur. In the cove below, Tennyson located his alternative version of Arthur's advent, with the baby being washed ashore and picked up by Merlin. Beside the cove is Merlin's cave—not Mary Stewart's, but another Merlin's Cave—said to be haunted by his ghost. It is a natural tunnel going right through the base of the castle promontory. The far end is lower than the near end, so that when the tide comes in, the sea surges up through the cave in a spectacular fashion. One can get into the cave to watch the phenomenon, however, only when the tide is still fairly well down and has a long way to go. Later, the cave fills with water and becomes inaccessible. I remember that some years ago an entire International Arthurian Congress arrived when the tide was high, so the group failed to reach Merlin's cave. A little bit of local knowledge, and the appropriate timing—a little bit of convergence, if you like—would have made so much difference to that excursion and to the image of Tintagel the members of the international congress carried home with them.

Let me draw your attention to a more serious matter, a major intersection of disciplines: examination of the Round Table in the castle hall at Winchester. The table (or, rather, the tabletop, inasmuch as the legs have vanished) is a disk of wood eighteen feet across and painted in segments with the names of twenty-four knights and a picture of the king. The painting was done during the reign of Henry VIII, and the king is Henry himself at about the age of thirty. Since then, while the paint work has been touched up, the design has not been altered. What about the table itself though? How old is it? Even by the mid-fifteenth century, it was old enough for its provenance to be forgotten, and people solemnly asserted that it was Arthur's original. The chronicler John Hardyng said it was, and so did Caxton. It certainly is not. A few years ago it was examined by archaeologists and by experts on medieval carpentry, dendrochronology, and carbon dating. After long debate, their findings, it was agreed, pointed approximately to the date 1300. It might be a few decades either way, but is unlikely to lie outside the late thirteenth century or the early fourteenth.

This conclusion, though interesting in itself, opens a further vista, because it suggests that this piece of furniture was made for a known type of aristocratic entertainment inspired by Arthurian Romance. Loomis lists several medieval "Round Tables," as they were called, where kings and nobles, not only in England but also on the continent, would dress up as Arthurian characters and joust and feast in appropriate style. In 1299, Edward I held such an entertainment to celebrate his second marriage, and the Winchester table may have been made for that occasion. Henry III is another royal candidate, though for at least part of his reign he seems to have viewed Round Tables with some disfavor. At any rate, by taking into account not only what medieval writers say about the Winchester object but what modern scientists have added— by putting everything together—we can better appreciate the strength of the Arthurian vogue among the nobility and thereby become better informed as to when the vogue might have been at its height.

Then again, there is a matter I myself have been concerned with, the relationship of Geoffrey of Monmouth's pseudo-history to real history and the enlightenment that can follow from laying them side by side and studying both attentively. Most scholars who have discussed Geoffrey have treated him essentially as a literary figure. They may try to establish his sources, but they seldom probe for the underlying facts. Certainly he is no historian; he cannot be trusted for facts in any direct way. Yet we can distinguish him from contrivers of pure romance, because he unquestionably *uses* facts. We can see him, for instance, drawing on Roman history, bringing in Julius Caesar, Claudius, Constantine, and other real emperors and portraying them as doing things with a vague resemblance to what they actually did. Geoffrey is not simply inventing, and that is one of the features of his work that makes him such a strange and challenging writer.

It has been my good fortune to discover that when Geoffrey tells his story of Arthur, his imagination is working much of the time on real events hitherto barely noticed. By following leads, I think I have been able to show in part where the Arthurian legend came from and what its roots are. That, however, is a large topic, and I must refer the reader to what I have published in other contexts.[2] My point is simply that I have looked at Geoffrey the pseudo-historian in conjunction with the records of the time when his Arthur flourished. In that way, it eventually became possible to see what Geoffrey was talking about, however wild his exaggerations and fantasies may be, and to elucidate at least in part who the original Arthur-figure was and on what historical character the king is based.

Now I would like to turn to a highly public convergence of disciplines, one that deserves to be recalled, a major coming together of diverse interests and varieties of expertise. The convergence began in the 1960s, arising from the excavation project at Cadbury-Camelot, Cadbury Castle in Somerset, still regarded as a must for Arthurian tourists. Of course, Cadbury never had a castle in the medieval architectural sense. The word is employed, as often as not in this part of England, to mean a hill-fort; the hill itself is the castle. Iron-age Britons settled on high ground and surrounded the settlement with earthwork defenses by putting up stockades. The result was a fortified hill, and to this day, the banks and ditches of the fortification systems remain well defined.

In the case of Cadbury, John Leland, who published an account of his travels through England in 1542, calls the hill "Camelot" and mentions Arthur. Moreover, local Arthurian folklore is abundant. Granted, we must be cautious even in discussing the identification. The Camelot of romance is a medieval dream-city; it would be futile to search for it anywhere. It could well be, however, that a fifth-century Arthur had a personal citadel of some sort, and this one might be counted as the real Camelot so far as anything ever was, the reality at the headwaters of the legend. It could be that the idea of Arthur having a capital of his own trickled down through the centuries until it began to flow into a tradition enlarged by the romancers.

Cadbury Castle is a hill surrounded by earthwork ramparts that enclose eighteen acres of grass rising to a summit plateau. Before excavation, the hill's owner plowed up part of the enclosure for crops. A local amateur archaeologist named Harfield used to stroll over the hill, walking her dog. Mrs. Harfield poked about in the upturned soil with the ferrule of her umbrella (a highly elementary form of archaeological tool) and collected fragments of pottery. Having taken these home and washed them, she showed them to Dr. Ralegh Radford, who had done the pioneer work at Tintagel. Radford recognized some of the pieces as pottery of a significant kind, used for such luxury goods as wine, imported from the Mediterranean area, and datable roughly to the time when Arthur is supposed to have flourished. The find showed the existence of a wealthy household in approximately the right period.

In 1965, the Camelot Research Committee was formed, with Radford as chairman. The archaeologist Sir Mortimer Wheeler was president; Leslie Alcock, now Professor Alcock, was director of excavations; and I was secretary. The committee brought together different forms of scholarship and different interests—the Arthurian-literary, the Arthurian-historical, the dark-age archaeological; Roman historians, British prehistorians, amateurs interested in the Arthurian legend. This convergence was quite genuine. Funds were raised from each area of interest as well as from the public. The site was excavated during each summer from 1966 to 1970, with an influx of volunteers from all over the world and with wide media coverage. One evening, my telephone rang and a voice said: "This is Warner Brothers. Where was Camelot?" I asked why they wanted to know. The voice at the other end explained that Warner Brothers was filming a musical and wanted to include a map showing Camelot. I said Camelot was in Somerset. In the movie, there actually is an almost subliminal moment when a weird-looking map of England is displayed . . . and Camelot is in Somerset. It is my one contribution to Hollywood.

At any rate, the results were remarkable. They are set forth in Leslie Alcock's book *Cadbury-Camelot*, though he has somewhat revised his interpretations since. Removal of the accumulated soil from the top rampart revealed a vast defensive system of stone and timber that had been superimposed on the older earthworks dating from approximately Arthur's time. This development has not been paralleled at any other hill-fort in Britain, though numerous other sites have since been excavated. Excavation indicates that the hill was the residence of a king with great resources of manpower and that it was occupied at more or less the right date. Professor Alcock now says he is agnostic about Arthur personally and prefers to discuss the site solely in archaeological terms. If, however, we discuss the historical question, the British king whom I, for my part, would propose as the original Arthur-figure is the only documented candidate for Cadbury's royal refortifier.[3]

History and archaeology each have their place in *The Quest for Arthur's Britain*, a book that emerged from the Cadbury project. Though now out-of-date in several respects, the book has not yet been superseded. As its editor and co-author, I tried to organize a multiple approach to the subject, which at the time was a gesture of defiance. Devotees of medieval literature tended not only to ignore everything else but to be slighting. To some extent, this still happens. Such critics, in effect, say: "We have the legend, which is immortal. Why dig around outside and behind it? In particular, why even attempt a historical approach? Why go grubbing about looking for some dark-age Arthur who is irrelevant or who even weakens the story by making it smaller and meaner and less interesting?"

The classic expression of this point of view is T. H. White's *The Once and Future King*, in which White insisted that Arthur was not a "distressed Briton hopping about in a suit of woad in the fifth century." I always thought White's attitude mistaken. In the first place, surely there is intrinsic value in looking for truth. Second, setting up two distinct Arthurs, a magnificent monarch of romance and an unrelated and uninspiring "historical" chieftain, is not even under consideration. I recall making the vital point when *The Quest for Arthur's Britain* was under discussion. The publishers wanted to call it *The Quest for Arthur*. I said it wasn't that. We were concerned then—and in rebutting the criticism I am mainly concerned now—with Arthur's *Britain*, the Britain with which his story must be associated, even if he himself remains elusive. All too little is known about the Britain of the fifth century. Yet, if we bring such facts as research discloses into contact with the legend, these facts illuminate it. To some extent, we can discern its roots and better understand why it took the shape it did.

As I have tried to suggest, that is true in detail as well as in general. We can at least make out an explanation for Geoffrey's picking out Tintagel for Arthur's origin. Tintagel was an inhabited place, and quite likely an important one, at about the right time. We can at least see an explanation for Arthur's Glastonbury grave being plausible, even if faked. Glastonbury apparently was the home of the first British Christian community, reputedly and perhaps truly ancient enough, with a sacred and spellbinding aura appropriate to a man involved with myth. We can see an explanation for the legend's crediting Arthur with a unique capital of his own: Camelot. So far as we know, Cadbury's romantic identification reflects a unique character among strongholds in post-Roman Britain.

Still more significant is the light shed by history on the legend's background and the image of Arthur as its central figure. Britain's fifth-century career actually was exceptional and special. Here was a land that had been Roman for more than three hundred years, part of a great worldwide civilization. Unlike any other province of the Western Empire, however, it became self-governing before the arrival of the Barbarians (in this case, the Saxons). Unlike other provinces, Britain fought back, with temporary success. That unparalleled patriotic rally was the original setting for Arthur's story. It explains why Britain alone created such a legend out of the final agony of the Roman West; it explains why an Arthur conceived as the rally's leader became a hero for the Britons' descendants, with the mythology of a heroic age clustered around him.

If we look at the way Geoffrey pictures this hero, and the terms he uses to glorify him, we can see how plainly, despite all the fantasy and updating, the legend bears the stamp of the late Roman milieu. Arthur is a British version of a figure who haunted the dreams of that dissolving society—the *Restitutor Orbis*, the World-Restorer, the ruler who would master the forces of chaos, expel or subjugate the encroaching barbarians, and establish peace and prosperity. Almost to the end of the Western Empire, we find its spokesmen voicing that hope and saluting successive emperors, however unpromising, as destined to fulfil it. The legend of the messianic King Arthur makes it come to life in one portion of the empire, which, though drifting off, was still imperial in its inheritance. Arthur is a *Restitutor* for Britain.

Geoffrey, indeed, carries the theme further. He makes Arthur an emperor himself, claiming to be an heir of the great Constantine and planning to reunite the empire around a new center. Even in Malory, where the original nature of Arthur's Britain is almost effaced, the king's early acts show him in much the same light, overthrowing would-be usurpers and bringing order out of anarchy. If we place Malory in millennial perspective, as the teller of a story springing from that tottering, yet still hopeful, world, we can see why, even in medieval guise, Arthur is recognizably a *Restitutor* such as Britain yearned for. I have shown elsewhere that if we assess in Late Roman terms what the "restoration" meant specifically, this interpretation of him can be sustained in some detail.[4]

To revert to what may be called the literary objection, which I challenged in *The Quest for Arthur's Britain*, it seems to me that events have supported me more directly. Historical and other approaches, in combination, have refuted the critics on their own literary ground. The research I speak of has not reduced the mythos; it has enriched and enlarged it. Without in the slightest disturbing the traditional Matter of Britain, this research has been the main inspiration for the phenomenon I mention above—the growth of a new "matter" which extends the tradition. Far from losing sight of the received legend, modern creative writers have looked behind it and tried to imagine how Britain might actually have been in Arthur's time, re-evoking the tradition or, so to speak, re-mythifying it in new, more historically authentic forms.

I mentioned Mary Stewart and Marion Bradley. I could add Rosemary Sutcliff, Douglas Carmichael, and other novelists. And not only novelists. The dramatist John Arden offers his astonishing play *The Island of the Mighty*. The poet John Heath-Stubbs has given us his prize-winning heroic poem *Artorius*, perhaps the only work composed in English in recent years that can fairly be called an epic. A new Matter of Britain, yes; and the primary impulse has come from people who, though they never lost touch with the legend, have explored more than literary contexts, enlisted a variety of disciplines, and sought ancient origins and modern implications.

I have asked, before now, why the Arthurian legend possesses such perennial fascination, such power to revive itself again and again. I explored the problem in a book called *Camelot and the Vision of Albion*, appraising the theme alongside others—literary, religious, even political. My impression was that certain patterns of belief and imagination kept recurring, among them the ancient, undying dream of a golden age tragically lost, and that this was the common factor in all Arthur's major manifestations. Consider the following. At one stage, his Britain embodies a splendid resurrection of civilization out of internal strife and Barbarian ravagings. At another stage—that is, with the early Welsh—it is a country of warriors and saints and bards and heroic adventures, the Island of the Mighty, centered on Arthur as its war leader, chief of its mighty men. In medieval Europe it becomes a sort of chivalric Utopia; Tennyson gives Britain an allegorical quality expressing the ideals of his time, while modern poets and novelists tend to portray it as a battleground where noble purposes, even if thwarted, at least raise the struggle above mere misery and endow it with an aspect of grandeur.

In every version, of course, the glory is doomed. Beyond the sorrow of Camelot departed, though, the prophecy of Arthur's return implies that the golden age is still somehow "there" and that it is recoverable. The Arthurian legend affords glimpses of a deep yearning in the human psyche, which has taken many other forms besides this, inspiring prophets, reformers, and revolutionaries. That theme is far too large to explore here; I must refer anybody who may be interested to *Camelot and the Vision of Albion*. Only one thing more need be said now about the vitality and recurrent rebirth of the Arthurian legend, its repeated evocation of glory in new shapes. Even here, we can detect the power of convergence.

The legend began in a matrix formed by the Roman Empire. It started because, in Britain alone, a provincial people achieved self-government and resurgence. This was at once a Roman phenomenon and a British one, a unique resultant of two forces. Among the Welsh, the tradition of Arthur as historical war leader migrated into realms of Celtic mythology, and the outcome of that blending was Wales' strange, wild Arthurian saga, set in the Island of the Mighty. The medieval cycle grew from the annexation of Arthur with his Celtic context by continental romancers of chivalry, love, and enchantment. As I remarked, the modern flowering is due mainly to reappraisal of the old story in light of new knowledge and could never have happened as it has without the work of historians, archaeologists, and others who, often without intending it, have provided creative writers with fresh insight.

Whatever we ultimately are dealing with here, it is a presence too vast and potent for any single mode of approach, or for any narrow expertise. Let me close by returning to the central figure around whom all of this turns, with words better than my own—those of a short poem by G. K. Chesterton. Though fascinated by Britain's history and legends, Chesterton never had much to say about Arthur. He wrote one poem, however, addressed to a certain scholar (whose identity I can only guess at), a specialist who had spoken of "the myth of Arthur" as something false and merely fictitious. Chesterton chides this scholar for failing to take into account larger common-sense human considerations which here give the word *myth*, if it is used at all, a richer and more exalted meaning. In "The Myth of Arthur" these lead to a characteristically barbed final twist:

O learned man who never learned to learn,
Save to deduce, by timid steps and small,
From towering smoke that fire can never burn
And from tall tales that men were never tall.
Say, have you thought what manner of man it is
Of whom men say "He could strike giants down"?
Or what strong memories over time's abyss
Bore up the pomp of Camelot and the crown.

27

And why one banner all the background fills,
Beyond the pageants of so many spears,
And by what witchery in the western hills
A throne stands empty for a thousand years.
Who hold, unheeding this immense impact,
Immortal story for a mortal sin;
Lest human fable touch historic fact,
Chase myths like moths, and fight them with a pin.
Take comfort; rest—there needs not this ado.
You shall not be a myth, I promise you.

Boethian Themes and Tragic Structure in Geoffrey of Monmouth's *Historia Regum Britanniae*

MAUREEN FRIES

While fictions associated with the Matter of Britain usually are divided into the categories "romance" and "chronicle," the term *tragedy* also has been used in referring to individual works.[1] For instance, Tatlock argues that the *Historia Regum Britanniae* (of which the story of Arthur forms the spiritual center) "recalls the structure of good tragedy," Matthews that the *Alliterative Morte Arthure* is a "tragedy of fortune," Peck that it is one of willful behavior, Wertime that the *Stanzaic Morte Arthur* is a "tragedy of consequence," and Lumiansky, Moorman, Vinaver, and others that Malory's *Morte Darthur* is "determined from first to last by the tragic clash of human loyalties."[2] What has gone unnoticed is that a paradigm for all Arthurian tragic *mythos* exists from the beginning of full-fledged Arthurian narrative, not in the shards of earlier Celtic and Latin sources but in Geoffrey of Monmouth's account of Arthur in his *Historia Regum Britanniae*. I shall argue here that this account is founded on themes first developed by Boethius in *The Consolation of Philosophy*, from which are derived structural elements persistent in subsequent Arthurian tradition.[3]

A problem for any structural examination of medieval tragedy, Arthurian or otherwise, is the vagueness about the genre that besets critical theory. Medieval definitions per se, from

Diomedes onward, normally emphasize only the high rank of the protagonist, the high style of the narrative, and the inevitable plot movement from joy to woe.[4] An implicit model for Geoffrey's narrative of the rise and fall of a great king, however, exists in Boethius' *Consolation*, the most influential philosophical treatise of the Middle Ages and, next to the Bible, its most frequently copied book.[5] From Boethius, Western thought got its first extended literary (as opposed to artistic) image of the Wheel of Fortune and of the concept of mankind's turning upon it.[6] To Boethius, too, we owe the addition of worldly glory to the list of external goods under Fortune's power.[7] Both the wheel structure—particularly in what Howard R. Patch has called the "formula of four"[8]—and the idea of earthly fame as one of Fortune's gifts figure as integral parts of Geoffrey's narrative.

As an educated man and an excellent Latinist, Geoffrey may have known Boethius' *Consolation*. Its direct influence certainly is evident in his immediate predecessors, his contemporaries, and his successors. Directly before he wrote, Honorius of Autun revived the traditional figure of Fortune's wheel apparently for the first time since Boethius wrote.[9] William of Conches (d. 1159), whose work in its impact has been compared to the *Sentences* of Peter Lombard, drew his moral extracts in part from Boethius, particularly as regards circumstance and Fortune. Geoffrey's successor as an Arthurian enthusiast, Giraldus Cambrensis, in turn, drew on William's work.[10] Obviously, the climate for Geoffrey's use of Boethian themes was fertile.

Boethius is not, of course, the only possible influence on Geoffrey's thought. Eusebius (b. 263) inaugurated the conflation of Christian and Roman history that was to figure prominently not only in the works of Geoffrey but also in those of his predecessors Gildas, Bede, and Nennius. Eusebius conceived both of the corporate salvation of an entire people and of the social or political hero connected with providence and national history.[11] His midwifing of Christian historiography was succeeded by Augustine's "biblical *theology* of history," with its lack of "concessions to the exigencies or attractiveness of mere political and social ideals, however Christian their expression," and Augustine's disciple Orosius's Roman-oriented history of salvation, with its synthesis of national and biblical history.[12] But such cyclical theorists differ from both Boethius and Geoffrey in their emphasis on *salvation* history. Moreover, Augustine rejects that Fortune which plays so prominent a part in the *Historia* and which Boethius was to define definitively.[13] As Robert W. Hanning has demonstrated, Geoffrey of Monmouth differs from his predecessor-historians of Britain mainly because his vision of the past is to a large extent "free of Christian assumptions"—a crucial difference from other exemplars that Geoffrey shares (perhaps only) with Boethius among his possible predecessors, as also his conception of Fortune.[14]

Whereas Hanning, in the subtitle of his chapter on Geoffrey ("Great Men on a Great Wheel"), seems implicitly to recognize this Boethian dependency, nowhere in *The Vision of History in Early Britain* does he mention the name Boethius or his work.[15] Yet the *Vision* clearly is informed by the spirit and the letter of Boethius, who supplies Geoffrey with literal as well as metaphorical ideas on kingship and tragedy, in both a personal and a national context. Long before Geoffrey wrote, King Alfred had seen and used Boethian formulations, especially about kingship.[16] Whether Geoffrey knew Alfred's work, he was able to translate both Boethian letter and analogue into concepts containing broad British historical significance. Boethius' climactic and (originally) unique addition of mundane fame to Fortune's "goods," as well as the elaboration of Fortune's wheel, influences a nexus of ideas on self-rule and the rule of others in Geoffrey's *Historia*.

From the beginning of the *Consolation*, Lady Philosophy argues that good persons have governance over themselves which evil ones lack: "'numerous exercitus, spernendus tamen est, quoniam nulle duce regitur, sed errore tantum temere ac passim lymphante raptatur.'"[17] Such self-possession is like citizenship in ancient Rome: one who chose it as his dwelling place could not be banished except by his own choice—"'An ignoras illam tuae ciuitatis antiquissimam legem, qua sanctum est ei ius exulare non esse quisque in ea sedem fundare maluerit?'" (I, *pr.* V). Self-possession is also the reflection in man of God as king and ruler of the universe, an idea expressed again and again in the *Consolation* (as, for instance, in Boethius' much imitated hymn to the Great Chain of Being [I, *met.* V]). Philosophy reminds her pupil often of this godlikeness, for instance, "'uos . . . deo mente consimiles'" (II, *pr.* V).

Such godlike self-rule produces stability and happiness, contentment with one's lot as though it were one's native country—or, as Philosophy puts it to Boethius, "'Hic ipse locus quem tu exilium uocas, incolentibus patria est'" (II, *pr.* IV). Faulty self-rule exiles one from one's true home: Philosophy sees this at once in Boethius' initial self-pity. When she first sees him weeping, she knows him to be in misery and exile (I, *pr.* V). But felicity is not to be sought abroad but within oneself: "'Quid igitur o mortales extra petitis intra uos positam felicitatem?'" (II, *pr.* IV). The only fame that counts is the glory achieved in one's own country: "'intra unius gentis terminos praeclara illa famae immortalitas coartabitur'" (II, *pr.* V).

Self-governance and stability, not fortune, thus are the true determinants of man's fate. The definition of tragedy as *casus* which "that monster" gives is actually an effect, and not a cause, of human unhappiness. This appears in her own contradictory speech—which, significantly, is so divorced from reality as to be impersonated by Philosophy and retailed to Boethius second-hand. For herself, Fortune claims the power to turn happy lives into tragic ones: "'Quid tragoediarum clamor alius deflet nisi indiscreto ictu fortunam felicia regno uertentem?'" (II, *pr.* II). This topsy-turviness she emblemizes in her wheel: "'rotam uolubili orbe uersamus, infima summis summa infimis mutare guademus'" (II, *pr.* II.) In the same speech, her only utterance in the *Consolation*, she reiterates Lady Philosophy's ideas about the necessity of self-governance in the image of God—"'Tamen ne . . . intra commune omnibus regnum locatus proprio uiuere iure desideres'"— and taunts man about his lack of ownership of the riches and dignities he so desires, adding that she will concede him anything proper to mortal men: "'si cuiusquam mortalium proprium quid horum esse monstraueris, ego iam tua fuisse quae repetis, sponte concedam'" (II, *pr.* II). Indeed, only ignorance of their own nature causes men to imagine that they can ascend her wheel without descending: "'Ascende si placet, sed ea lege ne utique cum ludicri mei ratio poascet, descendere iniuriam putes'" (II, *pr.* II).

Fortune's examples of such descents are Croesus and Perses, both kings; but her references to kingship as a social institution are, in the Boethian framework, far fewer than those to the proper kingship of oneself and the kingship of God. Boethius the Prisoner (as opposed to Boethius the Author) offers himself as an example of a good but not kingly ruler: he elected to carry out in public what he learned from Philosophy in private (I, *pr.* IV), which also allowed him to work for the common good although he constantly was foiled by evil men (I, *pr.* IV). The vices of petty rulers he cites are echoed in Philosophy's diatribe against the vanity of earthly dignities (III, *pr.* and *met.* IV). For the fullest treatment of actual human kingship, however, we must turn to Philosophy's speech to the prisoner that immediately follows this passage, concerning "'regna regumque familiaritas'" (III, *pr.* V).

Philosophy's argument—crucial for Geoffrey's *Historia*—is that the very nature of kingship is bound to be unhappy because of its natural limits: "'Qua uero parte beatos faciens desinit potestas, hac inpotentia subintrat quae miseros facit; hoc igitur modo maiorem regibus inesse necesse est miseriae portionem'" (III, *pr.* V). Nor can the king's power keep him from care and fear (III, *pr.* V). A similar failure of control over their fates infects kings' followers: "'Quos quidem regia potestas saepe incolumis saepe autem lapsa prosternit'" (III, *pr.* V). In the accompanying *metrum*, Philosophy stresses the necessity of the inner kingship, control over oneself, for the mighty ruler: "'Qui se uolet esse potentem / Animos domet ille feroces'" (IV, *met.* II). This is a theme to which she later returns when contrasting the outer pomp of wicked kings with the wretchedness of their lack of inner (or self-) kingship.

33

In his *Historia*, Geoffrey takes up and explores the Boethian idea that proper inner rule must inform political kingship and that tragedy results from the absence of such personal/societal integrity. The kingly imperative to guide weaker, less exalted beings corresponds to the control a person must exercise over himself and—on a different level—to the control God exercises over the universe. Throughout the work, Geoffrey reiterates themes that are to reach a crescendo in its Arthurian section; in particular, he explores a pattern in which a temporary British victory because of God's aid is marred by royal sinfulness, which in turn results in national tragedy, usually through renewed pagan attacks.[18] Geoffrey sees British history as essentially circular, like Fortune's Wheel, its natural contours determined by the rise and fall of its kings and the initiatives to their disasters determined by the actions of their queens (or quasi-queens) in the most striking cases.[19] This circular pattern of rise and fall (as in the actual life of Boethius) triggered by (non-Boethian) feminine influence reaches a spectacular climax in the career of Arthur—which may be schematized as a Boethian-Fortunite wheel.

Arthur's begetting by Uther Pendragon upon a vassal's wife is an indicator of a subsequent trend toward political disorder in which personal excesses are replicated politically by a ruler, to the detriment of his kingdom. At this juncture of the *Historia,* such an action offers a familiar paradigm. Among Geoffrey's earlier examples are the illicit passion of Locrine, Brutus' son, for his mistress, and Vortigern's lust-inspired and fatally mistaken marriage to Hengist's daughter Rowena: both are failures in self-rule followed by failures in governance over others. Most pertinent to Arthur's reign, the results of Uther's passion for Ygerna—his warring against her husband, his conceiving of Arthur upon her before her husband is killed, his wasting away from a mysterious illness, and his winning of a significantly indecisive victory over the Saxons before they poison him—show him and his country on the downward swing of the wheel he had mounted as king.

Uther's son Arthur, however, at first seems destined to avoid the vicious circle of British kingship. Geoffrey initially emphasizes both Arthur's youth and the remarkable self-possession that accompanies it, along with the love it inspires in his people: "Erat autem Arturus XV annorum juvenis, inauditae virtutis atque largitatis. In quo tantam gratiam innata bonitas praestiterat, ut a cunctis fere populis amaretur."[20] His combination of the virtues of valor and generosity—"in illo probitas largitionem comitabatur" (HRB, ch. 143, p. 229)—allows him to restore to the kingdom the order that had eluded his father Uther as he defeats first the Saxons and then his domestic enemies. Once he has achieved this order in the state—"cum totius patriae statum in pristinam dignitatem reduxisset"—he marries (HRB, ch. 152, p. 237).

In contrast to the bad precedents set by Locrine, Vortigern and his father Uther, Arthur does not mate unwisely. His marriage choice is appropriate to his estate and condition, not only in beauty (a superficial quality Guinevere shares with the wrongly chosen women) but also in his bride's high Roman ancestry and gentle upbringing: "ex nobili genere Romanorum editam . . . in thalamo Cadoris ducis educata" (HRB, ch. 152, p. 237). Notably, lust—the leading motive for mating in Uther, Vortigern, and Locrine—is unmentioned. In Boethian terms, Arthur has made a proper choice: Lady Philosophy twice describes as one of the lasting joys Boethius should remember his chaste, well-reared wife (II, pr. III and II, pr. IV). Like his initial display of the kingly virtues, Arthur's marriage to Guinevere seems a further metaphor for proper self-rule.

The allied themes of self-rule and rule of one's kingdom coalesce in the most remarkable set-piece of the Historia, Geoffrey's account of Arthur's re-crowning. Length alone commends this passage to the careful reader's attention: it occupies about a tenth of the entire account of Arthur's reign. After further conquests, the establishment of a world court that thrives in peace for twelve years and nine years of successful war, Arthur calls a plenary assembly at Caerleon. Everything necessary for a display of that worldly fame added by Boethius to the previous lists of Fortune's goods is present. Caerleon, recommended by Arthur's intimates, is a *locus amoenus*, where a thriving school of two hundred philosophers spends its time forecasting Arthur's great deeds. A significant number of summoned guests arrive from all over the known world. Geoffrey's most meticulous expense of narrative energy, however, devolves on the re-crowning of Arthur and the apparently initial co-crowning of Guinevere.

King and queen here experience a like dignity, separate but equal. As Arthur proceeds in pomp to the metropolitan see, the Church of the Martyr Aaron, Guinevere—crowned with laurel and led by archbishops and pontiffs wearing her ensigns—figures in a procession to the Church of Julius Martyr. The music from the two temples is so equally grand that the knights who are there do not know which to enter first: "milites qui aderant nescirent quod templorum prius peterent" (*HRB*, ch. 157, p. 245). The joining by Geoffrey of personal and political themes highlights the similar joining of the Boethian necessities of proper governance of self and society.

That Guinevere's Church of Julius Martyr is also dedicated to the nuns ("dictarum puellarum") attached to it initiates an emphasis on chastity for women, complementary to valor in men, which Geoffrey continues into his description of the feast that follows. The king's eating and drinking with the men along with the queen's feasting with the married women is a custom he ascribes (without precedent) to Trojan origin (*HRB*, ch. 157, p. 245). Undoubtedly, his purpose, rather, is to remind his reader that Vortigern was smitten with his Saxon Renwein, and Uther with Ygerna, at nonsequestered royal banquets. Sequestration prevents sexual temptation in intemperate circumstances and encourages Boethian self-possession.

That such self-possession is different yet complementary in men and women emerges in the next passage. Knights and their ladies wear matching heraldic devices, and the love of their women is the reward of the men's valor. Indeed, the females will love no one except those who have proved themselves three times in war. Arthur's courage and Guinevere's chastity, therefore, are multiplied in their society: "Efficie-bantur ergo castae quaeque mulieres et milites pro amore illarum nobiliores" (*HRB*, ch. 157, p. 246). Here, Britain seems to have reached the state Boethius described in a famous passage adapted, among others, by Chaucer in "The Former Age": blissfully peaceful, without foreign entanglements and the needless death of war (II, *Met.* V). Self-possession has been actualized and extended to the allied proper possession of rule over others.

Such integration, however, is but a fragile earthly good in Boethian terms—the fleeting top position on Fortune's ever-turning wheel—and may easily be lost. Arthur's response to the challenge from the Roman emperor, which follows immediately his minutely described four-day re-crowning, is to announce his intention that Rome pay tribute to him. This overreaching appetite for earthly glory causes Arthur to entrust the defense of Britain to his nephew, Modred, and his queen, Guinevere (*HRB*, ch. 164, p. 253). As it turns out, Arthur's abandonment of his country—counter to repeated Boethian warnings against wandering from home—precipitates his ultimate subjection to the Wheel of Fortune. Not surprisingly, since Boethius so consistently associates Fortune with sea imagery (II, *pr.* I; II, *pr.* II and *met.* II and III: II, *pr.* IV), a theme Patch designates of "unusual importance," Arthur crosses the Channel as he begins this downward swing. His sea-dream of a conflict between a bear and a dragon is variously interpreted. For Arthur it concerns a conflict with a giant; for his followers, the conflict with the Roman emperor. Such a double interpretation is highly suggestive in terms of Arthur's actions and of Gawain's that follow.

Arthur's victory over the giant, a subhuman who represents an unexplored aspect of the king's own psyche (the giant's prime sin is lust, a reminder of Arthur's adulterous origins which he now seems to have overcome), momentarily reaffirms his Boethian self-possession. By it, he seems to become a good ruler of others as well, not just over Britain but over its colony Brittany. Such rule over oneself and others, however, does not appear in the subsequent conduct of Gawain who, as king's sister's son, bears a shadow role to Arthur's own.[21] As part of the embassy the king sends to Emperor Lucius, the purpose of which is to make the latter either retreat from Gaul or meet the king the next day in a free trial of rights, Gawain displays un-Boethian lack of self-control. Angered by a taunt from Lucius's nephew (here, the narrative doubling is obvious), Gawain beheads him, and thus begins a general battle between imperial and British forces that destroys any chance of reconciliation.

Nor is Arthur exempt from the contagion of this abandonment of right rule over self and others. When he receives news of the sufficient prisoners and plunder Gawain and the others have deliberately taken to placate him, the king commends them, promises rewards and makes no further mention of peace: "Quibus ille congratulans et honores et honorum augmentationes promisit, quoniam eo absente tantam probitatem egernant" (*HRB*, ch. 166, p. 261). That Arthur honors his men for their gallantry "eo absente" puts his *imprimatur* on a decisive loss of control in both personal and societal terms. There is now no further chance of the Boethian-desired peaceable kingdom.

Underlining the ubiquitous theme of the dangers of wandering from home is Arthur's rallying speech before the great battle with the Romans. Noting that his followers have conquered thirty realms—"qui Britanniam ter denorum regnorum fecistis dominam"—and denigrating the fine years of his own peace as merely a life of ease—"Licet quinque annis inexercitati" (*HRB*, ch. 169, p. 265), the king paints a tempting picture of the worldly good his men will obtain. Significantly, he first announces here the conquest of Rome as his goal. In turning from a finely delineated peace to an absolute war, from defense of his own lands to conquest of others, Arthur takes the step that will prove decisive in his own tragic fall.

This fall is adumbrated by the decline in self-possession in the subsequent battle with the Romans. Here, neither Arthur nor Gawain exhibits self-control. Angrily crying to his men not to let one soul of the "womanish" Romans escape, Arthur dashes at the enemy (*HRB*, ch. 174, p. 272). Once the battle is won, he sends the emperor's corpse to Rome as Britain's only tribute (*HRB*, ch. 176, p. 274). His lack of measure is echoed by Gawain (passim). It cannot help but seem, in the Boethian context, directly related to the subsequent news of the traitorous and incestuous usurpation of kingdom and queen by Modred, Arthur's regent.

Modred—another narrative double for Gawain, as king's sister's son—performs a multiple-plot function in the *Historia*. As incest, his action represents the most extreme loss of self-control, a taboo act against both family and society and a prime stroke against Boethian personal and political mastery. Similar to but worse than earlier accounts by Geoffrey of relatives—cousins, father, and daughters and especially brothers—in irreversible combat, Modred's move destroys Arthur's marriage—his prime personal emblem of self-possession, as demonstrated above. It also, as seizure of the kingdom, mirrors Arthur's obvious abandonment of both his personal and his political responsibilities. Modred—like Gawain, his brother—is the shadow side of Arthur that the king has ignored at his peril. The multiple character of his act—at once bigamy, incest, and high treason—is a multiplication of the nuptial fraud by which Arthur was conceived and under whose shadow he lives. That the object of the act is seizure of a queen reminds us of Boethius' representation of Fortune as a fickle female monarch (II, *pr.* I), a characterization Patch repeatedly emphasizes (pp. 60, 134, 143).

Like Gawain's earlier disruption of the possibility of a permanent peace, Modred's deed reflects the wrong actions of an Arthur who has also, if less obviously, lost control of himself. Yet it portends as well, at least implicitly, the salutary function which, in Boethian terms, accompanies all adversity. As Monica McAlpine has demonstrated for Chaucer's *Troilus and Criseyde*, the Boethian argument not only posits a turn from good to bad deeds but also allows for a reverse turn, from bad to good.[22] An Arthur who has taken the halfway turn of Fortune's wheel—from absolute reign to no reign at all—now returns once more to fight a just war against a domestic enemy. Here, the circular path of the Boethian wheel is transparent. Arthur pursues Modred to Cornwall, the place where Arthur himself was conceived. Between their two main engagements (at Richborough, where Gawain dies, and the River Camel), Guinevere flees to the convent of Julius Martyr, where her co-crowning with Arthur seemingly had inalterably set the seal on personal and social just rule. Guinevere's vow of chastity in the convent reaffirms the virtue that marked her crowned glory and suggests the possibility of regaining integration. With just such illuminative returns, Geoffrey's tragic structure emerges.

Arthur achieves integration both directly and indirectly. Having defeated and then killed his shadow nephew Modred, he gives up the crown of Britain to Constantine, his grandnephew and the son of that Cador whose grandmother's seduction by Uther had led to his ambivalent conception. In other words, he rectifies the nuptial fraud of his begetting. Arthur's renunciation of the world and all its goods implies and echoes Lady Philosophy's speeches to Boethius on the speciousness of worldly pomp (III, passim). Again and again, she states the fallacy of one's thinking to possess anything sublunary. In his own way, Arthur has arrived (as did Boethius) at an understanding of the marvelous circle of the simplicity of God: "'mirabilem . . . diuinae simplicitatis orbem'" (III, *pr.* XII). His being borne away to Avalon to be healed is, of course, a complex analogue: a combination of the Celtic Otherworld, the supernatural life of ultimate Boethian desiring (as in the example of Hercules, to whom the earth yields the conquered heavens: "superata tellus / Sidera donat," IV, *met.* VII) and, perhaps, the Christian promise of eternal life. Arthur's eventual return—not mentioned in the *Historia* but taken for granted in Geoffrey's later *Vita Merlini*—seems to signify the full turn of the Boethian wheel, from *regno* to *regno*, from beginning to end to beginning. He has lived out Patch's "formula of four"—Regno, Regnavi, Sum sine Regno, Regnabo (pp. 164–66)—by reigning, having reigned, being without reign, and expecting to reign again.

40

In the space remaining, I can indicate only a few Boethian references in subsequent Arthurian literature which underscore the tragic structure implicit in Geoffrey's *Historia*. For example, Fortune's wheel appears as turning for all in Wace's *Brut* and specifically for Lancelot in Chrétien de Troyes' *Conte de la charette*. The French Prose Vulgate *Mort Artu* offers not only an influential dream of Arthur's, in which Fortune places him on her wheel and assures him (as, through the lips of Lady Philosophy, she had Boethius) that no one rises who does not descend, but also Arthur's remark toward the end of his career, to Girflet: " 'Fortune, who has been my mother until now, but has become my step-mother, is making me devote the remainder of my life to grief and anger and sadness.' "[23] The dream is repeated, with variations, in both the *Stanzaic Morte Arthur* and the *Alliterative Morte Arthure*, as well as in Sir Thomas Malory's *Morte Darthur*. Surely the ubiquitous presence of Fortune and her wheel (she is even called a wonderful wheelright in the fourteenth-century alliterative *Awntyrs off Arthure at the Tarne Wathelyne*) is proof of subsequent Arthurian authors' recognition of Geoffrey's implicit debt to Boethian thought.

Even more Boethian is the evolving shape of Arthurian tragedy in these and other works. In his seminal study of medieval tragedy, Willard Farnham says that "Boethius also [as well as Seneca] . . . shows all the possibilities of a *De Casibus* [tragedy]."[24] Upon Geoffrey's story later authors built the increasingly elaborate tragic structure, climaxing in the French Prose Vulgate and Malory, which has fascinated so many writers to this day. The loves of Lancelot and Guinevere, Lamorak and Morgause, even Tristram and Iseult (drawn irresistibly into Arthurian orbit) echo and multiply the original incest of Modred. The most masterly use of this theme occurs in the Prose Vulgate *Mort Artu* author's assignment of Modred's fathering to Arthur's incestuous relationship with his sister Morgause.

Such tragic structure reaches its peak in Malory's *Morte Darthur*, as I have shown elsewhere.[25] From the Vulgate—as well as from earlier Middle English sources, the *Alliterative* and *Stanzaic Mortes* as well as Hardyng's *Chronicle* (the latter squarely in the Galfridian tradition)—Malory wove together basically Boethian ideas contrasting personal and societal order, proper rule of one's self and others, with their opposites. His illustrations of individual knightly careers, the well-tempered ones of Lancelot and Gareth and the uncontrolled ones of Tristram and Gawain, added to his balancing of the (here, early and successful) Roman War against those internecine conflicts which sunder Arthur's kingdom, allow for a striking contrast between an early, self-possessed Arthur and a later, largely lost king—in the fully Boethian sense of the adjective. Both complement and contrast with the loss of Galfridian control of chastity exhibited in the love affairs. Malory's is a magnificent achievement. Like all other versions of Arthurian tragedy, however, it owes its themes and structure to the Boethian-inspired thought first applied in the twelfth century to an inchoate Arthurian tradition by Geoffrey of Monmouth, whose *Historia Regum Britanniae* left a lasting imprint on all Arthurian works that followed.

A
Possible Source
of Geoffrey's
Roman War?

MARY L. H. THOMPSON

Arthur's campaigns in Gaul, here collectively termed his Roman War, make up a part of Geoffrey of Monmouth's *Historia
Regum Britanniae* for which almost no historical evidence has
been forthcoming and which has thus been considered exclusively fictional. After his pacification of the region and a
period of nine years of peace, the king holds court at Paris; no
significant amount of time appears to intervene between that
court and the one held later in Caerleon at Whitsuntide.[1]
Since Geoffrey (XI, ii, 501) dates the fatal battle between
Arthur and Mordred as occurring in 542, for Geoffrey, all the
events of Arthur's war in Gaul seem to have taken place in the
second quarter of the sixth century. History, however, offers
no evidence of troop movements from Britain to the Continent during this period. Geoffrey Ashe has suggested a historical basis for such movements in the crossing of British
forces into Gaul in about 470, but the particulars of that expedition offer little correspondence with the persons and events
described in the *Historia*.[2] Nevertheless, it is my contention
that many points of resemblance exist between Geoffrey's
narration and a much earlier account of an invasion of Gaul
and of warfare between Celt and Roman: Julius Caesar's *Commentarius de bello Gallico*. These similarities indicate that
events of Caesar's campaign, in 58–50 B.C., might have been

43

included in an intermediary Celtic account that became Geoffrey's source for this part of the *Historia*. This hypothesis, that Caesar's Gallic campaigns underlie Geoffrey's account, is well worth exploring, for it might help refute charges that certain parts of Geoffrey's account, like the battle at Siesia— or, indeed, this entire section of the *Historia*—are purely imaginary. It would help substantiate Lewis Thorpe's brave conclusion that "Geoffrey did not invent it."[3]

Opinion differs whether Geoffrey might have known Caesar's *Commentary*. J. S. P. Tatlock feels that he must have, and Hans Keller agrees, on the basis of Tatlock's assertion that a certain "Gesta Caesaris" appears in many medieval library catalogues.[4] Still, as astute a critic as Edmond Faral thought Geoffrey could have had no direct knowledge of Caesar because, in describing military actions between Langres and Autun, the *Historia* gives place names not found in the *Commentary*.[5]

I have examined carefully the language of both Caesar and Geoffrey of Monmouth in the several cases of correspondence to be discussed in this essay. In none of them does Geoffrey appear to have borrowed phraseology from the *Commentary*, as he seems to have done when using Bede as a source. A typical example is the incident of the felling of trees for use as military fortification. Not one word of Geoffrey's Latin (including even prepositions and conjunctions) duplicates anything found in Caesar. To illustrate, the passage from the *Commentary* reads: "Caesar silvas caedere instituit, et ne quis inermibus imprudentibusque militibus ab latere impetus fieri posset, omnem eam materiam quae erat caesa conversam ad hostem conlocabat et pro vallo ad utrumque latus extruebat" (III, 29).[6] In contrast, Geoffrey writes: "Quod arturus intuens iussit arbores circa illam partem nemoris indici et truncos ita in circuitu locari, ut egressus eis abnegaretur. Uolebat namque ipsos inclusos tamdiu obsidere donec fame interirent" (IX, iii, 436). Judging from a comparison of all such relevant passages, there seems to be no stylistic evidence that Geoffrey knew Caesar's account in the original.

Nevertheless, Geoffrey definitely seems to have known of the events of Caesar's campaign. The idea proposed here—that Geoffrey may have had access to a Celtic version of these same events—leads me to conclude that Arthur's exploits are based in part on those of Gallic chieftains who resisted Caesar's advance.

There is an obvious objection to this theory: history records the Romans, not the Celts, as victors. Against this argument must be placed the argument that a Celtic tale would have preserved a somewhat different emphasis—at the least, a focus on both the virtues and the vices of Caesar's opponents. It should be remembered that the conquest of Gaul was neither quick nor easy. Caesar faced a series of revolts during his nine years in Gaul. During hostilities he was briefly a captive, and in 52 B.C. he was nearly defeated by an alliance of tribes under their best-known leader, Vercingetorix. Sporadic resistance to Roman rule continued for years, even under the empire. Caesar had, of course, written his self-laudatory commentary to establish his claim to military skill, but this aim did not preclude his mention of temporary Gallic successes or of the difficulties he faced owing to the valor of his opponents. Moreover, it is clear that Caesar's eventual victory was due not only to his own ability and to better Roman organization and discipline but to the lack of steadfastness of the Celts and especially to the long-standing enmity among the various tribes as well.

Aulus Hirtius notes (VIII, 25 and 48) that defeated Gallic chieftains (for example, Ambiorix, Commius) sometimes escaped and moved away from the expanding Roman sphere of influence. Others may have sought refuge in Britain. No matter where they went, migrating survivors no doubt took with them their own version of what had happened in Gaul in the first century B.C., probably emphasizing, as had Caesar for himself in his turn, their own successes and discounting their own defeats. Further, it is not unlikely that in later centuries, Gauls and Britons might have edited what they may have heard (or even read) of the Roman version of the conflict, in the process presenting a far more favorable picture of Celtic resistance—even to the point, perhaps, of turning defeat into stalemate or into something more favorable.

Because both the section in Geoffrey's *Historia* on Arthur's Gallic wars and Caesar's entire *Commentary* are about warfare, it is to be expected that certain verbal conventions in describing battle produced similarities. Nevertheless, the two accounts share so many details that, on balance, it is difficult to believe that Geoffrey did not draw on some version of Caesar's account. In another essay, I note how the two works seem to agree in certain particulars—the geographical locations of battles and the size of armies involved.[7] Here, the subject will be limited first to noteworthy parallels between Geoffrey and Caesar in the nature of military incidents, and second, to similarities in the names of principals involved. These are discussed in the order in which they occur in the *Historia*.

In Arthur's first expedition to Gaul (XI, xi, 446–51), four elements in Geoffrey have clear parallels in Caesar (Book VII of the *Commentary*) writing about Celtic resistance under the Gallic chieftain Vercingetorix: Arthur's ambition to secure dominion over a vast region; his laying waste of the countryside; his strategy of giving gifts to secure the cooperation of Gauls against Romans; and his ordering of a military action to the south under the command of a subordinate. Geoffrey says that Arthur's invasion of Gaul grew out of his ambition to conquer the whole of Europe. In like fashion, Caesar reports that Vercingetorix encouraged his supporters by declaring that, after winning over other Gallic tribes not yet in agreement with their aims, "he would create a single policy for the whole of Gaul. . . . With Gaul thus united, the whole world could not stand against them" (VII, 29).[8] Arthur is described as laying waste the countryside; Vercingetorix, unsuccessful in halting Roman attacks on Gallic towns, proposes to his council that now "the war must be waged in a quite different way than hitherto." To prevent the enemy from gathering food from barns and granaries, he declares that "all villages and isolated buildings must be set on fire in every direction from the Romans' line of march as far as foragers seemed likely to be able to reach" (VII, 14). A third parallel involves the use of gifts to gain allies. Geoffrey says that Frollo is unable to resist Arthur's invasion successfully, in part because the better part of the army of the Gauls was already in Arthur's service: he had bought them over by gifts (IX, xi, 448). Caesar also finds that tribes formerly loyal to Rome desert to join Vercingetorix, who used "every means he could think of to bring the other tribes into the alliance, even trying to seduce them with bribes and promises" (VII, 31). Finally, after his victory over Frollo, Arthur sends Hoel to Aquitania to force the Poitevins and Gascons to surrender (IX, xi, 450–51). Similar is the dispatch by Vercingetorix of a subordinate, Lucterius the Carducan, to induce or compel tribes in the south of Gaul to join the alliance (VII, 5 and 7). In each instance, Arthur's motives or actions strongly resemble those of the most renowned of the Celtic warlords of Caesar's account.

It seems possible that two of Caesar's campaigns provide elements used in Geoffrey's story of the battles between Arthur and the fictional Roman emperor Lucius. Especially important are Caesar's account of the revolt of the Eburones under Ambiorix (Book V) and that of the resistance of Vercingetorix two years later (Book VII). In Geoffrey's story of the skirmish at Autun (X, iv, 474–79), Arthur comes upon the Roman forces near the Aube and sends a delegation, including Gawain, to Lucius, demanding that the Romans either withdraw or meet the British in battle. For its part, the *Commentary* tells of a parley called by the Eburones, who have surrounded a Roman winter camp and who offer the garrison, in the person of its envoy, Gaius Arpineius, similar terms—either safe conduct to another camp or renewed attacks (V, 26–37). In Geoffrey's account, Gawain is angered by a slur made by a Gaius Quintillianus and beheads him; according to Caesar, the great Gallic revolt of 52 B.C. was initiated by an uprising in which several Romans were killed, including a Gaius Fufius Cita (VII, 3).

At this point in the *Historia*, Geoffrey is as uncomplimentary of the fighting spirit of these Britons as Caesar is about that of the Gauls in his *Commentary*. Geoffrey reports that, while the Britons yearned for a fight with all their heart and soul, once they began it, they did not care much whether they won or lost (X, iv, 477). This sounds like the references to the "fickleness" of the Gauls in the *Commentary* and to their "delight in fighting." Caesar says that "while the Gauls are quick and eager to start wars, they lack the determination and strength of character needed to carry on when things go against them" (III, 19). When consent has been given for an attack, they are "exultant; it was almost as if the victory was already theirs" (III, 18). Similarly, both authors praise the Romans for their cool professionalism under attack. When Geoffrey shows the Romans making a stand, he is careful to praise the Roman commander, saying that the Romans were carefully instructed by Petreius Cocta, good captain (X, iv, 477). Caesar's statement about the legate Lucius Cotta, who was in charge of the defense against the Eburones (note the similarity in names), has the same ring: "He did everything possible to save the army, calling on the men and encouraging them as a commander-in-chief would, and fighting in the line like an ordinary soldier" (V, 33).

In Geoffrey, entrapment of the Romans results in a victory for the Britons; he says the Romans were enfeebled and dispirited and ready to show their backs, for they had lost their captain (X, iv, 478). In Caesar's account of the Roman fight against the Eburones, Romans who had left their camp in a kind of panic nevertheless stand firm against Gallic ambush from dawn until mid-afternoon (V, 32–36). Then Sabinus, one of the Roman legates, goes to Ambiorix, chief of the Eburones, to ask for quarter and is treacherously killed. Having lost their commander, the Romans retreat to their camp at nightfall where, all hope gone, the survivors commit suicide (V, 37).

The largest part of the confrontation between Arthur and Lucius in Geoffrey's *Historia* is the battle of Siesia (Saussy?) (X, vi–xiii, 481–96). Arthur's tactics there approximate those chosen by Gallic chieftains in Caesar's account. Arthur occupies the valley, waiting for Lucius as he marches out of Langres. The advantage lies with the Britons, who descend from the heights on the Roman column; Morvid, Earl of Gloucester, who had been stationed higher up in the hills, attacks the Romans in the rear when they least expect it (X, xi, 494). In Caesar's account, in anticipation of the evacuation of the Roman camp, Ambiorix's men are positioned in a double ambush in the woods: "When the greater part of our column had descended into a deep defile the Gauls suddenly appeared at each end of it and began to harrass the rear-guard and stop the head of the column climbing the hill to get out" (V, 32). Arthur's speech to his troops in Geoffrey includes these words: "You have put the Romans to flight. . . . They have had to withdraw. . . . They must come through this valley on their way to Autun, where you will be able to fall upon them when they least expect it" (X, vii, 484). In Caesar's *Commentary,* Vercingetorix has a similar rallying speech: "The Romans are leaving Gaul . . . and fleeing to the Province. . . . [We] must attack them now, while they are on the march and encumbered by their baggage" (VII, 66). The two situations are similar in several respects—the Roman retreat, the surprise ambush from an elevated position, the urgency felt by the Celtic commanders to annihilate the Roman threat while they have the chance.

If Arthur seems modeled on the character of Vercingetorix, even the British king's last defeat bears some resemblance to the final failure of that Gallic leader. The key element is treachery, betrayal. Geoffrey recounts how, on his triumphant way to Rome, Arthur learns that Modred has made himself king. Modred is condemned in the strongest possible language: "treacherous tyrant," "traitor," "perjurer," and so on (XI, i, 496–98). In the story told by Caesar, Vercingetorix, like Arthur, is unable to attain his final goal—in this case, elimination of Roman influence from Gaul—and there is reason to believe that treachery on the part of his subordinates is responsible. For example, it is difficult to understand why the huge Gallic army raised to relieve the Roman siege of Alesia was not able to break through, unless it was because the disaffected Gauls failed to support Vercingetorix. A tribe called the Bellovaci, for instance, do not send their full quota of

49

men, declaring they will fight only at their own discretion and not under the command of anyone else (VII, 75). Caesar notes as well that another tribe, the Aedui, bitterly resented being rejected from the leadership of the Gallic campaign and that two of their cavalry commanders, Eporedorix and Viridomarus, "took orders from Vercingetorix" but "much against their will" (VII, 63). These and other glimpses of dissension among the Gauls could have given Geoffrey a key to help explain Arthur's lack of success against the Romans.

Whereas military motives, strategy, and tactics are always somewhat conventional, the foregoing account shows that the activities of the Gallic forces against the Romans (and, more particularly, of the main Gallic leaders Ambiorix and Vercingetorix) in many respects run parallel to those of Arthur and the British, who were fighting the same enemy in the same theater of operations. Such parallels become more convincing when the names of some of the principals in Geoffrey's *Historia* are compared with those in Caesar's account. In general, enough close resemblances occur to suggest that Geoffrey's cast of characters is roughly patterned after Caesar's.

The first Roman that Arthur encounters in Gaul is the tribune Frollo (IX, xi, 448). In the *Commentary*, the nearest equivalent is "Ollovico" (VII, 31), the name of a Gallic chieftain, not a Roman official. Yet Caesar reports that the Senate had granted him the honor of being called "friend of the Roman people." Although *tribunus* under the Republic denoted either an aide attached to a legion or an elected official at Rome, the word originally meant chieftain of a tribe. Possibly, Geoffrey uses *tribunus* in the latter sense when applying it to Frollo, for the last syllables of Ollovico, *-vico*, are found in the titles of other Gallic chieftains. Had the name used by Caesar also included a standard Gallic honorific prefix *vor-*, *ver-* in a Celtic source known to Geoffrey, the result would have been "Vorollovico" ([*Vor*]-*ollo-vico*), or, with the ending clipped, simply *V[o]rollo*.[9]

While Geoffrey is thought merely to have invented Latin-sounding names for his Roman generals, we find names in

Caesar's *Commentary* that could be the basis for several. According to Geoffrey, the Roman general killed in the skirmish at Autun was Vulteius Catellus (X, v, 474); the name could be the result of the faulty transmission, oral or written, of Caesar's "(Gaius) Volcatius Tullus" (VI, 29). Geoffrey's fight between Britons and Romans near the Aube, discussed above, is similar to the attack Caesar describes against the retreating Romans led by Lucius Arunculeius Cotta (V, 24–37); in the same battle died the standard-bearer Lucius Petrosidius. It is possible Geoffrey's Senator "Petrius Cocta" (X, iv, 477) is a conflation of these two Romans in Caesar's account.

Geoffrey's Roman emperor Lucius Hiberius is not found in history. The praenomen was a common Roman one; in Caesar's *Commentary* are ten persons of that name who play active roles. Among them are senior centurions, who would have taken a prominent part in battles; *legati* in command of legions; and one Lucius Caesar, who nevertheless appears only in command of forces in the Province (Gallia Narbonensis, in the south of France) (VII, 65). In addition, there are three consuls named Lucius, and Caesar refers to four Romans with this first name who were defeated by the Gauls in wars before 58 B.C. Any negotiations between the Gauls and the Romans would have featured prominently the names of the consuls, chief officers of the Republic.

The only person described by Caesar as a Spaniard *(hiberus)* is Quintus Junius, a negotiator sent by Sabinus and Cotta to meet with attacking Gauls under Ambiorix (V, 27). There is no indication of his fate, but one assumes that in the subsequent ambush he perished along with Lucius Petrosidius, Lucius Aurunculeius Cotta, and a Quintus Lucanius. It is possible that attempts to simplify confusion among these names of similar sound and spelling may have led to the creation of Geoffrey's "Lucius Hiberius," who is described first as procurator, then as emperor.

In Caesar's time, a procurator was simply an agent or deputy, but in the imperial period the term came to mean an official of the government. *Imperator* was the title of a general in charge of two or more legions, the designation indicating at basis the distinction of command as opposed to the duties of a soldier. The title was conferred on a general after an important victory and later was one of the titles of the successors of Julius Caesar as head of state—hence, also, the source of our meaning of "emperor." Thus it may be that "general" is a better translation of the title held by Geoffrey's "Lucius Hiberius."

Following the same line of argument, certain Celtic names in the *Historia* can be matched with those in Caesar's work. The name Dubricius, belonging to the bishop at the plenary court at Caerleon (*Historia*, IX, i, 432), recalls Diviacus (or Divitiacus), chief of the Aedui at the time of Caesar (I, 3). Gorbonian map Goit, listed among those in attendance at Caerleon (IX, xii, 454), is reminiscent of that of the uncle of Vercingetorix, Gorbannitio (VII, 4). And a Briton killed at Siesia, Riddomarcus (*Historia*, X, x, 491) could easily be based—onomastically—on the Aeduan cavalry commander Viridomarcus (VII, 38).

The most interesting connection between Galfridian and Caesarian nomenclature, however, may lie outside those names actually listed in the *Historia*. The meaning of the title by which the chief opponent of the Romans was known may bear particular importance for Geoffrey's understanding of the role of Arthur. Three of the Celtic chieftains appearing in Caesar's account provide a close connection with a title that must have been known to Geoffrey. Two are named Cingetorix, and the third is, of course, the illustrious Vercingetorix. Some Celtic scholars suggest that the meaning of *cing* is "people" or, alternatively, "champion." The root *get* (or *cat*) means "battle" or "warrior," while *rix* clearly is "chief" or "leader."[10] (The prefix *ver-* [or *vor-*], as above, retains its honorific value of "great.") Thus the actual meaning of *Vercingetorix* was something like "great leader of the people in battle" or, indeed, something close to the title Nennius says King Arthur himself bore—*dux bellorum*.

To conclude, reading Geoffrey's *Historia* after Caesar's *Commentary* is much like looking at the underside of a brightly woven cloth, where the patterns and figures seem oddly duplicated, though the design may be somewhat blurred and the colors grown faint. The congruence between the two works over "the war in Gaul" is never exact, but certain similarities are sufficiently intriguing to suggest the possibility that one "source" Geoffrey had access to for his account of King Arthur's exploits on the Continent—in no matter how distorted and attenuated a form it had come to him through more than ten centuries of transmission—was Caesar's *Gallic Wars*.

Transformations
of a Theme:
The Depoliticization of
the Arthurian World
in the
Roman de Brut

JEAN BLACKER-KNIGHT

The pervasive tendency of medieval vernacular writers to transform Latin texts into courtly versions suited to the tastes of their audience has long been recognized. Charles Muscatine observed that writers of Old French romances often used their Latin sources as points of departure for discussions of love and etiquette, ignoring much of the tone and often many of the conventions and themes of the originals.[1] More recently, Hans Ulrich Gumbrecht noted a similar tendency in modifications made by thirteenth-century Spanish romance writers on twelfth-century Old French romances which were themselves recastings of Latin texts. He assigns the variations in the derived texts to certain social factors, noting that the social function of the texts "determines the interpretation the texts undergo in their reworking, as well as their linguistic structure and modifications of content."[2]

To date, many of these critical observations have been confined to works considered by modern critics to belong to the realm of "imaginative literature." The temptation is to assume that such extensive altering of received material was peculiar to the transmission of fictional texts—the term *fiction* itself suggesting license on the part of a second author to depart from the original. Literary authors, however, were not

the only ones to "be so original that they handled no pre-
decessor without pouring new life into him and so unoriginal
that they seldom did anything completely new."[3] Histories as
well were in the public domain and, as a result, were subject
to being "translated" into the vernacular, often with what
seems to us blatant disregard for their political, social, or ideological aims. Geoffrey of Monmouth's *Historia Regum Britanniae*—extant in more than two hundred manuscripts, fifty
from the twelfth century alone—is one historical narrative
that was redone repeatedly in Latin—excerpted, adapted,
and occasionally copied nearly verbatim.[4] The *Historia* was
also "translated" into the vernacular many times over.[5]

Each version of the *Historia,* derivative yet unique, was
likely created in response to perceived audience needs and
expectations; and Wace's *Roman de Brut,* the earliest vernacular adaptation of the *Historia* extant, is no exception.[6]
Writing in Old French octosyllabic couplets, the poet-histo-
rian made imaginative use of his major Latin source, producing a work substantially different in political bias, tone, and
representation of character from Geoffrey's.[7] Indeed, the
changes Wace made in the Arthurian world as presented by
Geoffrey have implications not only for the history of the
transmission of Arthurian material into French verse but for
twelfth-century habits of translation and the mentality that
informed them as well.

The many differences between the *Historia* and the *Brut*
stem primarily from three factors: Wace's own view of translation; the change in the national political climate in England
in the twenty years between the writing of the Latin text and
its Old French "translation"; and a difference in the general
composition of the respective audiences. In this essay I argue
that the changes Wace made in characterization, arrangement of material, and, especially, the political import of that
material stemmed from a broad view of translation; an opportunity to present the work officially to the court during a
period of relative stability; and an audience of nonexperts.
His situation was very different from that of Geoffrey who,

though he wrote with an eye to those in power, operated within the tradition of Latin historiography, under the scrutiny of fellow historians.[8]

Even today, the term *to translate* has broad meaning, though it most frequently implies the goal of producing a "faithful rendering" of a text from one language into another. Whereas, in practice, "faithful rendering" often allows for interpretation or nuancing through word choice, it does not allow for wholesale addition, omission or alteration of material of the sort one finds in the "translations" composed by the three principal twelfth-century poet-historians of Old French—Gaimar, Wace, and Benoît de Sainte-Maure. The translations produced by these historians often included extensive revisions of sources, conflation of materials from multiple originals, and the incorporation of oral evidence wherever deemed appropriate, thus revealing a concept of translation hugely at variance with our own more narrowly defined "giving of the *sense* or *equivalent* of [the original] in another language."[9]

Wace often says he is translating a work from Latin into "romanz," implying a narrowly defined language-to-language transference of information; but in practice, he frequently used more than one source for his "translations."[10] In his earliest work, *La Vie de Sainte Marguerite*,[11] Wace says he has translated a work of Theodimus:

> Ci faut sa vie, ce dit Grace [*sic*],
> Qui de latin en romans mist
> Ce que Theodimus escrist.
> (740–42)

> (Here is his life, which Wace tells,
> Who put from Latin into *romanz*
> That which Theodimus wrote.)[12]

He implies that he has simply transferred the story he found in Theodimus's work from Latin to *romanz;* yet, as the editor of the *Sainte Marguerite* has shown, Wace's version merely emphasizes Theodimus's text, among others.[13] In the *Vie de Sainte Nicholas*,[14] Wace says he is creating an excerpted version of a Latin original:

> En romanz dirrai de sa vie.
> Et de ces miracles une partie
> En romanz voil dire un petit
> De ceo que nus le latin dit
> Que li lai le puissent aprendre
> Qui ne poent latin entendre.
> (39–44)

> (In *romanz* I will speak of his life
> And about his miracles a part;
> In *romanz* I want to tell a small bit
> Of what the Latin tells us
> So that the lay people can learn
> Who are unable to understand Latin.)

Here, too, however, "le latin" could refer to a single source or collectively to several; Wace never cites his source(s) by name.[15] He apparently thought his patron, Ralph Fitz Tiout,[16] would not care to know the exact sources involved in the compilation written for him so long as they were "trustworthy" and well-rendered into French:

> Qui fait le liure mestre guace
> Quil ad de seint Nicholas feit.
> De latin en romanz estreit,
> Al oës Robert le fiz tiout,
> Qui seint Nicholas mult amout.
> Mult auereit longes apenser,
> Qui en romanz voldreit conter,
> Et torner en consonancie,
> Les granz miracles et sa vie.
> Ne nus ne trouom pas escriz,
> Ne nus ne auom tost oïz.
> (1475–85)

(Master Wace who made the book
Who made it about St. Nicholas
From Latin into *romanz* he turned it
For the ears of Robert Fitz Tiout,
Who loved St Nicholas very much.
He thought about it a lot and long,
Who wanted to tell it in *romanz*,
And turn it into rhymes,
His great miracles and his life.
We won't find it written down,
Nor have we heard it all.)

Wace says it is the "story" of Nicholas' life—"les granz miracles et sa vie" he wishes to relate, as if the "story" existed independent of the various texts that contained versions of it. In many instances, it appears that Wace was more interested in transmitting a reliable account of a string of events than in transmitting all the contents of a particular text.

The opening lines of the *Brut* as well suggest that Wace was working from a single book; even so, only a modern critic would thus assume the preservation of that source's internal integrity:

Ki vult oïr e vult saveir
De rei en rei e d'eir en eir
Ki cil furent e dunt il vindrent
Ki Engleterre primes tindrent,
Quels reis i ad en ordre eü,
Ki anceis e ki puis i fu,
Maistre Wace l'ad translaté
Ki en conte la verité.
   Si cum li livres le devise . . .
          (1–9)

(They who want to hear and who want to know,
Of kings and kings, from age to age,
Those who were and those who came after,
Those who held England first,
What kings had come in order,
Who were the most ancient ones,

Master Wace has translated it,
Who tells the truth about it.
    As the book sets it forth . . .)

Despite the reference to "li livres" (9), the fact that Wace mentions oral tales about Arthur—". . . les aventures truvees / Ki d'Artur sunt tant recuntees" (9790–91) (the adventures composed / Which about Arthur were told so often)—and the fact that he includes information not found in any other written sources from the period (on the Round Table, for example), indicate that his idea of translation was fluid indeed, admitting the use of multiple originals which he blended together to form his own poems.

Although Wace did not think it necessary to confine his "translation" to a single source, nevertheless it is useful to view his poem against the backdrop of Geoffrey's *Historia,* for two reasons: the latter was the major Arthurian history predating the *Brut,* and Wace did, in fact, base the Arthurian portion of his poem (verses 8541–13,298 of the 14,866 total) primarily on Geoffrey.[17] The dependence of the *Brut* on the *Historia* renders Wace's depoliticization of the Arthurian world all the more worthy of critical attention; in fact, the conspicuous absence in the *Brut* of the *Historia*'s political and nationalistic intensity may be a contributing factor to the general assessment that Wace was simply trying to make Geoffrey's history more entertaining for the members of the courtly audience.[18] Although Wace appealed to the aesthetic sense of his courtly audience and to their desire to see themselves reflected in literature, it is misleading to infer that the majority of his adaptations were cosmetic in nature. Rather, Wace took Geoffrey's apologetic for the Britons in their strife against the Saxons—an impassioned plea for a strong, united rule in England—and created a dispassionate account of the shifts in power in pre-eighth-century Britain, with Arthur as the "courtly" rather than political hero of the drama of the Britons.

In essence, Geoffrey's purpose in writing his history of the rise and fall of British dominion in England was twofold: nationalistic and political (pragmatic). He aimed to show that, though the Britons once had legitimate claim to lordship over Britain through their Trojan ancestry, they lost control over the island because they continually fought among themselves. Geoffrey's story is filled with pairs of warring brothers, such as Belinus and Brennius, Archgallo and Elidurus; only Arthur, an only child whose conception was brought about through preternatural assistance, manages to achieve and sustain a lengthy period of peace, although this peace, too, ultimately is destroyed by a close family member, his nephew, Mordred.[19]

By means of this saga of internecine struggle, Geoffrey sought to impart a political lesson to his immediate audience—the Anglo-Norman ruling elite—and to posterity: present and future kings were to learn from the example of the beleaguered Britons that the only way to secure and sustain peace was through united rule. This lesson of strength and peace through unity was extremely timely, since Geoffrey was still writing the *Historia* (ca. 1130–38) during the early years of the civil war involving three claimants to the throne: King Stephen, nephew of Henry I, who seized the throne upon Henry's death in 1135; Matilda, Henry's daughter and heir-designate; and Robert of Gloucester, Henry's eldest, though illegitimate, son who fought on Matilda's side against Stephen.[20] Geoffrey undoubtedly wanted to catch the attention of those in power; most of the manuscripts from the first half of the twelfth century contain dedications to Robert of Gloucester, the most powerful English earl of the period, and to Waleran of Meulan, most likely the most powerful Norman noble; both men had originally been supporters of Stephen against Matilda, before going over to her side in 1138.[21]

In the *Historia*, Geoffrey set out to challenge current views on the passage of dominion from the Britons to the Saxons. As R. W. Leckie has pointed out, "Geoffrey extended the period during which the Britons constituted the dominant force in Insular affairs well into what was normally reckoned as belonging to Anglo-Saxon history [producing an] account [which] offered an alternative and decidedly British view of events in the fifth, sixth, and even seventh centuries."[22] Geoffrey's bias in favor of British dominion led him to consider the Romans, Anglo-Saxons, Scots, and Picts as enemies and to attach great importance to Arthur's having been a *British* hero who managed to conquer each of those peoples.

Wace, a Norman, did not share Geoffrey's British patriotism, nor did he embrace Geoffrey's didactic purpose, although he did preserve almost all of the major events in Geoffrey's narrative. In the *Brut*, the Britons are still the descendants of Aeneas (via Brutus); but, according to Wace, Trojan ancestry does not automatically confer privilege of rule. The Britons are just one in a series of peoples who occupied the island at one time or another, as had the Romans, Anglo-Saxons, Scots, and Picts; in this typical passage, etymology takes precedence over national sentiment or political analysis:

> Le language qu'il ainz parloent
> Que il Troïen apeloent,
> Unt entr'els Bretun apelé.
> Mais Engleis l'unt puis remué;
> La parole e li nuns dura
> Tant que Gormund i ariva;
> Gormund en chaça les Bretuns
> Si la livra a uns Saissuns
> Qui d'Angle Angleis apelé erent,
> Ki Engletere l'apelerent;
> Tuz les Bretuns si eissillierent
> Que unches puis ne redrescerent.
> (1189–1200)

> (The language they spoke then
> Which the Trojans named,
> Among themselves was called Breton.
> But the English changed it later;
> The speech and the name lasted
> Until Gormund arrived;
> Gormund chased out the Britons,
> He delivered England to the Saxons,
> Who were called English by the Angles,

Who called it England.
All the Britons exiled themselves;
They never set it right after that.)

As a result of his lack of intense fondness for the Britons, their demise at the end of the seventh century is of no great consequence to Wace and certainly no cause of consternation or grief.[23] For his part, Geoffrey expresses anger, dismay, even disgust at the self-induced fall of the Britons: "Supradicta namque mortalitas et fames atque consuetudinarium discidium in tantum coegerat populum superbum degenerare quod hostes longius arcere nequiverant" (XII, xix, 535) (For indeed the aforementioned plague and famine and the habitual dissension combined to cause this proud people to degenerate so much that they were unable to keep their enemies at bay).[24] Wace simply states:

Tuit sunt mueé et tuit changié,
Tuit sunt divers e forslignié
De noblesce, d'onur, de murs
E de la vie as anceisurs.
(14851–54)

(All were transformed and all were changed
All were different and realigned
In nobility, honor, and in mores
And in the lives of the ancestors.)

The tone of urgency in Geoffrey's work is absent in Wace's, where one finds instead disinterested acceptance, revealing no attachment to any party, and, if anything, a greater interest in etymology than in politics.

The message of the *Brut*—if there is one beyond the literal level of plot and character—is far removed from the explanations for the demise of the Britons put forth by Geoffrey. Wace presents historical events as if to convey the inevitability of change. In the rise and fall of peoples, the evolution of languages, and the rebuilding of towns and monuments, Wace seems to allude to the revolutions of the Wheel of Fortune. He describes the shifts of power that took place in ancient London, dwelling on the undulations of time rather than the implications of those shifts, in a typically aloof and rather melancholy tone:

> Par plusurs granz destruiemenz
> Que unt fait alienes genz
> Ki la terre unt sovent eüe,
> Sovent prise, sovent perdue,
> Sunt les viles e les contrees
> Tutes or altrement nomees
> Que li anceisor nes nomerent
> Ki premierement les fonderent.
> (1239–46)

> (Through several great destructions
> Which foreign peoples wrought,
> Who often held the land,
> Often taken, often lost,
> Were the towns and countries,
> All named otherwise
> Than the ancestors named them
> Who first founded them.)

The apparent melancholia need not be attributed to disappointment over the passing of a favorite king or people; Wace evinces little enthusiasm for any side.

In fact, Wace does not account for these permutations of history, nor does he comment on them; it is as though they defied interpretation. This is all the more curious, because he frequently is concerned to present the "facts" correctly, as any responsible historian would. For instance, he declines to speculate on Arthur's possible return, because he has no proof beyond what his source has offered:

> Maistre Wace, ki fist cest livre,
> Ne volt plus dire de sa fin
> Qu'en dist li prophetes Merlin;
> Merlin dist d'Arthur, si ot dreit,
> Que sa mort dutuse serreit.

Li prophetes dist verité;
Tut tens en ad l'um puis dutée,
E dutera, ço crei, tut dis,
Se il est morz u il est vis.
(13282–90)

(Master Wace, who made this book,
Does not want to say any more about its end
Than the prophet Merlin says about it.
Merlin says about Arthur, if he was right,
That his death would be in doubt.
The prophet does tell the truth,
[But] all the time since then, one has doubted it
And will doubt, I believe, all the sayings,
[Of] whether he is alive or dead.)

Wace implies as well a contrast between the veracity of his poem and the unreliability of tales currently in circulation:

Furent les merveilles pruvees
E les aventures truvees
Ki d'Artur sunt tant recuntees
Ki a fable sunt aturnees.
Ne tut mençunge, ne tut veir,
Tut folie ne tut saveir,
Tant unt li cunteür cunté
E li fableur tant flablé [*sic*]
Pur lur cuntes enbeleter,
Que tut unt fait fable sembler.
(9789–98)

(Marvels were performed
And adventures sung
Which are told about Arthur so much
That they have turned into fables.
Not completely lies, not completely true,
Nor all folly, nor all wisdom;
The tale-tellers have sung so much
And the fable-makers so "fabled"
To embellish their tales
That they have made them all seem like fables.)

64

Although Wace was concerned with the truth of his narrative and thus was reluctant to take a stand on unverifiable material, he did not need to interpret it analytically to do his job well. His aim was to inform nonexperts, not to edify fellow historiographers. Those nonexperts probably included Henry II and Queen Eleanor, as well as others among the Anglo-Norman aristocracy.[25] Wace sought to fulfill his role as purveyor of knowledge by offering his history of the Britons to an audience of laypeople similar to those who heard the *Saint Nicholas*. Lacking Latin, they nevertheless expected an authenticity not found in the "contes" which "Tant unt li cunteür cunté" (*Brut*, 9795) ("in the 'tales' which 'the tale-tellers' have told so much"). By structuring the *Brut* chronologically, "de rei en rei, de eir en eir," and by weaving together threads from both written and oral sources, Wace gave his audience what they could not have found in scattered oral legends, whether in French or Welsh: a vast, comprehensive network of "facts."

In addition to Wace's general reluctance to comment on the political ramifications of historical events, two other aspects of the *Roman de Brut* illustrate the depoliticization of the Arthurian material: characterization and the exclusion of Merlin's prophecies. Wace's characterization of Julius Caesar is an excellent example of the shift from polemic and partisanship to disinterested courtly narrative. Geoffrey had praised Caesar with a view to building up the Britons, not the Romans. On the subject of Caesar's challenge to the Britons after his conquest of Gaul, Geoffrey exclaims:

> O admirabile tunc genus britonum ipsum bis in fugam propulerat qui totum orbem sibi miserat. Cui totus mundus nequivit resistere illi etiam fugati resistunt parati mortem propatria et libertate subire. Hinc ad laudem illorum cenit Lucanus de Cesare: Territa quesitis ostendit terga britannis. (IV, ix, 318)

> (O how worthy of admiration that British race was then! Twice it had sent into flight that man who brought the entire world under his sway. That people, though even now driven from the

battlefield, are resisting him who the whole world could not withstand, prepared to die for their fatherland and for liberty. For this reason, Lucan spoke their praises when he said of Caesar: "He fled in terror from the Britons whom he had sought to attack.")

Wace, on the other hand, praises Caesar, but not to make the Britons look better for having defeated him. He introduces the Roman general with what could be called "reflex praise," complimentary phrases used by Old French authors almost automatically to describe any nonvillainous dignitary, to make that figure readily recognizable within a courtly context:

> Julius Cesar li vaillanz,
> Li forz, li pruz, li conqueranz,
> Ki tant fist e tant faire pout
> Ke tut le mund conquist e out.
> Unches nus huem, puis ne avant,
> Que nus saçom, ne conquist tant.
> Cesar fu de Rome emperere,
> Savies huem mult et bon donere,
> Pris out de grant chevalrie
> E lettrez fu, de grant clergie.
> (3833–42)

> (Julius Caesar, the valiant,
> The strong, the noble, the conqueror,
> Who did so much and was able to do so much,
> Who conquered and held all the world.
> Never has any man, before or after,
> Whom we know about, conquered so much.
> Caesar was Emperor of Rome,
> A very wise man and giver of gifts;
> He was possessed of great chivalry
> And was lettered, of great learning.)

Such superlatives were not calculated to paint Caesar as an unusually sympathetic figure. Rather, the description is part of Wace's plan to portray this famous individual from classical times in terms rapidly becoming characteristic of descriptions of heroes in virtually all twelfth-century narrative poetry: *vaillanz, forz, saviez, (sage),* and *de grant chevalrie* ("valiant," "strong," "wise," and either "having a great army" or "possessed of chivalric qualities" or both). These terms identify and define Caesar and are not meant as anti-British polemic; but by using them, Wace makes Caesar less an enemy of the Britons and more a participant in a courtly system of values with greater relevance to the poet's own age than to the British history he is recounting. Thus Caesar is rendered noteworthy not because he was defeated by the Britons but because he—like Arthur, among others—was worthy of being labeled "li vaillanz, li forz, li pruz, li conqueranz."

Arthur is also depoliticized and rendered "courtly." Because Wace does not alter the major events of Geoffrey's narrative, Arthur remains the world-conquering hero but not because, as a Briton, he had some special right to that honor. Instead, he conquers as a figure of unusual strength and organizational abilities who, even more than Caesar, transcends national allegiance and political context. In addition, although Wace does not completely reduce Arthur to a courtly figurehead, he does draw attention away from Arthur's military exploits by focusing on his social deportment. Unlike Geoffrey, who emphasizes Arthur's military victories, Wace overshadows those same victories by focusing on the king's reputation for courtesy.

Like other heroes in the *Brut,* such as Gawain and Julius Caesar, Arthur fulfills the roles of knight and leader to perfection, possessing the major attributes of a courtly role model in abundance:

> Les thecches Artur vus dirrai,
> Neient ne vus en mentirai;
> Cevaliers fu mult vertuus,
> Mult fu presanz, mult glorius;
> Cuntre orguillus fu orguillus
> E cuntre humles dulz e pitus;
> Forz e hardiz e conqueranz,

67

Large, dunere e despendanz.
(9015–22)

(I will tell you of Arthur's qualities,
I will lie about nothing concerning them.
He was a very stalwart knight,
He was very worthy, very glorious;
Against the haughty he was haughty,
Against the humble, tender and full of pity;
Strong, hardy, and conquering,
Generous, gracious with gifts, and magnanimous.)

Arthur is more eminent than others in his social refinement as well: as long as he lived and reigned, "Tuz altres princes surmunta / De curteisie e de noblesce / E de vertu e de largesce" (9029–32) (He surpassed all other princes / In courtesy and nobility / In strength and largesse). Geoffrey refers to tournaments sponsored by Arthur, where knights learned to excel at arms while ladies, wearing their colors, learned to encourage them by scorning any knight who had not proved himself at least three times in battle. To Geoffrey's description of these and other festivities at Arthur's plenary court (IX, xiii, 455–58), Wace adds details about the types of songs sung and instruments played, the clothing worn, and the gifts given—in all, devoting 424 verses to the festivities (10197–620). To this tableau of courtly decorum, Wace adds a reference to the Round Table, though with some reluctance. Ever conscious of his self-assigned role as a reporter of "facts," he protests: "ne vuil je mie faire fable" (10286–87) (I do not at all wish to make fables).

Of uncertain origin, the Round Table was likely part of a common stock of oral tales. Wace includes it in making a statement about conceptions of personal self-worth:

Pur les nobles baruns qu'il out,
Dunt chescuns mieldre estre quidout,
Chescuns se teneit al meillur,
Ne nuls n'en saveit le peiur,
Fist Artur la Roünde Table

Dunt Bretun dist mainte fable.
(9747–52)

(For the noble barons he had,
Of whom each thought he was better,
Each considered himself the best,
Nor did any know of the worst,
Did Arthur make his Round Table
Of which the Bretons tell many fables.)

The establishing of the Round Table, which could have served as a political statement regarding the equal status of Arthur's barons, functions here merely as a commentary on egoism. The order in which the knights are served at table is not shown to have a direct bearing on the execution of Arthur's administrative duties, except insofar as the egalitarian seating arrangement might have prevented quarrels over precedence from spilling over into a political context:

A table egalment seeient
E egalment servi esteient;
Nul d'els ne se poeit vanter
Qu'il seist plus halt de sun per,
Tuit esteient assis meain,
Ne n'i aveit nul de forain.
(9755–60)

(They were seated equally at table
And were served equally;
None of them was able to boast
That he was seated higher than his peer:
They were all seated equally
Nor was anyone excluded.)

Wace's emphasis on Arthur's reputation apparently pushed aside any treatment of political questions. Arthur has earned his renown not as a British leader feared by the Anglo-Saxons and others but as a magnanimous giver of gifts and sayer of *corteisies*. In the *Brut*, people do not come to Arthur's court to plead for justice, to pay taxes, or to ask that a new monastery be built, but:

> Tant pur Artur, tant pur ses duns,
> Tant pur cunustre ses baruns,
> Tant pur veeir ses mananties,
> Tant pur oïr ses curteisies,
> Tant pur amur, tant pur banie,
> Tant pur enur, tant pur baillie.
> (10331–36)

> (As much for Arthur, as much for his gifts,
> As much to know his barons,
> As much to see his dwellings,
> As much to hear his courtesies,
> As much for love, as much for his proclamations,
> As much for honor, as much for his guardianship.)

In the *Historia*, Arthur had appointed a bishop and two archbishops immediately following the dispersal of his plenary court at Winchester (IX, xv, 458–59). In the *Brut*, he gives gifts of a more baldly material nature, such as gold and furs rather than delegating power to his supporters (10597–616). Arthur's political dimensions are thereby greatly diminished; what we are left with is an image of kingship as spectacle, a picture of largesse and munificence reminiscent of many portrayals of his Frankish counterpart, Charlemagne.

Finally, in addition to incorporating numerous apolitical characterizations in the *Brut*, Wace omits an extremely important section of Geoffrey's narrative, the *Prophetiae Merlini*, which comprises Book VII of that work; this omission, in fact, is the most dramatic example of Wace's draining of political import from the material associated with Arthur.[26] Geoffrey had intended the *Prophecies* as a commentary on both the disorganization of the ancient Britons and the civil turmoil in his contemporary England. Not surprisingly, the *Prophecies* actually were read by historians of the period not so much as prophetic utterances referring to the seventh century and extending into the future but, rather, as predictions for the current time and the near future.[27]

Had Wace included the *Prophecies* without comment, they would have taken their place alongside much early material in the poem Wace included but declined to analyze. Wace excuses his decision to leave out the *Prophecies* by protesting that he does not know *how* to interpret them, implying that it would have been dishonest if he had reproduced them in ignorance of their meaning:

> Dunc dist Merlin les prophecies
> Que vus avez, ço crei, oïes,
> Des reis ki a venir esteient,
> Ki la terre tenir deveint.
> Ne vuil sun livre translater
> Quant jo nel sai interpreter;
> Nule rien dire ne vuldreie
> Que si ne fust cum jo dirreie.
> (7535–42)

> (Then Merlin uttered the prophecies
> Which you, I believe, have heard,
> Of the kings who were to come,
> Who were going to hold the land.
> I do not wish to translate his book,
> For I do not know how to interpret it;
> I would not wish to say anything about it,
> Lest it did not happen the way I would tell it.)

Honesty and trepidation notwithstanding, by stripping Merlin of his political predictions, Wace has removed a primary element in Geoffrey's characterization of the prophet-magician. Wace reports that Merlin was peerless as a diviner and engineer but affords only one glimpse of Merlin as a diviner— the scene where Merlin explains to Vortigern the significance of the two dragons battling under his tower (7501–7506, 7512–22). The apolitical Merlin is portrayed as an instrument used to enhance Utherpendragon's efficiency in numerous

71

arenas: through feats of preternatural engineering, Merlin moves the giant stones from Ireland to Salisbury Plain to create Stonehenge (8083–8178) and disguises Utherpendragon as Gorlois in order to trick and thereby seduce Ygerne (8691–8729). From this characterization, it was a short step to the portrayal of Merlin strictly as a magician—instead of as a sage—as seen soon after in such Old French prose romances as the thirteenth-century *Huth-Merlin*.[28]

Wace evidently assumed that his audience could easily do without the revelations contained in Book VII of the *Historia*. It would follow that, if Wace's assumption can be read as an accurate gauge of audience expectations, his audiences showed little or no interest in political issues, much less political controversy; they wanted the skeletal "facts" of history but had no desire to delve into the implications of those facts. Thus, while Wace preserved vestiges of issues of statehood and territorial dominion merely by including incidents from his sources that involved them, he did not feel obligated to preserve the sense of political commitment found in his sources or to invest the material with one of his own. In fact, King Henry and his court may have wanted the poet to omit this aspect of his subject, replacing political and administrative concerns with courtly descriptions as a reflection of themselves, not as a reflection of the ancient Britons whose cause Geoffrey had expended so much energy to champion.

What factors, then, enabled Wace to write a history in many ways at odds with his major source for the Arthurian section? He so frequently contrasts his work with "contes" and "fables," citing the need for veracity, that it is difficult to believe he merely wanted to tell a "good story," if by that is meant a fictitious narrative created primarily for entertainment value.[29] Audience expectations, not authorial whim, encouraged Wace to squeeze the politics out of Geoffrey's narrative; though interested in an "accurate rendition" and not just a diverting tale, Wace's audience cared little for the political implications of early British dominion in England. Wace wrote roughly twenty years after Geoffrey, following Henry II's ascent to the throne, under the comparative stability that the cessation of the civil war brought; he had little incentive to use the Arthurian story to warn against the pitfalls of internecine struggle, as Geoffrey had had. In addition, in times of new-found peace, the audience at court would have preferred to see a reflection of their king's strengths—in the guise of Arthur—than a worrisome suggestion of his possible future demise at the hands of his family. This would explain the emphasis on *prouesse* and *valor,* plus the omission of the sometimes triumphant but often gloomy political prophecies and of such administrative details as Arthur's granting of ecclesiastical office—the latter an extremely sensitive issue throughout the years of the investiture controversy.[30] Also, unlike Geoffrey, who anticipated that his work would be seen by other writers of Latin histories, Wace wrote for Henry and the Anglo-Norman court, whose members would not have missed the pro-Briton, anti-Roman and anti-Saxon references that Wace omitted.

To judge from the relatively large number of extant manuscripts of the *Brut*—nineteen in total, twelve clustered around the early to mid-thirteenth century—the poem was well received; its success may have prompted Henry II to give Wace a prebend at Bayeux sometime between his completion of the *Brut,* in 1155, and his starting to work on the *Roman de Rou,* in 1160.[31] The *Brut* was popular probably not just because it contained material about Arthur, who was gaining in popularity as a heroic figure, but, more important, because it presented a plausible, modernized, accessible rendering of Arthur's "life" and exploits set against the backdrop of early British history, a rendering that served to cement the Brutus–Arthur–Henry II connection without too many cumbersome details.

Wace's audience would therefore not have considered the apolitical nature of the *Brut* a disservice to the *Historia.* As "translator," Wace was not expected to duplicate *en romanz* Geoffrey's history or any other particular text; he was expected to make British and Anglo-Saxon history "de rei en rei, de eir en eir," readily available to an audience that could not read Latin or, if it could, had little access to texts or the time or inclination to pore over them.[32] Wace served as interpreter (as he says with apparent sincerity) between the Latin sources and the public, a go-between who was permitted to fill in any gaps he found in those sources with material from oral sources in order to complete an educational and entertaining picture.[33] For medieval readers and listeners, Arthur's "story"—or even Arthur's "history"—existed apart from the individual texts that contained it and thus was available for any writer to appropriate in his own idiom and reshape according to the needs of his audience, provided he tacitly agreed to preserve an unspecified, recognizable amount of the old tradition while creating a new one.

A Jungian Interpretation of Sexually Ambiguous Imagery in Chrétien's *Erec et Enide*

JAN A. NELSON

In the prologue to *Erec et Enide*, Chrétien de Troyes informs us that he has drawn a *bele conjointure* from a simple tale of adventure and in doing so has made use of his learning.[1]

> et tret d'un conte d'avanture
> une molt bele conjointure
> par qu'an puet prover et savoir
> que cil ne fet mie savoir
> qui s'escïence n'abandone
> (ll. 13–17)

[drawn from a tale of adventure a very beautiful composition by which one is able to prove and to know that he does not act wisely who does not make use of his learning.] Neither Chrétien nor any of his contemporaries have provided us with an explicit definition of *conjointure*. Its precise meaning continues to be debated.[2] Nevertheless it must refer in some way to the manner in which the various elements of the narrative have been put together; the word itself tells us that much. It seems clear, then, that Chrétien was conscious of his role as *trouvère*, or *inventor*, and that he selected and ordered the narrative elements of his composition for the purpose of expressing a definite idea. Were this not the case, the text would have no more than a literal sense; it would be no more than the simple *conte d'aventure* with which he began. In fact, repeated close reading of the romance reveals astonishing precision with respect to word choice, and aptness with respect to imagery as the sense of the romance emerges.[3] The validity of this statement can be demonstrated by an examination of four animal images that occur in the work. Two of these images, the ones built up around the sparrow hawk and the stag, are conspicuous; the other two, based on the goat and the leopard, are less so.

The narrative of Chrétien's *Erec et Enide* is organized as a series of three major movements, or phases. Each movement illustrates the relationship between Erec and Enide from a different perspective. The narrative, therefore, is not linear; it turns back on itself. It moves through a series of variations on a central intellectual conception that is revealed as the narrative exposes it from different angles. The rhetorical model for this kind of disposition of narrative elements received considerable theoretical treatment during the twelfth century and was well known to writers as *expolitio* or *interpretatio*.[4]

The first movement opens at Arthur's court where, against the protests of all present, the king has ordered the hunt for the white stag. In this ritual the knight who takes the stag thus wins the right (and the obligation) to kiss the lady whom he deems most beautiful, an act that cannot go without challenge and resultant mayhem. Erec chooses not to take part in this hunt and rides instead with the queen and one of her maids into the forest. There they hail a knight, his lady, and a dwarf whom they see approaching. The strangers, however, do not respond to the queen's greeting and Guenevere sends her maid to learn the knight's identity and to invite him and his party to court. First the maid, then Erec himself meets with verbal abuse and a lashing from the dwarf as the group rides past. Erec, who is unarmed and without his warhorse, sets out in pursuit, vowing not to return until insult and injury have been avenged. Arriving shortly at a neighboring castle, he finds preparations underway for an annual contest in which the participants determine in combat whose lady is the most beautiful. Twice now the victor has been Ydier, the discourteous knight whom Erec has sworn to bring to justice; twice in previous contests it has been Ydier who has presented his lady with the symbolic prize, a sparrow hawk. Erec recognizes his opportunity. He finds lodging with an impoverished but noble vavasor. When his host learns of Erec's resolve to challenge Ydier, he loans him the necessary weapons, a warhorse, and even his daughter Enide. The next day, in a long and exhausting fight, Erec defeats Ydier and claims the sparrow hawk for Enide. The episode closes with the departure of the couple for Arthur's court. There they will marry. They are in every way an ideal match. Erec has been established as a paragon of chivalric virtue, Enide as a model of feminine beauty. As Chrétien describes them, they are a complementary pair in perfect balance:

> molt estoient igal et per
> de corteisie et de biauté
> et de grant deboneretè.
> Si estoient d'une meniere,
> d'unes mors et d'une matiere,
> que nus qui le voir volsist dire
> n'an poïst le meillor eslire
> ne le plus bel ne le plus sage.
> Molt estoient d'igal corage
> et molt avenoient ansanble;
> li uns a l'autre son cuer anble;
> onques a deus si beles ymages
> n'asanbla lois ne mariages.
> (ll. 1484–96)

[Of noble birth were they, equal in courtesy and comeliness. So were they of one manner, one habit, and one substance. No one who would wish to tell the truth would be able to choose the better of the two, nor the more beautiful nor the more wise. They were of equal character and a most becoming pair. The one steals the other's heart. Never did religion or marriage bring together two such beautiful images.]

At court the two receive a warm welcome; but it is Enide,

still clad in her ragged clothing, who is the immediate object of attention. Guenevere takes her in charge, dresses her in an ermine-lined tunic and splendid mantle, and then announces that it is Enide who should receive the ritual kiss. Arthur and all present agree, and the honor of the white stag is bestowed on her without contest, an event itself without precedent. The sparrow-hawk contest affirmed Enide's character and defined her role as the feminine complement to Erec. The ritual stag hunt, as the frame of the romance's first major movement, then provides the means by which Enide is brought to prominence.

With the formal statement "ici fenist li premiers vers" [here ends the first verse (l. 1796)], the narrative movement turns back and begins the first variation on its theme. Within the economy of the romance, this second, or middle, section is at once of greatest length and greatest complexity. It begins with the marriage of Erec and Enide. Describing their union, Chrétien recalls the preceding movement by means of images developed from the animals that figured prominently there: the stag and the sparrow hawk.

> la reïne s'est antremise
> de l'atorner et del couchier,
> car l'un et l'autre avoit molt chier.
> Cers chaciez qui de soif alainne
> ne desirre tant la fontainne,
> n'espreviers ne vient a reclain
> si volantiers quant il a fain,
> que plus volantiers n'i venissent.
> (ll. 2024–31)

[The queen took charge of preparing their bed, because she loved them both very much. A hunted stag panting with thirst does not desire so much the fountain nor the hungry sparrow hawk come to the lure so eagerly as they came there.] On the surface, the stag and the sparrow hawk appear to be specifically and appropriately male and female. The stag, or *cers*, is, after all, the male of its species. And the sparrow hawk, or *espreviers,* is the female of its species.[5] Erec comes to the marriage bed as the hunted stag thirsting for water, and Enide as the hungry hawk to the lure.

Whatever Chrétien's source may have been for the ritual stag hunt, the image in which it here culminates is biblical. It is taken from Psalm 41: "Quemadmodum desiderat cervus ad fontes aquarum / Ita desiderat anima mea ad te Deum fortem, vivum."[6] [As the stag desires the waters of the fountain / So does my soul desire you, strong and living God.] Chrétien, however, has modified this forceful biblical image and rendered it specific to this text by adding the adjective *chaciez* [hunted]. The poet must have consciously effected this shift, since it creates a matched pair of images drawn from the real world of hunting that contrasts with a second pair, the goat and the leopard, which are drawn from the imaginary world of the bestiary. The images themselves reflect the broader narrative movement as it turns from the real to an experimental permutation of Erec's character.

The ideal marriage, the perfect psychic balance of the matched and complementary pair, is, of course, difficult to maintain. Erec is so taken by his wife's beauty, and he finds such solace in their intimacy, that he seems recreant. The social order that depends on the strength of his authority is threatened. His vassals, sensing their increasing vulnerability, become restive. More important, they blame Enide. One day, as Erec and Enide lie in bed, she begins to weep, lamenting her apparent contribution to Erec's psychic dysfunction:

> Lasse, fet ele, con mar fui!
> de mon païs que ving ça querre?
> Bien me doit essorbir la terre,
> quant toz li miaudres chevaliers,
> li plus hardiz et li plus fiers,
> qui onques fust ne cuens ne rois,
> li plus lëax, li plus cortois,
> a del tot an tot relanquie
> por moi tote chevalerie.

Dons l'ai ge honi tot por voir;
nel volsisse por nul avoir.
(ll. 2492–2502)

[Alas, says she, I wish I had never been born. What did I come seeking when I left my native land? The earth ought to swallow me up since the best knight, the bravest, the proudest, the most loyal, and the most courteous—even count or king—has completely given up chivalry because of me. Truly I am shamed. I would not have wanted it for anything.] Her tears fall on his naked chest; he awakens to hear her say: "Amis, con mar fus!" [Lover, I wish you had never been born (l. 2503).] He demands a clarification. She explains and then tells him:

Or vos an estuet consoil prandre,
que vos puissiez ce blasme estaindre
et vostre premier los ataindre,
car trop vos ai oï blasmer.
(ll. 2562–65)

[Now you have to come up with a plan for doing away with the blame and for recovering your reputation, because I have heard you criticized too often.] Erec replies that both she and the others are right. He then orders her to put on her very best dress and mount her palfrey. As Chrétien puts it:

Or est Enyde an grant esfroi;
molt se lieve triste et panssive;
a li seule tance et estrive
de la folie qu'ele dist:
tant grate chievre que mal gist.
(ll. 2580–84)

[Now Enide is really frightened. She rises sad and depressed. She gives herself a good lecture on the foolish thing she said and concludes with the proverb: A goat will paw the ground until it ruins its bed.] The proverb may perhaps be interpreted as: Look for trouble long enough, and you'll find it. As is well known, few ever looked for trouble more than François

80

Villon; and, in a moment of regret, he too applied this proverb to his own unfortunate situation. It is the opening verse of his "Ballade de Proverbes," a poem made up of thirty-two proverbs all meaning exactly the same thing.[7] Rarely do we have available so convenient and definitive a list of the possible narrative elements available to a medieval poet in a given situation. They prove just how apt is Chrétien's use of this particular proverb. The *chievre* [goat] is clearly and explicitly the female animal.[8] It applies immediately to Enide. And, most importantly, it evokes the marriage bed.

While Enide is busy following Erec's instructions, he orders that his weapons be brought:

> Puis s'an monta en unes loiges,
> et fist un tapiz de Limoiges
> devant lui a la terre estandre:
> et cil corrut les armes prandre
> cui il l'ot comandé et dit,
> ses aporta sor le tapit.
> Erec s'asist de l'autre part
> sor une ymage de liepart
> qui el tapiz estoit portraite.
> Por armer s'atorne et afaite.
> (ll. 2623–32)

[Then he went up and had a carpet from Limoges spread out before him. The one whom he ordered to do so ran to get his weapons and brought them to the carpet. Erec sat down opposite them on the image of a leopard that was worked into the fabric. He gets ready to arm himself.] Here the leopard must surely be understood as emblematic of Erec in some way. What does it tell us?

The bestiary tradition has little to say about the leopard, but what it does say is clearly pertinent to Erec's present situation. Saint Isidore, for instance, informs us: "Leopardus ex adulterio leaenae et pardi nascitur" and "sicut et Plinius in Naturali Historia dicit, leonem cum parda, aut pardum cum leaena concumbere et ex utroque coitu degeneres partus creari, ut mulus et burdo."[9] [The leopard is born of the adulterous union of a lioness and a pard. As Pliny says in his natural history, the lion mates with the female pard or the pard with the lioness and from either union there results degenerate offspring, like the mule and the ass.] Erec must indeed feel degenerate at this moment. The measures he undertakes are not meant to punish Enide, whose logic he has explicitly accepted, but to meet his wife's demand that he affirm his own identity.[10]

Erec now forces Enide to ride out alone ahead of him. He forbids her to speak to him or even to warn him of danger. There follows a series of combats not only between Erec and the opponents attracted by his lone wife but also between Enide's love for her husband and her obligation to obey his command that she not warn him of impending danger. Each struggle is more threatening than the preceding one: three thieves, five thieves, an evil count and his men; a dwarf knight, Guivret le Petitz, whose strength and nobility are characterized by the golden lions depicted on his saddle; two giants, and finally yet another evil count. In each situation, love and chivalry triumph to return the narrative to its point: Erec and Enide are a complementary pair, perfectly balanced. Neither can function well without the other. Character must be tested, but it is, after all, a permanent disposition of moral qualities. Like all epic figures, Erec and Enide do not become; they are.

The bestiary tradition adds unexpected precision to Chrétien's identification of Enide with the goat. Again, Saint Isadore describes these animals: "Morantur enim in excelsis montibus, et quamvis de longinquo, vident tamen omnes qui veniunt."[11] [They live on high mountains and, although from afar, nevertheless they see all who approach.] No image could be more appropriate to the role Enide plays in this part of the romance. She has been made to ride alone at a distance from her husband and told not to warn him of approaching danger. It is precisely her goatlike capacity to see from a distance the approaching enemy that provides the means of testing her character. When the three thieves attack, "Enyde vit les robeors: molt l'an est prise granz peors." [Enide saw the rob-

bers: very great fear seized her because of them (ll. 2827–28).]
When the five thieves attack, "Quand Enyde les ot veüz, tot li
sans li est esmeüz." [When Enide had seen them, her blood
ran cold (ll. 2959–60).] Then, when Enide and her exhausted
husband have fallen into the hands of the evil count Caolin,

> An une chambre recelee
> furent dui lit a terre fet:
> Erec an l'un couchier se vet;
> an l'autre est Enyde couchiee,
> molt dolante et molt correciee,
> n'onques la nuit ne prist somoil;
> por son seignor fu an esvoil,
> car le conte ot bien coneü,
> de tant com ele l'ot veü,
> que plains estoit de felenie.
> (ll. 3432–41)

[Two beds had been set up in a quiet bedroom. Erec goes to
bed in one, Enide in the other. She is very upset and angry.
She did not sleep any that night. For her husband she lay
awake, because she had recognized the count well as soon as
she had seen him, for he was full of treachery.]

When Count Caolin pursues the fleeing couple, "Enyde ot la
noise et le bruit de lor armes, de lor chevax, et vit que plains
estoit li vax. Des que cele les vit venir, de parler ne se pot
tenir." [Enide hears the commotion and the noise of their
weapons, their horses, and saw that the valley was full of
them. As soon as she saw them coming, she was unable to
keep from speaking (ll. 3538–42).] The Caolin episode is at the
center of the central movement of the romance, the third of a
graded series that is followed by a second graded series of
even more dangerous encounters: the first with the dwarf,
Guivret li Petitz; then with the two giants; and finally with
the Count of Limors. Erec, however, had recognized Enide's
loyalty to him in her behavior toward Count Caolin. "Or ot
Erec que bien se prueve vers lui sa feme lëaument." [Now
Erec hears very well that his wife is proving herself loyally to
him (ll. 3480–81).] That is, they are once again depicted as the

ideal couple whose example, significantly, has a therapeutic effect on Count Caolin, who says:

> Retornez tuit isnelemant;
> esploitié ai vilainnemant:
> de ma vilenie me poise;
> molt est preuz et saige et cortoise
> la dame qui deceü m'a.
> La biautez de li m'aluma:
> . . . . .
> que fos feisoie et deslëax
> et traïtes et forssenez.
> Onques ne fu de mere nez
> miaudres chevaliers de cestui.
> (ll. 3629–34, 3640–43)

[Everyone go home quickly. I have behaved very badly. The lady who tricked me is very worthy, wise, and courteous. Her beauty set me afire . . . so that I acted like a fool, a disloyal, treacherous madman. A better knight than this one was never born.] When Erec and Enide ride away, they are together. She is no longer the goat.

It should be clear by now that Chrétien made remarkably precise and appropriate use of stag, sparrow hawk, leopard, and goat in order to express the emotional states of both Erec and Enide as they move through the world of Arthurian romance. No artist, however, is in complete control of his or her subject matter. I suggest, in fact, that the meaning, the *sensus*, of this romance reaches far beyond Chrétien's interpretive power, his *scientia*. After all, as Marie de France stated in the prologue to her *Lais:*

> Es livres que jadis feseient,
> Assez oscurement diseient
> Pur ceus qui a venir esteient
> E ki aprendre le deveient,
> K'i peüssent gloser la lettre
> E de lur sen le surplus mettre.
> Li philesophe le saveient

> E par eus memes entendeient,
> Cum plus trespasserunt le tens,
> Plus serreient sutil de sens[12]

[In the books they (the ancient writers) wrote in the past, they spoke rather obscurely for the ones who were to come so that they might be able to study the text and bring to it their own interpretation. The philosophers knew it; among themselves, they understood that their meaning would become more subtle with the passage of time.]

Even a superficial reading of *Erec et Enide* suggests that Chrétien's intention was to exemplify an ideal relationship between husband and wife, a relationship in which the woman's contribution is as important as the man's. Thus the first part of the romance provides for our discovery of Enide, our recognition of her beauty, and our acceptance of her as Erec's equal. That much is stated explicitly:

> que nus qui le voir volsist dire
> n'an poïst le meillor eslire
> ne le plus bel ne le plus sage.
> Molt estoient d'igal corage
> et molt avenoient ansanble.
> (ll. 1489–93)

[No one who would wish to tell the truth would be able to choose the better of the two, nor the more beautiful nor the more wise. They were of equal mind and a most becoming pair.]

Chrétien understood that such terms as "cortesie, beauté, corage, bel," and "sage" were appropriate to either sex; he applied them equally to Erec and to Enide. Yet his imagery is implicitly more complex and leads beyond the socioeconomic relationship of the two sexes. Clearly, the stag and the sparrow hawk are male and female animals; but, on closer examination, they become ambiguous. For instance, the stag, which is Erec thirsting for Enide's bed as a soul thirsting for heaven, is also the stag pursued by the knights of Arthur's court as symbolic of the fairest lady. The image is sexually ambiguous. The sparrow hawk, which is Enide hungering for her master's lure, is also the dominant sex of her kind and a more eager, more effective huntress than her mate. Again, the image is sexually ambiguous. Erec is the stag, but the stag is suggestive of beauty and vulnerability. Enide is the sparrow hawk, but the sparrow hawk is suggestive of courage and violence. Erec is the knight, but the stag is the quarry. Enide is the lady, but the sparrow hawk is the hunter. The stag is a functioning element in Chrétien's Arthurian world precisely because appropriate female traits are present. Similarly, the sparrow hawk functions because appropriate male characteristics are present. Chrétien had at his disposal neither the Jungian terms *animus* and *anima* nor the concomitant concept of an essentially androgynous psyche; nevertheless, his imagery, at once ambiguous and unambiguous, derives its validity from and, in turn, explicates his postulate: Si estoient d'une meniere, d'unes mors et d'une matiere."[13] [So were they of one manner, one habit, and one substance (ll. 1487–88).]

Also, the chiasmatic structure of the sexually ambiguous imagery in the first section of the romance can be seen to extend to the second part. If Enide is symbolized by the sparrow hawk, or hunter, in one, she is symbolized by the goat, or hunted, in the other. Similarly, Erec, the hunted stag in part one, becomes the leopard or hunter in part two. This chiasmatic relationship has its source in the intellectual integrity of the romance and permits us to recognize the second part as a variation on or restatement of the first. If the first part is, as Chrétien termed it, a *vers*, then the second and third parts are too. The narrative movement folds back on itself; it consists of phases that repeat and vary the central intellectual conception: Erec and Enide are "d'une meniere, d'unes mors et d'une matiere." There is an active and a passive, a male and a female, aspect to both. Furthermore, the physiologically and socially dominant aspect cannot function in the absence of its opposite. Enide is brought out of poverty and obscurity to Arthur's court; she is brought into existence as the ideal lady by an Erec who sets out unarmed, against the background of the stag hunt. That is, Erec does not function fully as a knight until he discovers the impoverished vavasor and his daughter.[14] Nor can she emerge from obscurity without him. Again, in the second part of the romance, it is Enide exposed as prey who leads Erec out of degeneracy into the fullness of knighthood again. Yet there, too, her very existence depends on his prowess. Together, they form a whole, an ideal union of man and woman, knight and lady. As such, they themselves become images: "onques a deus si beles ymages / n'asanbla lois ne mariages" (ll. 1495–96). In fact, they are therapeutic images. This has already been seen in the Caolin episode, which significantly is located at the center of the romance; but in the third movement, the so-called Joie de la Cort, it is given even greater emphasis.

The central movement of the romance begins with Erec's marriage and his subsequent, debilitating fascination with Enide. The situation is that of a man possessed by his *anima*. In the Joie de la Cort, the situation is reversed. In this episode, Erec and Enide find themselves on an enchanted island inhabited by Enide's cousin and her giant lover, Maboagrins.[15] The two no longer function; rather, they must remain enclosed within the world of their enchanted island until Maboagrins is defeated in single combat. This is the situation of a woman who has been content to remain within the world of nature, to function more or less instinctively and without appropriate cultivation of the *logos*, the intellect, the *animus*. As a result her *animus*, abandoned in the unconscious and feeding on its energy, has become a gigantic, inappropriately dominant force in her life.[16] When Erec defeats Maboagrins, Enide's cousin is finally able to emerge once again into the world of Arthurian romance as a functioning lady. This is what restores the Joy of the Court.

From a Jungian perspective, Erec and Enide are best understood as representative of the male and female aspects of an essentially androgynous individual. They are the *animus* and the *anima* of the Arthurian knight, Erec.[17] Chrétien himself said that he was writing about Erec: "d'Erec, le fil Lac, est li contes." [Of Erec, the son of Lac, is the tale (l. 19).] He did not write: "d'Erec et d'Enide est li contes," which would have been an equally possible octosyllabic verse. The particular *sensus* or interpretive development that Chrétien brought to the apparently well-known tale of Erec must have had to do mainly with his discovery and validation of Enide as the necessary feminine complement within a sacramental union or, as we may now add, within a balanced male psyche. The effect of this discovery on Chrétien himself may well be revealed in his description of the golden cross Erec gives as an offering at the Mass following his marriage:

> et une croiz, tote d'or fin,
> qui fu ja au roi Costantin:
> de la voire croiz i avoit,
> ou Dame Dex por nos s'estoit
> crocefïez et tormantez,
> qui de prison nos a gitez
> ou nos estïens trestuit pris
> par le pechié que fist jadis
> Adanz par consoil d'aversier.
> (ll. 2325–33)

[and a cross of fine gold, which once belonged to Constantine. There was in it some of the true cross on which was crucified and tormented for us Our lord, who freed us from prison where we were being held by the sin that Adam committed through the devil's devices.] Unlike his contemporaries, Chrétien does not hold Eve, the feminine element, responsible for Adam's sin.

"Que nus qui le voir volsist dire" (l. 1489) now becomes a more heavily charged verse. In Chrétien's time the truth was, as it still is, difficult to accept. "When a man discovers his *anima* and has come to terms with it, he has to take up something which previously seemed inferior to him. It counts for little that naturally the *anima* figure, be it image or human, is fascinatingly attractive and hence appears valuable. Up to now in our world, the feminine principle, as compared to the masculine, has always stood for something inferior. We only begin at present to render it justice."[18] With the passage of time, the sense of Chrétien's romance has indeed become more subtle; the therapeutic value of his images even more potent.

"Now I Se and Undirstonde": The Grail Quest and the Education of Malory's Reader

STEPHEN C. B. ATKINSON

Since the appearance of Vinaver's *Malory* in 1929, critics dealing with the "Tale of the Sankgreall" have focused almost exclusively on Malory's relationship with his source. Many of
these critics—again, following Eugène Vinaver—have found
Malory's sixth tale disappointing in comparison with the
French *Queste*.[1] To earlier readers less preoccupied with its
source, the Grail material seemed a more appealing, more important part of Malory's accomplishment.[2] The contrast may
be accounted for by the difference in focus; earlier critics attended primarily to their own experience as readers of Malory's text, whereas Vinaver and his successors have diverted
their attention from the act of reading to the business of
source-study. Renewed attention to the experience of reading
Malory's sixth tale reveals elements of Malory's art to which
little commentary has been devoted but which are crucial to
the overall accomplishment of the *Morte Darthur*.[3]

Central to the Grail adventures is the education—or re-education—of the knights of the Round Table. Central to the experience of reading about those adventures is the education of
the reader. Here, the reader does not merely witness events, as
we do through much of the "Tristram," where we watch like
spectators at a vast tournament while the varieties of chivalric experience are played out before us. In confronting the

Grail material, we are urged to participate, forced to test our perception and judgment in company with the knights themselves. This effect is felt both by the reader of the *Queste*'s French and the reader of Malory's English, though Malory's condensation reduces the time spent by knights and readers alike passively listening to sermons; thus it proportionally increases the reader's active role. In one respect, though, Malory's readers are in a very different position from the readers of the *Queste:* they have in store Malory's seventh and eighth tales. My aim in this investigation is to suggest that in the "Tale of the Sankgreall," Malory is training his readers to approach more perceptively the great final sections of his work.[4]

The reader's induction into the Grail world depends first on the juxtaposition of its spiritual values with chivalric patterns of conduct familiar from Malory's "Lancelot," "Gareth," and "Tristram." When, for example, Melyas de Lyle asks to be knighted by Galahad and reveals himself as a king's son, he falls naturally into the pattern of Gareth, knighted by Galahad's father. When Galahad, having granted the request, tells him, "ye ought to be a myrroure unto all chevilry" (883.9), the words seem as much prediction as advice.[5] And when Melyas, at a fork in the road, asks leave to pursue his first adventure, our expectations of his success are likely to obscure Galahad's warning:

> "Hit were bettir," seyde sir Galahad, "ye rode nat that way,
> for I deme I sholde bettir ascape in that way, bettir than ye."
> (883.35–36)

At this point, we may take the warning as little more than the sort of skepticism faced by young, unproved knights such as Gareth or La Cote Mal Tayle.

The largely conventional nature of these events does little to prepare the reader for the abrupt conclusion of Melyas' inaugural quest. The casual ease with which a nameless knight overthrows him "that he felle to the erth nyghe dede" (884.22) marks a sharp departure from predictable patterns, a departure underlined by Galahad's unsympathetic words:

91

> "Sir Melyas, who hath wounded you? Therefore hit had bene
> better to have ryddyn the other way." (884.26–27)

Galahad's words recall for us his earlier warning, and to the extent that we overlooked it in favor of our optimistic expectations, we share Melyas' chagrin.

No such warning is available a few pages later when an event that seems a normal part of knight-errantry proves a gross violation of the standards of the Grail quest. Because they are knights of the Round Table, Gawain, Uwain, and Gareth are set upon by the knights who held the Castle of Maidens; they meet the challenge by defeating and slaying their seven attackers. Nothing in the conduct of the Round Table knights violates a single principle of chivalric conduct, so it is a shock when Gawain is told by a hermit that

> "had ye nat bene so wycked as ye ar, never had the seven
> brethirne be slayne by you and youre two felowys: for sir
> Galahad hymself alone bete hem all seven the day toforne, but
> hys lyvyng ys such that he shall sle no man lyghtly." (892.2–6)

This is the first occasion when an action entirely admirable in chivalric terms proves entirely reprehensible in the world of the Grail. The reader, whose expectations have now been thoroughly disrupted, is apt to proceed with a new sense of caution.[6]

That caution pays off as the reader approaches later events. Perhaps the clearest reversal of chivalric values in the entire Grail quest is Lancelot's experience at the tournament of the black and white knights. His decision to join the losing side is a stock chivalric response, and his subsequent defeat is the more galling because he is captured in spite of his great strength. In "the Tale of Tristram," Malory tells us that "sir Trystrams was called bygger than sir Launcelotte, but sir Launcelot was better brethid" (415.33). Here, Lancelot is taken by a tactic designed "for to tire hym and wynde hym" (932.2). The import of the event is underlined for us by Lancelot himself: "For never or now was I never at turnemente nor at justes but I had the beste. And now I am shamed" (932.16–17).

We may be distressed at this turn of events, but few readers, I believe, are surprised. One immediate clue, of course, is the black-white symbolism, a topic to which I will return. Another clue is the announcement of Lancelot's motive: "Than thought sir Launcelot for to helpe there the wayker party *in incresyng of his shevalry*" (932.24–25; italics mine). That this phrase should seem ominous shows the degree to which, only halfway through the tale, the reader has been weaned from the responses conditioned by "the Tale of Tristram." The caution bred by such early surprises as Melyas' downfall and bolstered by myriad later events has begun to give way to a new confidence, and the reader is again in a position to formulate expectations based now on the new standards of the Grail world.[7]

Reshaping our chivalric expectations in this way is only part of our re-education. In addition, we find that the Grail world differs from the world of knight errantry in its basic principles of operation and in how the significance of events is to be understood. In this sense, then, the most important and—initially, at least—bewildering feature of this new world is introduced when in a speech beginning "Sir, I shall telle you what betokenyth of that ye sawe in the tombe" (882.28–29), "a good man" expounds to Galahad the allegorical *significatio* of a recent experience.

Allegorical interpretation of this model accompanies most of the important tests the knights of the Grail quest face; the verb *betoken* grows as familiar to the reader as the monks, hermits, and recluses who expound the meaning of Grail world phenomena. At the outset, though, these interpretations contribute greatly to our sense of this new realm's strangeness. For example, to our surprise at reading of Melyas' abrupt defeat must be added our surprise at learning that we have been reading allegory:

. . . for the way on the ryght hande betokenyd the hygheway of oure Lorde Jesu Cryst, and the way of a good trew lyver. And

the other way betokenyth the way of synnars and of mysse-
belevers. . . .   (886.12–15)

Not only the landscape but the characters as well are allegorical:

> . . . And so, sir Galahad, the holy knyght which fought with
> the two knyghtes, the two knyghtes signyfyeth the two dedly
> synnes whych were holy in thys knyght, sir Melias; and they
> myght   nat withstonde you, for ye ar withoute dedly
> synne.   (886.26–30)

The reader's effort to adapt to this new feature of Malory's
narrative is further complicated by two problems. First, the
allegorical is not clearly marked off from the literal; it is not
restricted, for example, to a dream world. There are, of
course, allegorical dreams in the tale, but they coexist on apparently equal terms with allegories embodied in waking vi-
sions and in real events of the flesh-and-blood world. The
second problem is equally disorienting: figures take on and
shed allegorical status without warning. Thus the hermit who
shelters Gawain rebukes him for slaying the seven knights
from the Castle of Maidens in the passage quoted above. In
chivalric terms, this reproach is remarkable enough, but the
hermit now shifts suddenly into interpretation:

> Also I may sey you that the Castell of Maydyns betokenyth the
> good soulys that were in preson before the Incarnation of oure
> Lorde Jesu Cryste. And the seven knyghtes betokenyth the
> seven dedly synnes that regned that tyme in the worlde. And I
> may lyckyn the good knyght Galahad unto the Sonne of the
> Hyghe Fadir that lyght within a maydyn and bought all the
> soules oute of thralle: so ded sir Galahad delyver all the may-
> dyns oute of the woofull castell.   (892.7–14)

Although this sudden exposition gives a new and unexpected
dimension to the episode, it remains unclear what connection
the allegory has to Gawain's own experience with the seven

knights. The interpretation ends as abruptly as it began, and the hermit concludes:

> "Now, sir Gawayne," seyde the good man, "thou must do pen-aunce for thy synne."   (892.14–16)

Attempts to sort out the status of the seven knights are futile. As Galahad's opponents, they are allegories; yet, when Gawain and his companions kill them, they have not overcome the seven sins but have murdered real men.

The recluse who interprets for Lancelot the meaning of the tournament raises the same problem when she tells him "that turnamente yestirday was but a tokenynge of oure Lorde. And natforethan there was none enchauntemente, for they at the turnemente were erthely knyghtes" (933.14–17). Further, these "earthly knights" (here, the term clearly means knights of flesh and blood—that is, not apparitions) are engaged in what appears to be an unremarkable chivalric exercise: "The turnamente was tokyn to se who sholde have moste knyghtes, of Eliazar, the sonne of kynge Pelles, or Argustus, the sonne of kynge Harlon" (933.17–19). Yet, the recluse goes on, "Eliazar was all clothed in whyght, and Argustus were coverde in blacke. And what thys betokenyth I shall telle you" (933.19–21).

In the elaborate explanation that follows, the trappings of these earthly knights apparently are the vehicle of an allegory whereby their tournament represents the Grail quest and their two parties its followers, an allegory staged for the testing of Lancelot:

> The day of Pentecoste, whan kynge Arthur hylde courte, hit befelle that erthely kynges and erthely knyghtes toke a turnemente togydirs, that ys to sey the queste of the Sankgreall. Of thes the erthely knyghtes were they which were clothed all in blake, and the coveryng betokenyth the synnes whereof they be nat confessed. And they with the coverynge of whyght be-tokenyth virginite, and they that hath chosyn chastite. And thus was the queste begonne in them. Than thou behelde the

synners and the good men. And whan thou saw the synners
overcom thou enclyned to that party for bobbaunce and pryde
of the worlde, and all that muste be leffte in that queste; for in
thys queste thou shalt have many felowis and thy bettirs, for
thou arte so feble of evyll truste and good beleve. Thys made
hit whan thou were there where they toke the and ladde the
into the foreyste.   (933.22–934.5)

The reader must struggle to keep literal and allegorical elements distinct in the course of reading the passage, especially
since the term *earthly* has reverted to its more usual, moral
meaning. The "erthely knyghtes" (that is, real knights) of the
tournament represent the "erthely knyghtes" (that is, sinful
knights) of the Round Table; but they represent "the good
men," the prospective Grail knights, as well. The reader is
driven eventually to some such formulation as this: Eliazar
and Argustus are engaged with their followers in a straightforward tournament; but in some manner their trappings embody an esoteric meaning relevant only to Lancelot's quest
and understood only by the recluse. Even this scheme immediately proves inadequate when the recluse continues. "And
anone there apered the Sankgreall unto the whyght knyghtes,
but thou were so fyeble of good beleve and fayth that thou
myght nat abyde hit" (934.6–8). Clearly, this tournament was
not a simple chivalric contest after all. Any hope for a neat
division between literal and allegorical dies here as Eliazar's
literal knights take a literal part of their own in the Grail
quest even as they betoken its workings allegorically.

More than any other element of "The Tale of the Sankgreall," the sudden emergence of allegory is what forces readers into a more active role. The allegory appears to have three
effects, each dependent on the preceding one. The first is that
of simple confusion. We are forced to change our entire approach to Malory's narrative; lack of a clear demarcation between the phenomena that bear concealed meaning and those
which do not prevents the reader from easily adapting to this
new world. Kept off balance, we feel at times the same baffle-
ment and frustration that the knights themselves feel. The

disorienting effect of Melyas' immediate defeat, violating our expectations concerning chivalric narrative, is deepened immensely when his conqueror proves an embodiment of Melyas' own sin.

The second effect of the plunge into allegory develops from the first, as we are forced to rely on the explanations of hermits and recluses. In general, allegorical representation of meaning implies a self-conscious mind at work, hence the successful marriage of allegory and dream-vision. As we read such an allegory, we are able to refer its design to the continuing presence of the author-dreamer—Guillaume de Lorris, William Langland, even John Bunyan. The knights from the Castle of Maidens, however, are not characters in a dream; no visible figure is responsible for endowing them with abstract meaning. Certainly, the hermit who explains their significance to Gawain did not create them to represent the deadly sins. Similarly, Lancelot's recluse can interpret the events of the tournament, but she did not manipulate the black and white knights. Thus the design of these allegories must be attributed to an unseen creator whose medium is the material world, and the second effect of the tale's allegorical episodes is to make us feel the presence of God directly governing the world of the quest and deliberately staging its events.

Our perception of God's role in the events of the tale means that their significance is not haphazardly conceived but is instead rational, consistent, and, ultimately, intelligible. This conviction leads, in turn, to the allegory's final effect: the reader becomes an active participant, an interpreter of events. Just as we move from surprise at Melyas' defeat early in the tale to the later anticipation of Lancelot's, so we move from bewilderment at the first appearance of allegory to a response that seeks to understand the allegorical meaning even as the literal events unfold. Testing of the knights of the Round Table provides the occasion for testing the reader. The basic pattern of these tests remains the same: obscure or misleading events are followed, often some pages later, by authoritative interpretation. In the interim, the reader is challenged first to perceive the problematic nature of the episode, then to uncover its true significance. Because the pattern is essentially unvarying, the effect of repeated tests is, to some extent, cumulative. We become more acute readers, sensitive to hints of trouble (more sensitive, often, than the knights themselves). We become more adept at interpretation through repeated exposure, as the underlying reality of successive episodes is revealed to us. Our increasing sophistication as readers, however, is largely matched by the increasing complexity of the material we are required to deal with. A comparison of key moments in the testing of Percival and Bors will illustrate most of these features of the reader's experience.

In the adventures of Percival, the problems of chivalric expectation and the allegorical nature of events come together most vividly in the climax of Percival's temptation. The appeal for aid from the disinherited gentlewoman dovetails with the provision of the Round Table oath enjoining the knights "allwayes to do ladyes, damesels, and jantilwomen and wydowes socour, strengthe hem in hir ryghtes" (120.20–22). The gentlewoman explains her plight:

> "Sir," seyde she, "I dwelled with the grettist man of the worlde, and he made me so fayre and so clere that there was none lyke me. And of that grete beawte I had a litill pryde, more than I oughte to have had. Also I sayde a worde that plesed hym nat, and than he wolde nat suffir me to be no lenger in his company. And so he drove me frome myne herytayge and disheryted me for ever, and he had never pite of me nother of none of my counceyle nother of my courte. And sitthyn, sir knyght, hit hath befallyn me to be so overthrowyn and all myne, yet I have benomme hym som of hys men and made hem to becom my men, for they aske never nothynge of me but I gyff hem that and much more. Thus I and my servauntes werre ayenste hym nyght and day, therefore I know no good knyght nor no good man but I gete hem on my syde and I may. And for that I know that ye ar a good knyght I beseche you helpe me, and for ye be a felowe of the Rounde Table, wherefore ye ought

98

nat to fayle no jantillwoman which ys disherite and she be-
sought you of helpe." (917.12–19)

The reader's response to this speech is both conditioned by
elements of the passage itself and informed by our recollec-
tion of previous events in Percival's quest and in earlier portions of the tale. The speech contains too many puzzles,
incongruities, and danger signals to be accepted as naively
even by a first reader as it is by Percival; above all, at this late
stage of Percival's adventures, the emphasis on Round Table
chivalry is apt to elicit skepticism from the reader. His persistent troubles, especially with horses, in the earlier portions
of his quest, and the revealing moment when "he kest away
shylde, helme, and swerde" (911.13–14), reinforce the doubts
developed by such earlier adventures as Melyas', leaving us
uneasy about wholehearted appeals to a chivalric tradition
that repeatedly has proved inadequate.

Distrust of this blatant appeal to traditional chivalry leaves
the reader confident that Percival faces a trap. The precise
nature of the trap, however, is elusive; no one is likely on a
first reading to develop any such complete interpretation as
the hermit later provides. What the reader does notice are
moments when the literal elements of the gentlewoman's account seem vague or implausible—especially, perhaps, the
turning point of her story: "Also I sayde a worde that plesed
hym nat, and than he wolde nat suffir me to be no lenger in his
company" (917.15–17). When the hermit at length provides us
with a comprehensive interpretation, this and several other
puzzles are resolved:

> "A, good knyght," seyde he, "thou art a foole, for that jantill-
> woman was the mayster fyende of helle, whych hath pousté
> over all other devyllis."
> Than he tolde sir Percivale how oure Lord Jesu Cryste bete
> hym oute of hevyn of hys synne, whycch was the moste
> bryghtist angell of hevyn, and therefore he loste hys
> heritaige. (920.3–5, 7–10)

Having read this explanation, we are compelled to recall—or

even turn back to—the gentlewoman's speech; and now, a number of features—some of which we may scarcely have noticed at the time—fall into place. Few readers, I imagine, are suspicious initially of the language of chivalric fealty employed by the gentlewoman. Now, however, "I have benomme hym som of hys men and made hem to become my men" emerges as a grim euphemism for damnation, and our passing curiosity as to the identity of "the grettist man of the worlde" gives way to embarrassment at our failure to realize just who was meant. In retrospect, the clearest clue of all is the gentlewoman's statement: "he *mayde* me so fayre and so clere" (917.13; italics mine). How could we have missed so obvious a reference to the Creator? When Percival's hermit concludes, "Now, sir Percival, beware and take this for an insample" (920.12), his words seem in part addressed to the reader. Indeed, Percival's ordeal is largely over at this point; but the reader must go on to later portions of the tale, hoping to approach them more intelligently after the experience of following Percival's quest.

In the testing of the second Grail knight, Bors, the reader is challenged by many of the same elements that appear in Percival's adventure and in other, earlier portions of the tale. Here, though, the demands on the reader are intensified. The plot is far more complex, and deliberate echoes—such as the appearance of another disinherited gentlewoman—frequently are misleading. Most difficult of all for the reader is Bors' dream of the black and white birds. Malory has been at some pains since the beginning of the Percival section to establish a clear pattern of black-white symbolism. Percival's aunt describes the Grail knights as "three whyght bullis" (906.32).[8] The horse ridden by the nameless knight who kills Percival's mount is "blacker than ony bere" (910.5), and the fiendish horse Percival escapes from is "inly black" (911.31). The ship in which the good man arrives is "coverde within and without with whyght samyte" (914.22–23); the ship carrying the gentlewoman is "coverde wyth sylke more blacker than ony bere" (915.34–35). The pattern continues through the material intervening between Percival's adventures and those of Bors, surfacing in Lancelot's encounter with the black and white knights and again in Gawain's dream of the black and white bulls.[9] In every case, white is associated with figures either promoting or enjoying success in the Grail world, black with figures opposed to such success or denied it. Indeed, in his interpretation of Gawain's dream, Nacien the hermit enunciates part of this pattern as if it were a principle: "And by the bullys ys undirstonde the felyshyp of the Rounde Table whych for their synne and their wyckednesse bene blacke; blackenes ys as much to sey withoute good vertues or workes" (946.17–20). It is in these terms, then, that we are obliged to read Bors' dream:

> And anone as he was alsepe hym befelle a vision: that there cam two birdis, that one whyght as a swanne and that other was merveylous blacke; but he was nat so grete as was that other, but in the lyknes of a raven. That the whyght birde cam to hym and seyde,
> "And thou woldist gyff me mete and serve me, I sholde gyff the all the ryches of the worlde, and I shall make the as fayre and as whyght as I am."
> So the whyght birde departed. And than cam the blacke birde to hym and seyde,
> "And thou serve me to-morow and have me in no dispite, thoughe I be blacke. For wyte thou well that more avaylith myne blacknesse than the odirs whyghtnesse."
> (957.35–958.11)

Of all the traps set for the reader in the sixth tale, this one appears, in retrospect, the most deliberately planned. The reference to blackness in the raven's speech must recall Nacien's words, and thus consolidates our reaction to the dream's symbolism. When we learn later how mistaken we were, it is crucial for the full effect of the experience that we recall the significant hints we overlooked, the clearest of which is the rival swan's promise to give Bors "all the ryches of the worlde"—a distinctly false note in the Grail quest.

The reader's dilemma is dramatized in the text itself, where, for the first time, a false interpretation of events is offered within the tale. In the Percival section, the gentlewoman opens her campaign by denouncing the old man in the ship as "an inchaunter and a multiplier of wordis" (917.1–2); here, though, we are given a full-scale exercise in interpretation designed to subvert the allegory of Bors' dream. The interpretation put forward is hardly satisfactory, however; its resemblance to earlier passages is superficial and short-lived:

> . . . The whyght fowle betokenyth a jantillwoman fayre and ryche whych loved the paramours and hath loved the longe. And if thou warne hir love she shall dy anone—if thou have no pite on her.   (963.28–31)

The orthodox "betokenyth" is quickly undercut by the courtly terms *paramours* and *pite,* and the rest of the passage deteriorates into obscure syntax and implausible matter.[10] It fails completely to mention the black bird, and its clearly perverse values—promoting kinship and downplaying chastity and virginity—leave us unconvinced.

Our dissatisfaction with this interpretation brings us no closer to a better one, and our continuing uncertainties about this and other elements of Bors' quest must wait until near the end of the section, when the abbot provides a comprehensive reading of all Bors' adventures, including the dream of the two birds:

> And by the blak birde myght ye understande Holy Chirche whych seyth, "I am blacke," but he ys fayre. And by the whyght birde may be undirstonde the fynde, and I shall telle you how the swan ys whyght wighoutefurth and blacke within: hit ys iposcresye, which ys withoute yalew or pale, and semyth withouteforth the servauntis of Jesu Cryste, but they be withinfurthe so horrible of fylth and synne, and begyle the worlde so evyll.   (967.23–31)

Again, this is somewhat humiliating. Early in the tale, we learned not to rely on previous portions of Malory's work for help in understanding the Grail world. Now our faithful reliance on the sixth tale's sytem of black-white symbolism is itself undercut. The key to the symbolism of Bors' dream is not Malorian but Scriptural: the raven's "though I be blacke" (958.10) should have referred us to *The Song of Songs'* "Nigra sum sed formosa" (1.4), while the whiteness of the admittedly suspect swan should have recalled the whited sepulchers of Matthew 23:27.

Although the sixth tale continues to challenge our skill as readers and, as here, to defy easy comprehension, we can take satisfaction in the progress we have made. Our earlier chagrin at failing to anticipate Melyas' fate may seem matched by our present chagrin at failing to recognize the raven of Bors' dream; but, in fact, our reaction to the two episodes could hardly have differed more. In the case of Melyas, our blunder resulted from thoughtless confidence in traditional patterns, complacent enough to override Galahad's explicit warning. By the time we get to Bors' dream, our entire attitude has altered. Far from being overconfident, we tend to feel help-less, caught within a network of seemingly inconsistent echoes, references, and suggestions. In the first instance, we were unobservant and unthinking; in the second, we are if anything hyperobservant, eager to fit all the phenomena into an appropriate pattern but frustrated in our attempt. When we hear the explanation of the abbot, we are in the classic position of the reader of whodunits, watching unfounded sus-picions evaporate and each piece of the pattern fall neatly into place.

As the reader proceeds to Malory's seventh and eighth tales, failure to interpret Bors' dream correctly is not particularly important; what *is* important is our chagrin at failing to do so. We emerge from the sixth tale as active, questioning, con-cerned readers, and we bring new skills and attitudes to the material that now follows. Indeed, it is in the mind of the active reader Malory has trained that his final tales achieve their success. Much of this success derives from the reader's sympathy with Lancelot, who emerges as a complex figure torn between conflicting demands—a far more vivid and so-phisticated portrait than is offered of him in the pre-Grail material. The reader's sympathy stems less from memories of his chivalric achievements in the third and fifth tales than from sharing—quite literally—his spiritual struggles in the Grail world. There, like the reader, and more dramatically than any other character, Lancelot moves from the expected patterns of chivalric narrative—such as the knighting of Galahad, who initially appears as a traditional *bel inconnu*—through radical disruptions of those patterns, especially his overthrow by Galahad and the later loss of his horse and armor. Like us, Lancelot confronts the allegorical nature of the Grail world, most disturbingly in the tournament of the black and white knights. It is not so much in the events of Lancelot's quest that Lancelot and the reader are linked as it is in his attitude toward the whole undertaking.

Lancelot is earnest but only intermittently successful in his attempts to meet the challenges and avoid the pitfalls of the Grail world. His frequent setbacks have little effect on the effort he brings to the quest, and that effort largely mirrors our own. Percival and Bors survive all the traps laid for them, but neither tries to understand the significance of events before their meaning is formally expounded. Only Lancelot struggles (as does the reader) to understand events as they occur. Early in his quest he is denied admission to a chapel, lies helpless during a miracle of the Grail, has his horse and armor taken, and is driven off by a mysterious voice. Although the words of the voice are later explicated in detail, Lancelot has by then drawn the moral. "For tho wordis wente to hys herte," Malory writes, "tylle that he knew wherefore he was called so" (895.32–33). He has Lancelot describe at length his own spiritual condition in the sort of speech otherwise reserved for hermits and priests.[11]

> My synne and my wyckednes hath brought me unto grete dishonoure! For whan I sought worldly adventures for worldely desyres I ever encheved them and had the bettir in every place, and never was I discomfite in no quarell, wer hit ryght were hit wronge. And now I take uppon me the adventures to seke of holy thynges, now I se and undirstonde that myne olde synne hyndryth me and shamyth me, that I had no power to stirre

nother speke whan the holy bloode appered before me.
(896.1–9)

In this effort to "se and undirstonde," Lancelot and the reader
are united.

If our fundamental sympathy for Lancelot in the final tales
derives largely from the sense of shared enterprise in the
Grail quest, it is part of the complexity of those tales that the
fruits of the enterprise—a heightened sensitivity to deceitful
language and a new sense of God's unseen workings—should
on several occasions shake our sympathy for Malory's hero.
Nowhere in the final tales is this effect clearer than in Lancelot's great speech on returning Guenevere to Arthur
(1197.4–27). The reader's reaction to Lancelot's eloquence on
the grandly staged occasion is complex, but all the elements
of that reaction are traceable to the experience of the sixth
tale. Whereas our sympathy for Lancelot persists to some degree throughout the speech, it is soon mingled with suspicion,
then open dismay. The sixth tale teaches us to be suspicious of
what is omitted from important speeches—the unspecified
"worde" of Percival's damsel, the silence concerning the raven
in the false interpretaion of Bors' dream. We quickly sense
something missing when Lancelot protests: "And sytthyn hyt
pleased you at many tymys that I shulde feyght for [the
queen], therefore mesemyth, my good lorde, I had more cause
to rescow her from the fyer whan she sholde have ben brente
for my sake" (1197.16–19). The crucial difference between the
earlier instances Lancelot refers to and his latest rescue of
Guenivere is the nature of the current charges against her,
which he alludes to but disguises with his "brent for my
sake."

Just as we recognize the source of our hesitation, Lancelot
appears to answer it: "For they that tolde you tho talys were
lyars, and so hit felle uppon them: for by lyklyhode, had nat
the myght of God bene with me, I might never have endured
with fourtene knyghtes, and they armed and afore purposed,
and I unarmed and nat purposed" (1197.20–24). Although it

forestalls momentarily our first objection, this claim raises a far more serious one. We are compelled to recognize in these lines a fraudulent appeal to the idea lying behind judicial duels: victory is a God-given sign of innocence. Under the present circumstances, Lancelot's invocation of this belief strains our sympathy to the limit, because the idea he exploits here for rhetorical advantage is one in which we as readers have a real stake.[12] Central to our experience of the sixth tale is the sense of God's presence as the designer of the allegorical patterns of the Grail world. That sense is the tale's most important legacy as well. Although no later episodes emerge as full-fledged allegories, we are repeatedly urged through the final tales to consider the possibility of divine intervention and thus to weigh the actions of characters in the seventh and eighth tales directly against the standards of the Grail world. In the present instance, the sense of God's presence thoroughly undercuts Lancelot's authority and reveals to us (though not to the weeping onlookers—another situation familiar from the sixth tale) how far he has come from "the promyse and the perfeccion that he made in the queste" (1045.11–12). The same sense served a similar purpose earlier, giving substance and impact to what otherwise would have been empty bluster: Melyagaunt's warning to Lancelot that "yet shulde ye be avysed to do batayle in a wronge quarell, for God woll have a stroke in every batayle" (1133.27–28). God strikes no open blow for Melyagaunt, but the comment, reinforced by our recollections from the Grail quest, echoes through all Lancelot's subsequent invitations to trial by combat. Melyagaunt has reminded us of how the Grail world operated, and he has made Lancelot, despite his prowess, appear vulnerable.

This sense of the unseen workings of God is most important in a reading of Malory's great, original contribution to "The Healing of Sir Urry," the story of the Round Table's decline. Here, Lancelot's inexplicable tears at what appears to all observers a triumph make sense in terms of the sixth tale. In Urry's miraculous cure, recalling the various healings and exorcisms of the Grail quest, we encounter evidence that God

106

still intervenes in human affairs and that the Grail world has not been left entirely behind. No hermit arrives to expound the allegory, and we are not drawn to see the episode in those terms. Its purpose, however, is clearly instructive; Lancelot's tears prompt us, recalling our active role in the sixth tale, to consider the meaning of this strange event. For Lancelot, as for us (we are once again linked), the entire experience is a reminder of the Grail quest. In particular, Urry's recovery is vivid evidence of God's benevolence, thus is the most direct reminder possible of Lancelot's backsliding. He weeps at this bitter reproach, "as he had bene a chylde that had been beatyn" (1152.35–36).[13] Beyond its immediate significance, for the reader, the key to the episode is the revival halfway through the final tales of the reader's own Grail-world experience, a renewed sensitivity to the unseen. This sensitivity allows the reader to judge with discrimination the deceitful elements of Lancelot's speech during the reconciliation scene while allowing the reader to reenter easily the world of miracles, when Lancelot earns the reward for his renewed repentance and is seen by the bishop at the gates of heaven: "And I sawe the angellys heve up syr Launcelot unto heven, and the yates of heven opened ayenst hym" (1258.7–10).

As important as "The Tale of the Sankgreall" may be thematically for the *Morte Darthur* as a whole, it is equally important as an educational experience for the reader. It would be easy to enumerate multiple examples of how readers' training during the sixth tale is brought to bear on later material. We have been taught, in following the Grail quest, to read with a new wariness, a heightened attention to detail, a sharper ear for nuance. Most important, we have been trained to look behind events for their true significance, to be aware of the hidden manipulations of their architect. If this educational function is part of what makes the sixth tale important, it is much of what makes it enjoyable as well. When Vida Scudder writes that the account of the Grail quest "satisfies a restlessness which neither delight in arms nor love of woman nor loyalty to mortal king has been able to assuage,"[14] I wonder if the restlessness may not have been her own. After the extended pageant of "The Tale of Tristram," the Grail quest offers Malory's reader a field for new activity and a share in the testing process by which the knights are proved. Some readers will find this an exciting experience; no reader going on to the last stages of Malory's history will proceed unchanged.

Prophecy and Nostalgia: Arthurian Symbolism at the Close of the English Middle Ages

CAROLINE D. ECKHARDT

English society at the close of the Middle Ages was characterized by both great change and great continuity. It was characterized, too, by an intense interest in Arthuriana, both political and literary. Let us take the short span of years, 1480–86, as an example. These years include the end of the reign of Edward IV, the brief reign of Richard III, and the beginning of the reign of Henry VII. In 1480, William Caxton printed a version of the *Brut* chronicle, in which Arthur is the central heroic figure. About 1480, Arthur Plantagenet, illegitimate son of Edward IV, was born. In 1482, Caxton printed another edition of the *Brut*, and in 1483 and 1485, two further editions of the work appeared from presses other than Caxton's. In July 1485, Caxton printed Malory's *Morte Darthur*. In August 1485, Henry VII took the throne, claiming to fulfill the prophecies of Merlin. In September 1486, Henry's heir, a son, was born and was named Arthur.

Several aspects of the late medieval Arthurian enthusiasm in England have been studied in detail; others are discussed below.[1] My intention here is to demonstrate that different uses of the Arthurian legend at this time—specifically, in the fourteenth and fifteenth centuries—illustrate two different concepts of historical change. One such concept emphasizes the typological nature of historical events. In this perspective,

109

what has happened in the past is likely to occur again in the present or the future, though in a form somewhat changed to accord with new circumstances. The other concept emphasizes, in contrast, the inevitable movement of history toward its apocalyptic conclusion. In this perspective, what is past remains finished and will not come again. These two concepts correlate with two different attitudes toward the meaning of King Arthur as a symbol and his (supposed) historical era as an ideal. The first concept, which accepts—in fact, expects—the return of Arthur, lends itself to prophecy and political manipulation. The second concept, which assumes the determinate completion of the Arthurian story in its original temporal setting, lends itself instead to literary nostalgia. Arthur is a double figure, representing, on the one hand, the potential for historical recurrence, and, on the other, the foreclosure of that same possibility.

Why was it Arthur in particular who was given this double role? Obviously, a claim that he alone had the potential for interpretation within both historical perspectives would be unsound. Social history is full of surprises, and medieval thought was notoriously eclectic and likely to merge, substitute, and redefine its heroes. The Vergil we know as the classical poet was transformed, in the medieval imagination, into Vergil the magician; the goddess Diana became identified with the Virgin Mary. These are but two examples of the metamorphic energy that created and re-created the legends of the times. In all probability, no trait or quality attributed to a specific hero was attributed, or "had" to be attributed, *uniquely* to that hero. Nevertheless, in the English tradition in this period, it is difficult to identify another legendary figure who filled the same complex functions as Arthur.

For example, there seems to have been relatively less political and literary exploitation of the legend of Brutus. His tale, too, offered an inherent theme of rebirth and renewal—out of the ashes of Troy there came a new civilization, with Brutus as its link to Britain—and might therefore have been suitable for latter-day popular development. Perhaps Brutus was not so easy to present as a symbol to the general public, because

110

the centuries intervening since his story was told in Geoffrey of Monmouth's *Historia Regum Britanniae* (c. 1135) had failed to establish an active literary tradition for him. He had remained a fact in the legendary history, if one might use that paradoxical description; but he had not become evocative. He was not a "character." He had no widely known personality or generally celebrated set of individual experiences, emotional and private as well as public, as Arthur did. Thanks to the poets, everyone knew about Arthur's wife Guenevere, but there had been no comparable poetic recountings of Brutus' relations with *his* wife, whose name, according to Geoffrey, was Innogen. And the manner of Brutus' death, unlike Arthur's, was not invitingly obscure. It is, of course, true that Brutus and other early kings such as Cadwalader sometimes were mentioned in genealogical arguments and similar contexts. Edward IV, for instance, was linked to both of those names, being presented as true heir to the line of Cadwalader and as restorer of the name of Britain (the name of Brutus) to the island.[2] There was, however, no widespread enthusiasm about such figures as these. The absence of a full poetic and narrative tradition about them in the earlier medieval centuries, and therefore their less central place in the public imagination, would have made them less immediately functional as public symbols in the period we are discussing here.

Merlin might have been another possibility, for there was certainly an active and long-continuing popular tradition associated with him. In fact, pamphlets that brought Merlin's prophecies up-to-date were still being produced into the Renaissance and beyond. Still, the figure of Merlin tended not to represent an entire way of life, a dream of civilization, as did the figure of Arthur. Perhaps this is because in the dominant forms of his legend, Merlin was not a king. Although, in early Celtic poems, he was depicted as both king and warrior, those functions tended to drop away once he became absorbed into the Arthurian orbit. His characterization was at once diminished and enhanced: diminished, for he served the king rather than being the king; enhanced, for in his specialized roles as prophet, magician, and prankster, he acquired a distinc-

111

tive reputation that prevented him from being blended inconspicuously into the general background of secondary or helping figures. Correspondingly, Lancelot and Gawain could distinctively represent courtesy, or Galahad piety. Only Arthur—the king himself, and a king to whom the poetic tradition had already accorded special status from the twelfth century onward—seems to have been able to carry the full weight of both of the major historical perspectives examined here.

In late medieval England the name *Arthur* itself was politically significant. The best-known and -documented instance is that of Henry VII's heir, who, so named, was celebrated in pageant and poetry as the fulfillment of Arthurian prophecy, as the ancient hero returned, as "Arthur the second."[3] During the prince's short lifetime, the Arthurian connection was reinforced again and again. When he died at the age of fifteen and his younger brother became King Henry VIII, the Arthurian expectation, rather than being abandoned, was simply—and, to us, somewhat illogically—transferred: the antiquary Leland addressed the young Henry as Arthur revived and the Tudor use of Arthurian imagery continued unabated.[4] Henry VIII had King Arthur's supposed Round Table redecorated with new Tudor symbolism; Elizabeth, like her grandfather Henry VII, used a coat of arms displaying the legendary history of Britain, with Arthur an evident part of the design.[5] Other examples abound.

In naming his heir Arthur, Henry VII was building upon, rather than newly establishing, a pattern. A king who had reigned shortly before him, as well as a near-king earlier in the century, also had a son named Arthur, though neither of them came quite so near the throne.

The Yorkist king Edward IV, who, like Henry VII, achieved the throne by conquest, had a son known as Arthur Plantagenet, born in about 1480. Though illegitimate, he was acknowledged.[6] According to some accounts, his mother was one Elizabeth Lucie. It is not known why her child was given the name Arthur; in fact, little is known about her altogether and there remains some doubt as to whether Elizabeth Lucie, or another Elizabeth, or even the ill-famed Jane Shore, was the mother of Edward's son. The king's two legitimate sons, born in 1470 and 1472, bore famous names of the house of York: Edward, the name given to the elder, was the name of the king himself; Richard, the name given to the younger, was the name of Edward IV's father (who had claimed the throne but died before achieving it), and also the name of Edward's younger brother. These were significantly evocative names, and one might assume that the new child's name, despite his illegitimacy, was also chosen for its evocative value. As events turned out, Arthur Plantagenet was the only son known to have survived Edward IV by more than a few months, since the king's legitimate sons, "the princes in the tower," apparently were murdered shortly after Edward's own death.

After the change in dynasty, Arthur Plantagenet evidently was taken into the household of the new king Henry VII; for in 1509 he attended Henry's funeral as "Master Arthur," squire of the king's bodyguard. It might seem odd that Henry VII would have retained, as a personal attendant, this young man who was the last surviving son of Edward of York as well as the nephew of Edward's brother Richard III, the king Henry had ousted from the throne. Henry, however, had married Arthur Plantagenet's half-sister, Elizabeth of York, and wished to present himself as unifying the division between York and Lancaster; perhaps it was for these reasons that he accepted (or commanded) Arthur's service. Under Henry VIII Arthur had a reasonably successful though undistinguished career—serving in various military capacities, accompanying Henry to the Field of the Cloth of Gold, becoming (through a fortunate marriage) Viscount Lisle, and being elected Knight of the Garter. Toward the end of his life he was briefly arrested on suspicion of treason. Restored to favor, Arthur died in 1542.

Earlier in the century, Humphrey Duke of Gloucester, son of Henry IV and brother of Henry V, also had a bastard son named Arthur.[7] Less is known about this person, who was called Arthur or Arteys de Cursy. His birthdate is uncertain;

but, since he was adult near the middle of the century, he probably was born no later than 1425–30. After 1435, Duke Humphrey was next in line of succession and presumably would have become king had Henry VI died without issue. Arthur was Humphrey's only son. At the time of the duke's dramatic fall from favor and his sudden death in 1447, several members of his household were accused of having plotted to kill Henry VI so that Humphrey would in fact have succeeded to the throne. Arthur and four others were condemned to death, being pardoned at the very last moment by the king's intervention: they had already been hanged, and, still living, cut down for disembowelment when the royal pardon arrived.[8] Apparently what became of them afterwards is unknown.

Whether Arthur de Cursy ever intended to unseat Henry VI is doubtful; yet, even if the charge against him were a complete fabrication, it implies that he was regarded as dangerous. Though illegitimate, he was acknowledged to be the duke's son, and the legendary King Arthur had also been of dubious birth. An illegitimate Arthur was not necessarily an insignificant one. In addition, the contemporary power of the Beaufort family, legitimated after the fact, perhaps tended to make legitimacy seem a somewhat adjustable concept.[9] Therefore, Humphrey's enemies may have thought it politically advisable to get Arthur out of the picture.

There were other Arthurs, though none so near the throne. Duke Humphrey had a French stepbrother Arthur, who was Constable of France, styled himself Earl of Richmond, and became Duke of Brittany near the end of his life.[10] James V of Scotland had a son named Arthur, despite the hostility of some of the Scottish chroniclers toward Arthur and their partisanship for Mordred.[11] Nevertheless, the name is relatively rare in this period. It seems to have been associated primarily with royalty and near-royalty and "did not come into general use," according to the *Complete Peerage*, "until modern times."[12] It seems likely that, to the public mind, any royal offspring with this name would have been associated with King Arthur.

114

As important as the name of Arthur are the prophecies of Merlin. In Geoffrey of Monmouth's *Historia Regum Britanniae,* Merlin the prophet is placed not in King Arthur's reign but in the preceding one.[13] Nevertheless, his prophecies mention Arthur (under the metaphoric guise of the "Boar of Cornwall"). Later versions of the British history, including the *Brut* chronicle, show Merlin as prophesying to Arthur himself. Therefore, Merlin's prophecies form part of the Arthurian legend in the broad sense, whether Arthur is specifically mentioned or not. The most politically influential of these prophecies concerned the restoration of a Celtic dynasty, which was to occur at an indefinite time when the Saxon and Norman eras would have ended. In Geoffrey's *Historia,* Merlin does not predict that King Arthur himself will return, only that a descendant of the last Celtic ruler, Cadwalader, will come to power.[14] However, since Arthur was said to have disappeared mortally wounded but not exactly to have died, a second or revived Arthur, as well as some later descendant of Cadwalader, was a ready candidate for (re)appearance as king. Henry IV, Edward IV, and Henry VII—the three late medieval kings to take the English throne by conquest—all made use of the Merlin prophecies to give authenticity to their claims.

In 1399, when Henry of Lancaster returned from exile to claim first his Lancastrian rights and then the throne, he and his party drew on several of the traditional prophecies. Otterbourne's Chronicle reports that Henry declared himself to be Merlin's "Boar of Commerce," who, it was predicted, would unify the divided populace. The French metrical history of Richard II explains that one of Henry's companions applied to Richard another Merlin prophecy, a prediction concerning a king who was to be removed (like that king, Richard was indeed to be removed). Adam of Usk, describing Henry's landing, records a third prophecy of Merlin that Henry's group evidently circulated. The association of the Merlin prophecies with Henry had begun even before Henry's birth: Froissart recounts a peculiar incident about a prophecy told at court in 1361 (Henry was born in 1366) which predicted that the heir of Lancaster would become king.[15] It is quite possible that this prophecy helped bring the Lancastrian dynastic ambitions to fruition, or was planted by them, or, in interlocking fashion, both.

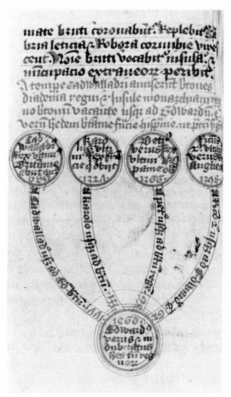

MS Bodley 623, folio 23v. Reproduced by permission of the Curators of the Bodleian Library, Oxford. The diagram illustrates the claim that Edward IV was true king of England because he was descended from Cadwalader. At the top of the folio occurs an excerpt from Merlin's prophecies. In the upper left circle appears the name Cadwalladrus; *this circle is joined to the lower circle, in which appears the name* Edwardus, *showing the continuity of the lineage. (Edward is also said to be true heir of Charlemagne and other kings identified in the remaining circles.)*

The effort to provide legitimacy for the claim of Edward IV, who took the throne from Henry's grandson, involved a different selection from Merlin's traditional prophecies, for Yorkist partisans asserted that in Edward IV lay the promised restoration of Celtic rule through the line of Cadwalader. Ed-

116

ward was explicitly presented in genealogical rolls as the descendant of Cadwalader and therefore the true king of Britain.[16] The same claim for Edward's descent occurs in such political miscellanies as MS Bodley 623 in the Bodleian Library, which includes a diagram associating Edward with a series of "good" or valid kings whose names are drawn from Merlin's prophecies and related lore; and associating Henry VI, whom Edward deposed, with a series of "bad," or invalid, kings.[17] Other Yorkist prophetic collections exist, suggesting a concerted effort to establish a connection between Edward's claim to the throne and the Arthurian prophecies. A political poem of 1471 explicitly compares Edward to Arthur himself:

> Of a more famous knyght I never rad
> Syn the tyme of Artors dayes.[18]

In this light it would certainly have been expedient—and, perhaps, virtually necessary—for Henry VII to prepare his own version of Arthurian propaganda when he too unseated the current ruler. In claiming descent from Cadwalader, he was merely appropriating the claim made earlier for Edward IV. Similarly, the red dragon on Henry's banner might have been chosen partly to challenge the Yorkist identification of Edward IV as the *rubeus draco* of Merlin's prophecy and Welsh tradition.[19] It would have been a reasonably natural outgrowth of this chosen Arthurian context to go further than his predecessors and use the name Arthur himself for the heir—which Henry, of course, did—in naming his first son. I would like to propose, though tentatively, that this further step might have been suggested to Henry in part by the existence of his wife's surviving half-brother Arthur Platagenet, perhaps even by the presence of Arthur Plantagenet in the new king's own household, if the then-six-year-old lad had joined the royal entourage by the time of Prince Arthur's birth (we do not know exactly when Arthur Plantagenet's attachment to the Tudor household began). If Edward's lineage had produced an Arthur, perhaps it was wise for Henry's to do so, too, and in the legitimate line. At any rate, Henry's emphatic exploitation of Arthurian associations can be seen as a continuation and a culmination of the political policies used by the two previous English kings who had taken the throne by conquest. The military triumphs attributed to the legendary King Arthur, and the fact that he too needed to establish the validity of his rule over the objections of his enemies, made him a particularly apt hero for a challenger of the throne to invoke; yet we should not forget that it was the entire traditional appeal of the Arthurian story that made effective its repeated use as political propaganda.

In general, the late medieval political uses of the Arthurian legend reflect an underlying concept of history as typology, or, to borrow R. W. Southern's term, history as prophecy.[20] This understanding of the course of events, which the new-made rulers repeatedly called upon, assumes the recurrence of human experiences and situations: events at one time virtually call forth or compel corresponding events at later times, in order to fulfill a necessary overarching pattern. The direction of historical sequence is not simply linear but touches back upon itself, echoes itself, conducts as it were a conversation with itself, an interaction in which people and episodes take part of their meaning from their earlier or later manifestations. A familiar example in religious history is the relationship between Eve and Mary. Mary is the new Eve, the counterpoint to Eve, both Eve's fulfillment and Eve's correction or denial. It is Eve's action of sin that makes Mary's action of redemption historically necessary. The two women are linked, as type and antitype, in a profound way that at once spans and negates the historical distance between them. The biblical prophets were understood as identifying such links between Old Testament and New Testament times. More broadly, prophecy as a phenomenon both sacred and secular was regarded as a primary means of grasping the connections between past, present, and future events.

In such a context, the Arthurian names and associations represent not primarily the past-ness of the past but, instead, its potential for re-creation in the present and the future. Merlin had foretold the restoration of Celtic rule and the return of a descendant of Cadwalader; to suggest that an Arthur would reign again would have reinforced the linkages between *then* and *now*, as, indeed, many lesser symbolic reenactments of the past, such as the use of the dragon banner, served to do. Arthur's role in this function did not emphasize his human uniqueness. On the contrary, to the extent that he participated in the general expectation of historical typology, with its assumed relationship of (pre)figuration and fulfillment, Arthur would have ceased to be a wholly individual "historical" personality and approached in stature those other somewhat larger-than-life personalities simultaneously located within history and beyond it. Like the biblical Jonah, whose three days spent in the belly of the whale were thought to foreshadow Jesus' three days' delay between the crucifixion and the resurrection, within the context of prophetic history Arthur became one of the great series of people whose stories would remain incomplete until later events provided, as one medieval commentator put it, their "declaracion" (clarification, fulfillment).[21]

This is a radically optimistic view of history, since it implies that the glories of the earlier Arthurian age can be recovered, or perhaps even surpassed, as Mary surpassed Eve or Jesus surpassed Jonah. This can, at the same time, be a radically pessimistic view of history, however, for it accepts the possibility that earlier disasters can be repeated in present time. Thus it is an inherently unstable and manipulable attitude toward historical development. Certainly, several late medieval English kings manipulated it in their favor. The esoteric nature of prophecy, secular as well as biblical, entails a need for expert interpretation, which each political party seems to have been willing to supply.

Let us turn from political events to the literary context. The last century and a half of the English Middle Ages saw a sustained enthusiasm for Arthurian poetry and prose, as well as Arthurian prophecy and royal symbolism. Twenty-three of the approximately thirty extant English Arthurian romances belong to the second half of the fourteenth century or later. *Sir Gawain and the Green Knight*, finest of the English verse romances, dates from the end of the fourteenth century; two other Arthurian masterpieces, the *Alliterative Morte Arthure* and Malory's *Morte Darthur,* span much of the fifteenth century between them.[22] Perhaps even more indicative of the general popularity of the Arthurian legend are the frequent brief references to Arthur in non-Arthurian literary works of many kinds. It is not necessary to tell his story, only to invoke his name or that of the Round Table. This wealth of Arthurian literature and reference ranges in tone from the high seriousness of epic to the low comedy of farce. Correspondingly, it is characterized by great variation in its depictions of the king.

A valuable complement to the political Arthuriana is provided by one aspect of the literary material—that aspect which shares the assumption that Arthur is an ideal figure but which reflects a somewhat different understanding of the nature of historical change. Many of the literary references to King Arthur convey primarily a sense of nostalgia for a lost, ideal world that will not return. They situate Arthur in a medieval version of a Golden Age, an imagined time when all the virtues of chivalry (but none of its vices) were practiced, when there was no impediment to the realization of the highest desires, and when Britain was the most powerful country among her sister nations.

The poem *Reson and Sensuallyté* (c. 1410) complains against the corruption of the present age and describes the Arthurian ideal by contrast:

> . . . trouthe and feyth ben al agoo.
> Yt was not wont for to be soo
> In tyme of the kyng Arthour,
> The noble, worthy conquerour,
> Whom honour lyst so magnyfye,
> For of fredam and curtesye,
> Of bounté, and of largesse,
> Of manhode, and of high prowesse,
> To remembre alle thinges,
> He passyde al other kynges.

120

. . . . .

> For love was tho so pure and fre,
> Grounded on al honeste
> Without engyn of fals werkyng,
> Or any spot of evel menyng,
> Which gaf to knyghtes hardynesse,
> And amended her noblesse,
> And made hem to be vertuous.[23]

Similarly, Arthur's conventional position as one of the Nine Worthies brought him into association with the great heroic figures of the past. In 1455, for example, Queen Margaret was entertained by a Nine Worthies pageant in which the actor impersonating Arthur addressed her thus:

> I Arthur kynge crownyd & conquerour
> That yn this land reyned right rially
> With dedes of armes I slowe the Emperour
> The tribute of this ryche reme I made downe to ly
> Ihit unto you lady obey I mekely
> as youre sure servande plesur to your highnesse
> for the most pleasaunt princes moral that es.[24]

In this vein, too, sometimes a brief reference suffices. In the poem *The Floure and the Leafe*, of about 1450–75, Arthur and the other Worthies represent a generalized ideal of noble behavior: "Tho nine crowned by very exemplaire / Of all honour longing to chivalry."[25]

The presentation of Arthur's reign as a distant, ideal Golden Age reflects a pervasive concept of history as a series of declining eras, a downward descent from an original heroic condition that cannot now be revived, for human nature has inherently deteriorated and the world itself has grown old.[26] Thus, Sir Thomas Malory laments that in his modern times people were no longer capable of faithful and patient love, as they were in Arthur's days:

> . . . nowadayes men can nat love sevennyght but they muste

121

have all their desyres. That love may nat endure by reson, for where they bethe sone accorded and hasty, heete sone keelyth. And ryght so fareth the love nowadayes, sone hote sone colde. Thys ys no stabylyté. But the olde love was nat so. For men and women coude love togydirs seven yerys, and no lycoures lustis was betwyxte them, and than was love trouthe and faythefulness. And so in lyke wyse was used such love in kynge Arthurs dayes.[27]

Such an attitude toward historical change clearly owes a great deal to ancient concepts of the Five Ages of the World, symbolized by the sequence of gold, silver, copper, iron, and clay as reflected in Dante's *Inferno*, canto xiv; or in other versions, by a similar series of increasingly weaker and more corruptible substances. Medieval elaborations on the older scheme included the theories of Joachim of Fiore, who postulated a number of stages, or "states," that would take place in secular history before the end of the world; and various millenarian or chiliastic movements, which anticipated the end point of historical time at some specified date (though Robert Lerner and other scholars use such terms as *chiliasm* and *millenarianism* more broadly, to refer to the viewpoint that there will be a temporary improvement in earthly conditions before the Last Judgment arrives).[28] The common ingredient in these philosophies of history is the assumption of the decline of the world, visible in an attendant diminution of human strength and virtue, with or without remissions before the closure of human time.

Christianity introduced a potential reversal of this general pattern. The Incarnation permits individuals to erase, as it were, the ill effects of the Fall and return to a state of inherent personal goodness. Nevertheless, Eden itself cannot truly be regained in this world. Redemption is ultimately personal, not universal, and the end point of history is the Apocalypse. In May McKisack's terms, "the medieval view of this world was, on the whole, pessimistic"; medieval rulers may have thought of themselves "as men living at the end of an age—of the great age of Greece and Rome, of Brutus and Arthur,

whose unworthy inheritors they were—or, under the shadow
of an apocalypse that must bring the temporal order to an
end."[29] A (non-Arthurian) macaronic poem of the late fourteenth century openly states the decline-and-fall mentality:

> Englond sum tyme was
>   regnorum gemma vocata;
> Of manhod the flowre
>   ibi quondam floruit omnis;
> Now gon ys that honowr,
>   traduntur talia somnis.[30]

Within this fundamental assumption of a downward movement, redeemable in individual but not collective terms, the
Christian tradition involves a further complication: from the
very beginning, the Golden Age was impure; for the serpent,
too, lived in the Garden. Malory, as one of the more profound
Arthurian writers, depicts the Arthurian realm as harboring
(like Eden) the source of its own downfall. To Malory, this original flaw, which he saw as also afflicting his own era, was the
human tendency toward instability:

> . . . by [Arthur] they were all upholdyn, and yet myght nat thes
> Englyshemen holde them contente with him. . . . Alas! thys ys
> a greate defaughte of us Englysshemen, for there may no
> thynge us please no terme. . . . And the moste party of all
> Inglonde hylde wyth sir Mordred, for the people were so new-
> fangill.[31]

With or without the complicating ingredient of vulnerability or evil within the Golden Age, this aspect of the late
medieval Arthurian tradition is primarily one of nostalgia
and distance. The Arthurian world represents a glorious British past radically different from the present corrupt world
that cannot be expected to return. Its rhetorical value is primarily one of contrast, as in the modern cliché "the good old
days." Chaucer's Wife of Bath, in fact, uses nearly that phrase
(c. 1390):

123

In th'olde dayes of the Kyng Arthour,
Of which that Britons speken greet honour,
Al was this land fulfilled of fayerye.
. . . . .
I speke of manye hundred yeres ago.
But now kan no man se none elves mo.[32]

The main components of the Arthurian Golden Age are, first, the predominance of Britian over the other nations, with Arthur depicted as an international conqueror in a way modern political conditions would not permit; and, second, the triumph of the arts of civilization, with Arthur's kingdom shown as adventurous yet decorous, graced with music and feasting and physical comeliness, open to magic and marvels and the jolly dancing of the elves, open even to tragedy in an appropriately formal and moral sense: a lost dreamworld of power, beauty, and noble relationships.

Both the prophetic and the nostalgic concepts of history are susceptible to optimistic and pessimistic interpretations. As has been mentioned, prophecy permits the return of evil as well as of good, and the theory of the declining ages permits the idea of a temporary remission or establishment of an improved society. Nevertheless, it would not be inaccurate to say that in an Arthurian context, the prophetic viewpoint was primarily optimistic, the nostalgic viewpoint pessimistic, insofar as expectations for present and near-future events were concerned. In a complex fashion, the two concepts of historical change could also be combined, producing an image of history as a series of stages proceeding inexorably toward the Apocalypse but punctuated by recurrences of the past and by things foreseen. Such a combination of perspectives is evident, for example, when Caxton remarks that the "ensamples of thynges passyd" can show his readers and listeners "what thynge is to be desyred" in the conduct of modern life: to Caxton, who regarded the historical and prophetic aspects of the Arthurian legend with some skepticism, the ideal things of the past could not be expected to come again; yet their depiction nevertheless could serve as a guide to our present desire.[33]

Caxton thus achieves a kind of synthesis, but in Arthurian terms, prophetic and nostalgic perspectives are sometimes uneasy companions, since the prophetic or typological expectation—but not the nostalgic appreciation—invites a strongly nationalistic linkage of the legend to current events. The Arthur who nostalgically represents a past Golden Age is a widespread and broadly shared ideal, as is shown by his presence in the international group of the Nine Worthies and by the many allusions to him in continental literature and the arts. The Arthur who might return, however, is an ideal specific to the British Isles, since, outside Britain (or perhaps Brittany also), a reappearance of Arthur the conqueror of the European nations would hardly be a popular event. As the Renaissance chronicler wrote of the name of Prince Arthur, Henry VII's son, "Englishmen nomore reioysed [at the choice of name] than outwarde nacions aħd foreyne prynces trymbled and quaked, so muche was that name to all nacions terrible and formidable."[34] Obviously, Hall exaggerates; but the claim that Arthur would return (or had done so) certainly reinforced other partisan and nationalistic trends in late medieval England.

In this period, a reference to Arthur—whether as the Golden Age hero who will not return, or as the conqueror who will—inevitably carries historical implications. The prophetic and nostalgic concepts are simultaneous, not sequential, reflections of the legend; despite the paradox of their contrast, they coexist. Their twin presence at the close of the Middle Ages, or near the conventional dividing line between the Middle Ages and the Renaissance, should caution us against perceiving the late medieval era as a time of almost unrelieved pessimism while assuming that it was the Renaissance, in a rebirth of hope, that looked affirmatively to the future.[35] The varied treatments of Arthur indicate that *context* is the great determiner of the connotations of the legend. Where the situation calls for the backward glance of nostalgia, Arthur's name will serve; where the situation calls for optimism and action, Arthur's name will serve there, too. The comprehensive appeal of his story, thoroughly developed in the poetic tradition, embracing public and private life, with religious and secular overtones, made him readily available to function as a double symbol of past and future: *rex quondam rexque futurus*, as Malory put it, in a splendid phrase whose Latinity suggests ancient historical records and whose semantic content points toward the modern era and beyond.

"An ancient idea of Chivalric greatness": The Arthurian Revival and Victorian History Painting

DEBRA N. MANCOFF

In the latter half of the eighteenth century, the quest for national identity was ubiquitous in Europe. It was an intensive, corporate soul-searching, closely allied to the Romantic movement and aimed at achieving a distinctive portrait of national character. Cultural interest turned inward, and the mythology and history of each country enjoyed unprecedented attention in literature and the arts. The new hero was the national hero, a symbol for those special qualities that distinguished a nation; new, national truths were sought with which people hoped to chart the course of their nation—past, present, and future. This new body of material was swiftly seized on by the pictorial arts. On the continent, especially in France and Germany, it was used to inform grand, allegorical cycles of history painting in fresco that were expressive of patriotic sentiment; in England, however, it was not until the Victorian era that national subjects found a grand vocabulary.

The Gothic Revival in England ignited strong archaeological interest in the literary and material remnants of the nation's medieval past. Artifacts of earlier glory were regarded as romantic curiosities until the early decades of the nineteenth century, when medievalism came to be used to inspire contemporary audiences rather than simply to entertain them. Chivalry, redefined as the inheritance of English manhood, became a dynamic force in the shaping of modern values. It was this new understanding of an ancient institution that allowed the painters of England to transform the archaeological reconstruction of the past into a direct and lucid allegory for the present. In light of this new understanding of chivalry, Arthurian subject matter, absent from the pictorial arts since the Middle Ages, reentered the British painter's repertoire. Between 1848 and 1864, William Dyce designed and executed a cycle of frescoes in the Queen's Robing Room in the new Palace at Westminster, which lauded the strengths of British character as they were personified in the heroes of Arthurian legend. The painter was not trying to narrate the saga of Arthur and his champions but striving to find a pictorial language for what he called "an ancient idea of Chivalric greatness."[1]

Meticulous reconstructive research into Britain's medieval past during the middle years of the eighteenth century heralded the commencement of the Gothic Revival. Attempts to assemble complete catalogues of the artifacts of the medieval era—including architecture, costumes, and weapons—preceded and in many ways made possible the more familiar escapist phase of the revival that produced such architectural fantasies as Strawberry Hill and gave birth to the first "Gothick" novel, Horace Walpole's *The Castle of Otranto*. Handsomely illustrated, these compendia served as a pictorial guide, not only documenting the appearance of "ancient" objects but giving the image of the medieval world a material reality. Thus, through study and classification, an image of the medieval world was pieced together.[2]

In this spirit of archaeological interest, the Arthurian legend was revived. Thomas Warton's *Observations on the Faerie Queene* (1754) marks the first attempt to analyze a work of "medieval" literature on its own merit. In his *Letters on Chivalry and Romance* (1762), Richard Hurd continued Warton's efforts, stating: "When an architect examines a Gothic structure by Grecian rules, he finds nothing but deformity. But the

Gothic architecture has its own rules, by which when it comes to be examined, it is seen to have its merit. . . . The same observation holds of the two sorts of poetry."[3]

Fragments of Arthurian poetry were presented in Thomas Percy's *Reliques of Ancient English Poetry* (1765), a compendium ranging from Scottish border ballads to Jacobean broadsides, taken from an old folio Percy claimed to have found "lying dirty on the floor in a bureau in the parlor."[4] George Ellis devoted a full volume of his *Specimens of Early English Metrical Romances* (1805) to the legend, presenting his tales in clear, modern language; he offered the fullest account of the chivalric saga to the widest circle of the general public, including young readers. As James Merriman has observed, "little wonder then that for the generation that was young in 1805, 'George-Ellis-specimens' could be used almost as a synonym for chivalric romance."[5]

Sir Thomas Malory's version of the legend was not available to the general public until the second decade of the nineteenth century. Out of print since 1642, *Le Morte Darthur* was known only by scholars with access to old texts. In the early nineteenth century, both Walter Scott and Robert Southey mounted and abandoned projects to edit and re-publish Malory's work; but it was not until 1816 that not one but two new editions of Malory appeared in print. The following year, Longmans published a luxury edition, edited by Southey and based on the standard Caxton text of 1485.[6]

When painters embraced the new subjects of national heritage, they adopted the methodology of literary and material archaeologists as well. As early as 1730, William Kent used an authentic portrait of King Henry V to lend veracity to his depiction of the monarch's meeting with the queen of France.[7] Robert Edge Pine, John Hamilton Mortimer, and Gavin Hamilton were among the artists who worked in this historical genre. Outstanding among them was Benjamin West, whose seven-part cycle on the life of Edward III, painted for Audience Hall at Windsor in 1787–89, typifies the era's pictorial interpretation of history. Determined to work with a historical vocabulary of absolute accuracy, West drew heavily on illustrated compendia and extant objects of the era.[8] As a result, he achieved a thorough re-creation of the weapons, costumes, and trappings of the mid-fourteenth century; but the noble actions of his medieval monarch were drowned in a wealth of archaeologically correct detail. West's cycle reduces to historical reportage, becoming merely a large-scale rendition of illustrations in contemporary popular historical publications. In this way, the use of historical subjects in painting reflected developments in historiography; it is possible that the pictorial arts in this period ignored the Arthurian legend precisely because it was viewed as non-historical.[9]

Accurate, detailed illustrations of historical events, though they did not conform to accepted definitions of history painting, enjoyed genuine popularity with British audiences. The concept of *istoria* can be traced to the writings of the Italian Quattrocento, but the placement of history painting at the apex of the hierarchy of subject matters had its genesis in the French academic tradition of the seventeenth century. Between 1666 and 1668, the art theorist André Félibien des Avaux—in his *Entretiens sur les vies et sur les ouvrages des plus excellens peintres anciens et modernes*, a treatise written as a handbook for training young painters at the Académie Royale—defined and elevated the status of history painting. Félibien's definition stated that history painting was more than the simple narration of a past event; it was the depiction of the nobility of human nature, expressed in examples of heroic action and based on the historical or mythological past. History painting was to serve as an exemplar of the potential greatness in the human soul and was meant to inspire the viewer to emulate in life the heroic endeavors and virtues depicted in painting. Félibien then drew a hierarchy of subjects, declaring without equivocation that the highest achievement in the realm of the fine arts was the exclusive domain of the painter of history.[10]

The Philosophes of the eighteenth century reaffirmed Félibien's definition and emphasized its didactic value. Such writers as Abbé Jean-Bernard Leblanc and Jean-Baptiste d'Argens urged painters to consider the importance of the empathetic response to painting; for, as La Font de Saint-Yenne explained, "le Peintre Historien est seul le Peintre de l'ame, les autres ne peignent que pour les ieux."[11] In his *Essai sur la peinture* (1766), Denis Diderot suggests that exhibitions of painting can become schools of virtue, inspiring for the high-minded viewer but chastening for the wicked, whose base desires and loathsome thoughts will be overpowered by the sterling examples of human action before them. In later writings, Diderot reiterated the moral import of the fine arts and exhorted artists to "paint as they spoke in Sparta."[12]

The advocacy of the Philosophes was rewarded by grand pictorial statements, most notably in the work of Jacques Louis David, whose stirring *Oath of the Horatii* (1784; The Louvre) speaks of loyalty, courage, and sacrifice in the cause of patriotism. In his depiction of the three sons of the Roman citizen Horace swearing to defend their homeland against three champions of Alba, historical detail is sparse and the setting is austere. Only the powerful action of the sons declaring their oath on the swords held aloft by their father is portrayed. David uses a story from the history of early Rome as a metaphor for French sentiment, as well as to veil his own Republican sympathies. His message would have been clear enough, however, for the narrative could have been known through the exposure of the audience to classical history or their familiarity with Corneille's tragedy *Horace*, presented at the Comédie Française two years earlier.[13] David presented a story well known to his public, eliminating the need for extraneous narrative detail and thus allowing the morality of the action to dominate the composition.

A German interpretation of high-minded historical painting emerged soon after 1800. During the year 1810 a small group of disaffected students from the Vienna Academy of Art moved to Rome and settled in an abandoned monastery, there to devote themselves to painting pure, ennobling subjects.[14] By the end of the decade the Nazarenes, derisively so-called for what some viewed as pious posturing, had adopted both a

131

grand and a simple approach to composition, and the heroic, sculpturesque figure style of the Renaissance master Raphael, for the depiction in fresco of subjects from the Bible and from medieval literature. This monumental mode of expression caught the attention of Ludwig, Crown Prince (later king) of Bavaria, who invited the best of the Nazarene painters to join him in Munich. Peter Cornelius accepted Ludwig's offer in 1819 and undertook a scheme of frescoes for the new Glyptothek. Julius Schnorr von Carolsfeld, who followed in 1827, was entrusted with a prestigious commission: the design and execution of frescoes for the Königsbau, five rooms in the Munich Residenz. The subject was the national epic, the *Niebelungenlied*.[15] Grand and powerful figures here enacted virtues of the mythic past; in the work of Schnorr von Carolsfeld, history painting drew directly on the German heritage, abandoning classical metaphor for subjects of immediate national significance.

British theorists were eloquent in their pronouncements on the supremacy of history painting; but theoretical advocacy was not borne out in visual demonstration. In his yearly *Discourse* to the students of the Royal Academy of Art, Sir Joshua Reynolds delineated the virtues of what he called the "Grand Style." In his *Third Discourse*, delivered 14 December 1770, Reynolds emphasizes that the painter should strive for a greater goal than verisimilitude: "The wish of the genuine painter must be more extensive: instead of endeavouring to amuse mankind with the minute neatness of his imitation, he must endeavour to improve them by the grandeur of his ideas." He continues his argument in the *Fourth Discourse*, of 10 December 1771. Urging that subjects be chosen for their ability to stir the viewer, he suggests, as a general example, "some eminent instance of heroick action or heroick suffering. There must be something either in the action, or in the object . . . which powerfully strikes the public sympathy." Reynolds warns against excessive detail and specificity once more: "A History-painter paints man in general; a Portrait-Painter, a particular man and consequently a defective model."[16] Despite these declarations echoing the sentiments of the French Philosophes, Reynolds earned his fame as a painter of elegant society portraits.

The strongest voice raised in favor of history painting in Britain was that of the painter James Barry. In 1775, Barry warned the artists of his nation: "History painting and sculpture should be the main views of any people desirous of gaining honour by the arts. These are the tests by which the national character will be tried in the after ages, and by which it has been, and is now tried by the natives of other countries."[17] Barry, however, in praising the achievements of David and other French masters, was alone in his assertion that continental painters surpassed their British contemporaries in the realm of history. He attributed this success to patronage, which was generous in France but nearly nonexistent in England.[18] Barry had the opportunity to demonstrate his ideas in a cycle of murals executed for the "Great Room" in the Adelphi, the new quarters of the Society of Arts. When his work was unveiled in 1783, however, it met with a reserved reception. In his allegorical program *The Progress of Human Culture and Knowledge*, Barry employed such a complex and esoteric iconography that his meaning was incomprehensible even to the most erudite.[19] Despite the protestations of theorists, history painting remained buried under narrative detail, love of verisimilitude, and unintelligible allegory. Until a forceful, lucid language and an equally direct mode of expression were found, history painting in Britain was condemned to languish.

The new allegorical language was found in chivalry but only after decades of reevaluation and transformation of the concept. The first advocate for the ancient institution was Richard Hurd, who, in his *Letters on Chivalry and Romance* (1762), described the chivalric character in romantic terms. The real transformation, however, began early in the nineteenth century, when romantic qualities defined by Hurd were personified in the heroes of novels by Sir Walter Scott. The bold knights of *Ivanhoe* (1819), *Quentin Durward* (1824), and *The Talisman* (1825) spoke in clear, simple language and exhibited the sensibilities of modern men. Scott's medieval heroes struck a familiar chord with their audience, who, in turn, began to see an affinity between themselves and chivalric knights and were inspired to emulate their noble deeds and romantic sentiments. No longer was chivalry regarded as an arcane institution but as the natural instinct of every red-blooded, patriotic Englishman. As Ivanhoe declares to Rebecca:

> Chivalry! Why, maiden, she is the nurse of pure and high affection, the stay of the oppressed, the redresser of grievances, the curb of the power of the tyrant. Nobility were but an empty name without her, and liberty finds the best protection in her lance and sword.[20]

It was in the writings of Kenelm Digby, though, that chivalry was most successfully translated into the modern idiom. In his *Broad Stone of Honour, or Rules for the English Gentleman* (1822), seven chapters of lofty, quotation-laden prose, Digby draws parallels between the medieval knight and his modern descendant, bridging the historical distance between knight and gentleman. Through his didactic method of teaching (as history painters did) by example, Digby sought to raise the moral spirit of the nation. His text enjoyed enormous popularity; it was in a second edition by 1823, and in 1829 it appeared as an extended, four-volume opus.[21]

By the 1830s, modern chivalry had reached the status of a cult, as aristocratic young gentlemen, Digby's most loyal readers, sought to put his teachings into practice. Perhaps the most substantial proof of his influence was the formation of the Young England party, led by Lord John Manners and dedicated to serving the weaker and less privileged in society. More popular were the sometimes frivolous conceits of chivalry: armor collections flourished in London and on country estates; valiant knights appeared at fancy-dress balls; and young men had their portraits painted in full armor. The height of pretense was reached in 1839, when thirteen young aristocrats donned armor to joust at the Eglinton Tornament, only to be defeated by a Highland rainstorm.[22]

With Queen Victoria's accession, the new chivalry turned solemn. The intoxication of the enthusiastic cult gave way to a mood of sober, moral interpretation. Nowhere is this better demonstrated than in such early Arthurian works of Tennyson as *Sir Galahad* (1842), in which courage becomes moral courage and strength, strength of will. Tennyson employed Digby's didactic method with far greater skill and subtlety. By the 1840s, the British audience for chivalric literature were learning to take inspiration from metaphorical example; their most cherished symbol was the valiant knight.

It was during the 1840s, too, that British painters were given an opportunity to compete on a grand scale with their continental counterparts in history painting. On 16 October 1834, a fire on the north bank of the Thames destroyed the conglomeration of buildings that for centuries had served as the seat of Parliament. The immediate need for a new palace at Westminster was answered with unprecedented speed and generous patronage on the part of the government. The sheer scale of the new palace, designed by Barry and Pugin, presented the chance for monumental fresco decoration in the interior; and a vast program of history painting was initiated. A parliamentary committee was formed in 1841 to direct the project, and Prime Minister Peel invited the young Prince Albert to serve as president of the new Fine Arts Commission. Peel's choice was an acknowledgment of the prince's own interests in art. Well educated and well traveled, Albert was aware of the best in continental history painting and was a great admirer of the achievements in Germany. His support of high-minded didactic painting lent credence to the British endeavor.

To prove to a skeptical public that British artists were equal to this vast undertaking, Prince Albert proposed a series of public competitions. The earliest of these resulted in monetary awards rather than commissions; for the most part, they served to stimulate public enthusiasm for the project. The competitions also served to demonstrate the new, symbolic import of chivalry. The competitors were asked to choose their own subjects from either national history or literature, and an overwhelming preference for the Middle Ages appeared in the submissions. Yet it was not the archaeologically reconstructed past of the previous century that found endorsement, but a new and direct allegorical interpretation of the virtues of that past. This new allegorical iconography can be seen in Daniel Maclise's competition design of 1845, later realized as *The Spirit of Chivalry* in the House of Lords in 1848. There, Lady Chivalry, a noble Raphaelesque woman, is shown accepting homage from her protectors and disciples: the mighty knight, the earnest aspirant, the troubadour, and the cleric. So profound were the associations stirred by this simple presentation that Charles Dickens was moved to exclaim: "Is it the love of Woman, in its truth and deep devotion that inspires you? See it here! Is it glory, as the world has learned to call the pomp and circumstance of arms? Behold it at the summit of its exaltation."[23]

The competitions also revealed the strong stylistic influence of German Nazarene painting, which by the 1840s was well known and much admired in England: large, powerful figures presented their inspiring messages in strong, clear gestures. Compositions were simple and stark, unburdened by the weight of historically correct detail. The strong presence of the German style may have been due in part to Prince Albert's taste; but many prominent British artists had visited Rome and Munich in the previous decade and were adherents of the Nazarene style well in advance of the start of the project at Westminster.

The new mode of British history painting quickly matured as the work at Westminster began in earnest. In 1846, William Dyce was awarded the first fresco commission, a depiction of *The Baptism of Ethelbert,* to hang in the House of Lords. Dyce was the most "German" of contemporary academic artists, and his manner—austere, sober, monumental—had been developed through years of diligent study of Italian Renaissance and Nazarene fresco painting on the Continent. In 1841, he had reported on the technique of fresco before the Fine Arts

General view into Queen Victoria's Robing Room, *frescoes by William Dyce.*
(British Crown Copyright—reproduced with permission of the Controller of Her
Britannic Majesty's Stationery Office)

Commission and had participated in the competitions of 1844
and 1845. By mid-decade, Dyce had become Prince Albert's
favorite painter. His cold, dignified style set the precedent for
subsequent work in the new palace.

It was Dyce who gave the new history painting its most eloquent national vocabulary. In 1847, while discussing with
Prince Albert potential subjects for the queen's Robing Room
in the new palace, the painter observed: "The stories of King
Arthur, and in particular Sir Thomas Malory's 'Morte
d'Arthur,' would supply to English Painters subjects of legendary history, which for their great interest, their antiquity,
and national chivalrous character, would surpass those of the
'Niebelungenlied,' of which so much has been made by the
Germans."[24] For Dyce, Arthurian legend exemplified British
national culture and thus was the ideal source for allegory. Up

137

to then, the legend had been ignored by the Westminster competitors, who, presumably, regarded it neither as history nor as literature but as mythology. Dyce surmounted this last obstacle to the creation of a distinct British expression in history painting by suggesting a legendary source in the form of native epic material that belonged to no particular period of history. Thus the need for extremely accurate historical reportage was obviated, and meaning could take precedence over the mode of illustration.

It is clear that Prince Albert agreed with Dyce's equation. Through Albert's efforts, the Fine Arts Commission invited Dyce to design and execute a cycle of seven frescoes illustrative of cultural virtues and drawn from the Arthurian legend. The prince had been firm on his choice of painter; in Dyce, he saw a probing turn of mind and a scholarly approach to painting, traits necessary in the transformation of a popular romantic narrative into an official allegorical statement on national heritage.

Dyce's scholarly preparation before submitting his designs to the commission helped substantiate the claim of the *Art Union* that he was "one of the few British painters who may be described as learned."[25] His sources were Davies' *Mythology of the English Druids* (1809), Dunlop's *History of Fiction* (1814), and Herbert's *Britannia after the Romans* (1836). Dyce demonstrated no interest in the compendia of the previous century; the sources he did employ suggest he sought moral lessons from the legend, not an evocation of its elusive setting in the distant past. Ultimately, he turned to the legend in the canonic version, Sir Thomas Malory's *Le Morte Darthur*, in the Southey edition of 1817.[26]

In 1848, in a letter to Charles Eastlake, secretary of the Fine Arts Commission, Dyce presented his findings. He explained that there were two modes of interpretation, the allegorical or "chivalric" as opposed to the more literal or "historical."[27] The latter might introduce infidelity, betrayal, and failure—factual events that had doomed the order of the Round Table. By adopting the former mode, Dyce could consider the companions of the Round Table as personifications of certain

138

moral qualities which make up the ancient idea of chivalric greatness. He left little doubt as to which view he preferred. In his conclusion, Dyce writes: "We have two views . . . the one mythological, the other Chivalric. . . . The one possesses interest for the Antiquary; the other belongs to all time." In his proposal for a selective editing of the legend, Dyce differentiated the interests of the history painter from those of the illustrator and thus resolved the theoretical dilemma that had troubled artists for nearly a century. The Fine Arts Commission accepted Dyce's proposal, and in 1849, work began in the Robing Room on the first Arthurian subjects to be painted in Britain since the Middle Ages.

Dyce's plan for the Robing Room was designed in compliance with then current theories of history painting. In each fresco a single chivalric virtue is personified in the actions of a hero from the Arthurian legend. Dyce chose those virtues which he regarded as national characteristics, essential to the chivalric knight but cultivated by the modern gentleman as well. Each personification exemplifies the specific virtue by presenting an incident from the legend; the actions of the figures were so clear in expression and gesture, however, that prior knowledge of the narrative was not essential. Like his predecessors in France and Germany, Dyce considered empathy the essential response elicited by history painting. For example, in the first completed fresco, *Religion: The Vision of Sir Galahad and His Company* (1851), Dyce portrays the rewards of chastity and simple faith. He was inspired by the incident described in Book XVIII, Chapter IX, in Malory, where Sir Galahad, Sir Bors, and Sir Percival share a vision of the Savior and a theological revelation in a rustic chapel. Dyce presents only the vision, with Galahad springing toward it in a burst of physical enthusiasm that invites the same emotional embrace of faith from the viewer.

Dyce regarded the next three virtues he addressed as specific facets of chivalry. In *Generosity: King Arthur unhorsed, spared by Sir Lancelot* (1852), Dyce lauds the magnanimity, respect for authority, and sense of justice essential to the character of Arthur's finest knight. In *Courtesy: Sir Tristram*

Generosity: King Arthur unhorsed, spared by Sir Lancelot. *1852 fresco by William Dyce. (British Crown Copyright—reproduced with permission of the Controller of Her Britannic Majesty's Stationery Office)*

harping to La Belle Isolde (1852), the knight's refined behavior with the Irish princess is balanced against his skill in the manly arts, symbolized by a falconer and a huntsman in the

140

background. A gentleman with the ladies but a fearsome opponent in the field, Tristram embodies an ideal equipoise in the chivalric character. *Mercy: Sir Gawaine swearing to be Merciful and never be against Ladies* (1854) is the culmination of the series of events presented in *Le Morte Darthur* Book II, chapters V through VIII, in which Gawaine's rash temper and lack of reason cause him to be brought to trial before Guenevere and her ladies. In a blind rage, the knight had dealt a fatal blow to the well-meaning wife of an opponent who inadvertently had stepped between the two men. Dyce chose to show only the moment of the knight's chastisement—as a lesson for all those who disdain women, even if their manifestation of that disdain does not match the enormity of Gawaine's crime.

The final work in the ensemble, *Hospitality: The Admission of Sir Tristram to the fellowship of the Round Table,* was Dyce's response to Prince Albert's request for a general illustration of the court.[28] He used this illustration to express a message of good fellowship and trust among men of equal status and skill. *Hospitality* was unfinished at the time of the artist's death in 1864 but was completed according to the original design by C. W. Cope. The remaining frescoes, *Courage: The combat between King Arthur and the five Northern Kings* and *Fidelity: Sir Lancelot rescuing Queen Guenevere from King Meliagaunce,* were abandoned at Dyce's death. They are mentioned in his correspondence, but designs for them have not survived.[29]

Dyce's method of translating narrative into allegory may be better understood through analysis of the fresco *Generosity.* The heroic image of Lancelot refusing to allow the slaying of the fallen king was based on Book XX, Chapter XIII of Malory. Lancelot has rescued Guenevere from death and given her sanctuary in Joyous Garde, whereupon Arthur is required to lay siege to reclaim his queen, though lacking the will to punish her or to face his friend in battle. Arthur falls from his horse in the conflict, and Sir Bors makes ready to slay him:

and so he alyght and drew hys swerde and seyd to sir Launcelot, "Sir, shall I make an ende of thys warre?" (For he mente to have slayne hym.)

"Nat so hardy," seyde sir Launcelot, "uppon payne of thy hede, that thou touch hym no more! For I woll never se that moste noble kynge that made me knyght nother slayne nor shamed."[30]

Mounted again, Arthur regards Lancelot and is consumed by sorrow, "thinking on the great courtesy that was in Sir Lancelot more than in any other man." Thus ends the tragic battle between the king and his finest knight.

Dyce's eloquent expression of Lancelot's compassionate generosity has a meaning beyond the literary narrative. His design is concise, well suited to the limited space of the virtical compartment in which it resides. Lancelot on a white steed dominates the composition. As he rides up to Bors, his cloak flying behind him, he raises his hands to halt the action. Bors stands astride the fallen king, his sword nearly pulled from its sheath before he turns to heed Lancelot's warning. Arthur is an essay in empathy: he sprawls heavily on the ground, hauberk torn from his now vulnerable body, vainly attempting to raise up the massive bulk of his torso. Without Lancelot's forceful intervention, the king will perish. It is the generosity of an opponent that saves him.

In *Generosity*, Dyce asserts his dramatic voice through simple, direct means. The tightly wrought composition and the fine visual differentiation of character focus the viewer's attention while a contrast between the physical gestures of Lancelot's beneficence and Arthur's collapse and impending defeat evokes a stirring emotional response. The fresco's narrative content is almost superfluous, for, to a generation schooled in the glorification of chivalry, the action of staying a sword to protect an unarmed, defenseless adversary was already charged with meaning. As if in accord with Reynolds' dictum on universality in history painting, Dyce exemplifies the generous treatment, not of Arthur in particular but of all those defeated. He shows heroic man acting nobly, a testament to the potential for great generosity in everyone's soul.

The importance of Dyce's achievement for the course of history painting was recognized in his day. Charles Eastlake declared the Arthurian frescoes equal or even superior to any work on the Continent; T. J. Gullick proclaimed that they represented "everything that is to be desiderated in monumental painting."[31] At last, a British artist had succeeded in the realm of high-minded history painting by creating an allegory thoroughly national in source and content, one that celebrated the ideals of an ancient institution with force and clarity.

Dyce's Arthurian frescoes were the first major monument in an Arthurian revival in the visual arts. By treating the national epic with respectful sobriety as a moral paradigm for the modern world, Dyce anticipated Tennyson's approach in *Idylls of the King*. Of central importance was his allegorical conception whereby "an ancient idea of Chivalric greatness" was taught by example. History painting was now securely set in mythological time; freed from historiographic elaboration, it could express national sentiment by appealing to a shared cultural inheritance. The quest for a national allegory came to a successful conclusion, and Dyce's achievement, seminal both for history painting and for the Arthurian revival, remained influential to the end of the century.

Malory's Expurgators

MARYLYN JACKSON PARINS

It is often remarked in modern Malory studies that Sir
Thomas Malory's work was not appreciated in the nineteenth
century.[1] For an unappreciated work, however, it was published a great many times, in volumes ranging from complete
scholarly editions to selections, modernizations, and adaptations. In the latter three forms, the *Morte d'Arthur* was most
often expurgated as well. The forms such expurgation took,
and the justifications for it, provide interesting insights into
nineteenth-century attitudes toward the value of Malory's
work.[2]

William Caxton, as Malory's first editor, revised Malory
mainly in Caxton's Book V, the section on Arthur's Roman
War, which Malory had drawn from the *Alliterative Morte
Arthure*. Obviously, Caxton's revisions, including his assignment of book and chapter divisions, were made on stylistic
rather than moral grounds, since his preface makes it clear
that the book can be read with profit. Wynkyn de Worde
added a famous passage beginning "O ye mighty and pom-
pous lords," praising the virtuous teaching of the book, and
the sixteenth-century editions of Copland (1557) and East (c.
1578) reprinted de Worde. Of the same period is Roger
Ascham's famous aside to his denunciation of "bawdie bookes

translated out of the Italian tongue," in which he said of the *Morte d'Arthur:*

> the whole pleasure . . . standeth in two speciall poyntes, in open mans slaughter, and bold bawdrye: In which booke those be counted the noblest Knightes, that do kill most men without any quarell, and commit fowlest aduoulteries by sutlest shiftes: . . . This is good stuffe, for wise men to laughe at, or honest men to take pleasure at. Yet I know, when Gods Bible was banished the Court, and *Morte Arthure* received into the Princes chamber. What toyes, the dayly readyng of such a booke, may worke in the will of a yong ientleman, or a yong mayde. . . .[3]

In 1634, William Stansby printed a new edition, and the editor, perhaps Jacob Blome, felt obliged to modernize the text of circa 1578. In addition, as he announced in the preface, Stansby "either amended or quite left out" phrases wherein "king Arthur or some of his knights were declared in their communications to sweare prophane, and use superstitious speeches."[4]

The eighteenth century produced no editions of Malory, the nineteenth a great many. Two inexpensive editions of 1816, both poorly edited, used Stansby's text. One of them, to enhance sales, claimed to have made the text more fit for the eyes of youth. There were then, as now, only two known copies of Caxton's text; the expensive 1817 edition introduced by Robert Southey was based on the incomplete one, which is missing several leaves at the end. Therefore, William Upcott, the textual editor, interpolated from other editions to fill in the gaps. Aside from this necessity, Upcott attempted a faithful rendering of Caxton. Most editors of the early nineteenth century saw no need to expurgate, nor did Thomas Wright, who preferred Stansby to Caxton for his complete edition of 1858, not because the Stansby edition had modified the swearing but only because its less archaic language and "modernized" spellings rendered it more accessible.

Alfred Lord Tennyson did not, of course, edit the *Morte*

d'Arthur, but he was an influential reshaper of its familiar stories in a form not universally admired. "Prudery is one of the principal counts in the modern indictment of Tennyson," wrote O. F. Christie in 1927. "He is accused of bowdlerizing the Arthur of Malory into the Arthur of the *Idylls*."[5] Christie cited Harold Nicolson, among others, as participant in this indictment; had he written later, he might have added T. S. Eliot. Eliot expressed ironic admiration for "the skill with which Tennyson adopted this great British epic material—in Malory's handling hearty, outspoken, and magnificent—to suitable reading for a girls' school: the original ore being so refined that none of the gold is left."[6]

Walter Houghton has pointed out that the wholesale condemnation of Victorian prudery oversimplifies or ignores deeply held convictions—in Tennyson, as in many of his contemporaries—that sexual immorality was, in fact, a corrupting evil and "unbridled sensuality," a danger to society. Nonetheless, Houghton points out as well that it is "only by keeping vividly in mind the merging influence of the Puritan revival, the exaltation of the family, and the acute fear of sex, that an age like ours . . . can . . . avoid finding Arthur more of an insufferable prig than an ideal man."[7]

Complaints about Tennyson's bowdlerizing of Malory, however, are not a modern reaction exclusively. Swinburne's attack on the "Morte d'Albert" is but one admittedly extreme example. Other Victorian critics compared Tennyson and Malory with less sympathy for the former than might be expected. F. J. Furnivall professed his great admiration of Tennyson, saying "[he] is to me personally more than all the other English poets put together, save alone Chaucer."[8] Nevertheless, in his edition of the French *Queste del Saint Graal*, Furnivall included this comment on Tennyson's version of Arthur:

> . . . as to Arthur's relation to Guinevere, I cannot feel that the modern representation is the truest one. To any one knowing his Maleore,—knowing that Arthur's own sin was the cause of the breaking up of the Round Table, and Guinevere's the means

only through which that cause worked itself out, . . . then for one so primed to come on Mr. Tennyson's representation of the king, in perfect words, with tenderest pathos rehearsing to his prostrate queen his own nobleness and her disgrace; the revulsion of feeling was too great.[9]

As a young barrister, William Blake Odgers, later an authority on the law, read a paper in the winter of 1871 to the Bath Literary and Philosophical Association, entitled "King Arthur and the Arthurian Romances."[10] In a section comparing Tennyson and Malory, Odgers notes that in Malory, Arthur "is not a 'blameless king,' he is flesh and blood like the rest of us; not an ideal of the sinless man." With Tennyson's Arthur, however, he says: "We can sympathize with Guinevere when she cries—'I could not breathe in that fine air / That pure severity of perfect light.'"[11] Odgers clearly prefers Malory's flesh and blood to Tennyson's sinless ideal.

William Minto and Frederic Harrison were among other critics and authors who compared Tennyson and Malory with apparent preference for Malory. Minto, for example, admires in Malory "the inexorable vengeance of an iron law that accepts no plea of ignorance" by which Arthur is punished "by the fruit of his own involuntary crime."[12] Tennyson, he thinks, "wipes off this blot of incest from . . . his spotless hero" and finding the motive for Mordred's treason in "simple depravity of nature," abandons the tragic aspects of the story at some peril.[13] Harrison, having noted that Malory's "tale of the death of Arthur, Guinevere, and Lancelot . . . may stand beside the funeral of Hector," adds of Malory's Arthur: "Beside this simple, manly type of the mediaeval hero the figures in the *Idylls of the King* look like the dainty Perseus of Canova placed beside the heroic Theseus of Phidias."[14]

The *Idylls* began appearing in 1859. Kathleen Tillotson has pointed out that Victorian authors before the 1860s were free to be relatively outspoken. In the 1830s and 1840s, she says, there were few "instances of squeamish editors," and those earlier decades also produced "fewer protests from readers and critics."[15] Both Tillotson and Houghton agree, though,

147

that the 1820s and the 1860s were "high points of squeamishness."[16]

Therefore, it is not surprising to find that, from 1862, Malory's *Morte d'Arthur* became the object of that expurgating thought necessary to make the book fit for boys, family reading, and the common man. Tennyson's treatment of the story thus had a dual effect; it created a popular market for quite a large number of new, often abridged editions of Malory; and, despite the critical demurrals noted above, it encouraged editors of the 1860s and later to produce versions morally more in keeping with Tennyson's.

Editorial statements justifying expurgation on moral grounds—many of them citing Tennyson as an exemplar—varied little when they appeared, and the details selected for expurgation, though not the thoroughness of suppression, follow an obvious pattern in dealing with passages of a sexual nature. James T. Knowles, an architect and later the founder of the periodical *Nineteenth Century,* brought out in 1862 a popular abridgement of Malory, with occasional additions from Geoffrey and elsewhere. Knowles' preface offers three justifications for modernizing and abridging Malory's work. One is the "antiquated spelling and quaint style" which have made the work "a treat for scholars rather than for the general reader"; therefore, Knowles modernized the text somewhat. Second, the general reader would find the original "too long, too monotonous, and too obscure"; therefore, the many tales were arranged "into a somewhat clearer and more consecutive story." Finally, the book was not "fitted for boys, who would probably become the principal readers of the Arthur legends in a popular form." Thus the editor has endeavored, he says, "to follow the rule laid down in the 'Idylls of the King'; and has suppressed and modified where changed manners and morals have made it absolutely necessary to do so for the preservation of a lofty original ideal."[17] Obviously, Knowles did see that lofty ideal in Malory; that is why he is presenting the work or, as he hopes, "paving the way for such a popular revival as is its due."[18]

Knowles claimed he did "little but abridge and simplify"

148

Malory; actually, his changes were substantive and materially altered the story. Here, for example, is his account of the begetting of Arthur:

> And it befell at a certain great banquet and high feast which the king made at Easter-tide, there came . . . Gorlois . . . and his wife Igerna, who was the most famous beauty in all Britain. And soon, thereafter, Gorlois being slain in battle Uther determined to make Igerna his wife. But in order to do this, and enable him to come to her—for she was shut up in the high castle of Tintagil . . . the king sent for Merlin, to take counsel with him and to pray his help. This . . . Merlin promised him on one condition—namely that the king should give him up the first son born of the marriage. . . .[19]

The next paragraph has Uther, now "happily wedded," approached by Merlin to arrange for the child's nourishing by Sir Ector. As several abridged editions would do, this version creates some confusion in motivation and in cause and effect.

Similarly, we find early on that Arthur's half-sister, the wife of Lot (Knowles, after Tennyson, calls her "Belisant") came to Arthur's court with her four sons. "And the king, not knowing that she was his half-sister, made great court to her; and being full of admiration for her beauty, loved her out of measure, and kept her a long season at Caerleon," arousing the increased enmity of King Lot.[20] There is no mention of the child Mordred, however. In Malory, Merlin, disguised as an old man, tells Arthur soon after this episode that Arthur has begotten Mordred on his own sister and that Mordred will destroy him; but in Knowles, again, there is no mention of Mordred in the corresponding passage, only the vague statement (from Malory, too) that Arthur has done something "for which God is displeased." Surprised indeed must be the reader who discovers some 260 pages after Belisant's visit to Arthur's court that Mordred was King Arthur's son by her.[21]

The Reverend Edward Conybeare's expressed aim in bringing out another "abridged and revised" edition in 1868 was "to put into a more popular form one of the least appreciated works in the English language."[22] The *Morte d'Arthur,*

Conybeare says, deserves greater popularity; but he, like Knowles, feels that "in its original form" it "could never be a general favourite at the present day. Its great length, the confusion and want of system in the divisions, and the occasional coarseness are insuperable obstacles to popularity," despite the renewed interest in Arthurian romance which the *Idylls of the King* has attracted.[23]

Conybeare hoped to "obviate . . . this unpopularity" by much abbreviation, by new book and chapter arrangements, and by cutting out the "coarse passages." He apologized, though, for the omissions to "those who, like himself, are lovers of this noble romance in its original form" and hoped his work would lead to a reading of the book in "its integrity."[24]

Although Conybeare's account of the begetting of Arthur is longer than that of Knowles, it simply omits any mention of Uther's desire for Igraine. "It befell in the days of the noble Uther Pendragon . . . that there was a mighty and noble duke . . . that held long time war against him; and this duke was named the Duke of Tintagil." The next sentence introduces his wife, Igraine, as a "right fair lady," and in the next, Uther is besieging Tintagil with a great host. Clearly, the implication is that his act is a response to Gorlois' holding long-time war against him; there is no mention of a feast, of Uther's infatuation, of Igraine's speech to her husband about being dishonored, or of their departure for Cornwall. All we learn is that the Duke was slain in a sally from the castle and that the barons thus begged Uther to make Igraine his queen. So they were married and in due time Igraine bore a son, and so on.[25]

Conybeare, however, apparently decided that what was not permissible in Uther was acceptable for Lancelot. Tennyson, after all, had shown Guinevere as faithless, and Conybeare allows Lancelot to be discovered by Mordred, Agravaine, and the others in "the Queen's chamber." He also left in the lines describing Lancelot's return to loving the queen after the quest of the Holy Grail, although he changed "they loved together more hotter than they did toforehand" to "loved together more than before."[26]

In Malory, Lancelot's madness occurs as a result of Guinevere's furious outrage when she hears his chattering of their love in his sleep, like a jay, while he is in the bed of Elaine, having been lured there—a second time—by Brisen. In Conybeare, both occasions of sleeping with Elaine are glossed over in the sentence, "And so by enchantment she won the love of Sir Lancelot, and certainly she loved him again passing well."[27] When "noise" of this came to Guinevere, she rebuked Lancelot, he swooned, and upon awaking leaped, mad, out the window. Nowhere is the conception of Galahad mentioned, though he is later said to be Lancelot's son. Similarly, Conybeare skips the episode in which Lancelot, at Meliagraunce's court, plans an evening rendezvous with Guinevere, takes a ladder to her window, passes some time in talk with her, rips out the iron window bars to get to her bed, cutting his hand in the process, and then bleeds on the bed. In Conybeare, the evening's events do not occur; Meliagraunce simply comes into the queen's chamber "on the morrow," wishing for a way to hide his own misdeeds, and accuses her of treason to the king.[28] No evidence is presented to support his accusation; neither the bed nor the ten wounded knights lying about are referred to as Lancelot challenges Meliagraunce.

Edward Strachey was undoubtedly the most careful examiner of Malory texts before Sommer began working on his scholarly edition. Strachey discovered Upcott's interpolations in the 1817 edition and noted an estimated 20,000 variations between Caxton's text and that of Stansby; for his own edition of 1868, he drew on the bulk of the 1817 edition, which he had found reliable, aided by collation with both texts of Caxton. His intention was to establish an accurate text but one that would not be printed as established. "What is wanted," Strachey said, "is an edition for ordinary readers, and especially for boys, from whom the chief demand for this book will always come."[29] His edition, therefore, is a "reprint of the original Caxton with the spelling modernized" and with "unintelligibly obsolete" words replaced by other old but still recognizable forms. His aim was to make the book "readable," and for the same reason, he added, "such phrases or passages as are not in accordance with modern manners have been also omitted or [he seems to apologize] replaced by others which either actually occur or might have occurred in Caxton's text elsewhere."[30] Strachey objected when Sommer referred to his edition as both modernized *and* abridged; but the fact is, he did leave out words, phrases—even, here and there, entire sentences. Nevertheless, it is not an abridgement in the usual sense of the word.

In his introduction, Strachey deals earnestly and at length with the question of the morality of Malory's book. The book did not, he says, "deserve the unqualified denunciation" of Ascham, but, he adds, it does exhibit a "picture of society far lower than our own in morals, and depicts it with far less repugnance to its evil elements . . . than any good man would now feel."[31] Nonetheless, compared to earlier works, Strachey finds in Malory evidence of an "upward progress in morals"; whereas Malory is not as great as Chaucer, still, the "brutish animal coarseness" of some parts of Chaucer has "dwindled to half its former size." Further, Strachey concludes his remarks on the textual alterations with this stirring (and defensive) passage:

> I do not profess to have remedied the moral defects of the book which I have already spoken of. Mr. Tennyson has shown us how we may best deal with this matter for modern use, in so far as Sir Thomas Malory has himself failed to treat it rightly; and I do not believe that when we have excluded what is offensive to modern manners there will be found anything practically injurious to the morals of English boys . . . while there is much of moral worth which I know not where they can learn so well as from the ideals of magnanimity, courage, courtesy, reverence for women, gentleness, self-sacrifice, chastity, and other manly virtues exhibited in these pages.[32]

To his credit, Strachey does not leave as many misleading conclusions to be drawn as had his predecessors. He does leave the conception of Mordred obscure and tones down passages describing Mordred's relationship to Arthur; "your own sone begoten of your sister" becomes "your sister's son," and the passage "for kyng Arthur lay by kyng lots wyf the whiche was Arthurs syster and got on her Mordred" becomes the much less specific line, "for the wrong king Arthur did him."[33] For the most part, Strachey does not attempt to alter the facts as presented by Malory; he changes mainly the language, to avoid any mention of explicit physical contact. That is, Uther visits Igraine disguised as her husband, and Arthur is conceived; Lancelot spends the night with Elaine, and Galahad is to be born; Gaheris strikes off his mother's head while she is entertaining Lamorak. Words like "bed," "begat on her," and "naked," however, were either changed to innocuous phrases or were deleted. For example, in the book's opening episode, when Merlin agrees to help Uther get into Igraine's castle, Caxton's Merlin says, "the first night that ye shall lie by Igraine ye shall get a child on her"; but Strachey's Merlin says, "after ye shall win Igraine ye shall have a child by her."

Similarly, in the dreadful episode in which Gaheris surprises his mother in bed with her young lover, Strachey omits any mention of the bed. Gaheris "came unto them all armed," not "to their bedside all armed," as in Caxton. After he has beheaded his mother, Gaheris refrains from killing Lamorak because, in Strachey, he is "unarmed" while in Caxton he is "naked," which in this context comes to the same thing. Strachey, though, also omits the delightful line that occurs after Lancelot realizes he has just spent the night with Elaine, not Guinevere. In Malory, Elaine "skipped out of her bed all naked, and kneeled down afore Sir Launcelot" to ask mercy; for, as she points out, "I have in my womb him by thee that shall be the most noblest knight of the world." In Strachey she does not skip; she is not described as naked; and we have not been told that there was a bed in the room. Elaine merely kneels before Lancelot and asks mercy saying, "I shall have a son by thee."

As Strachey noted, these expurgations do not affect the morality of the book; the language is less explicit, but the liaisons do occur and the results are the same. The sole editor of the 1860s, 1870s, and 1880s who used unexpurgated language was B. Montgomerie Ranking, in 1871. Using Stansby, perhaps through Thomas Wright's edition of 1858, Ranking's edition of *La Mort D'Arthur: The Old Prose Stories whence the "Idylls of the King" have been Taken* presented only limited portions of Malory's work; but those portions were not altered except for the spelling, which was modernized. Ranking is an enthusiast; his introduction declares that "no man, having a man's heart, could know the old romance literature and despise it; since a man's heart holds in reverence such faith, such true-heartedness, such purity, as ennoble the records of chivalry."[34] Nowhere does he apologize for "coarseness" or justify omissions or paraphrase on that ground. Ranking's intention is to present the old stories "whence Mr. Tennyson has drawn his inspiration."[35] He does so by providing from Malory (and from the *Mabinogion*, for "Geraint and Enid") the portions that correspond to Tennyson's *Idylls*. Ranking's notes call attention to some of the differences between Tennyson's and Malory's versions. Ranking shortens the "Holy Grail" section a great deal and omits "Tristram" and most of "Lancelot." Throughout, his plan necessitates elimination of many passages other editors either expurgated or left out on moral grounds; but he does not tamper with the wording of what he included. Uther did desire "to have lain by" Igraine, did in fact "lie" with her and "begat on her Arthur the same night." Perhaps Ranking adhered to his text so closely because he admired Malory's prose too much to alter it. As he says in the introduction: "It is not given to all to read in the French romances, or to explore the 'Mabinogion'; but surely every Briton might know the most perfect specimen of his own language."[36]

However, in the *Life and Exploits of King Arthur . . . A Legendary Romance*, a work published in 1878 and, for good reason, anonymously, the case is quite different. This work, based loosely on Geoffrey and Malory, is a retelling of stories of Arthur and Britain. It resembles a bad historical novel whose characters are given speeches and sentiments inconceivable in the supposed setting. The author's introduction says nothing about morals or about his plan for the work that follows. The only intimations of what is to come are his noting of an anecdote he has read in an old number of *Blackwood's*, which showed that Malory had been and is popular among schoolboys, and a somewhat condescending remark: "To the school-boy the tale is one of infinite delight and wonder, and to those of mature age the exploits of Arthur have something akin to the interest created by the inimitable 'Punch' . . . the incorrigible puppet" who always raises "an inward laugh at his expense."[37]

Given this apparent analogy of a Punch and Judy show to Malory's *Morte d'Arthur*, one is surely justified in having an inward laugh at this author's expense. It is not difficult. Here is the account of Arthur's begetting; the information is not given initially but in a flashback, as Merlin provides an explanation of his parentage for the young King Arthur:

> Then the king [Uther] . . . sent for the duke to come to court, and to bring with him his fair young wife, Igerna. They came, and smitten by her beauty, King Uther loved her, and conspired against her husband's life. . . .
>
> "I blush at such dishonour, unworthy of a churl—much more unworthy of a king!" said Arthur, reddening.

Merlin continues the sordid story to the point where "a furious sally was made by the duke from Castle Terrabil, in which he was slain by Sir Ulfius. Then the king sought the fair Igerna, and, by my enchantment, wrought it so that she, though a constant and virtuous lady, at first sight loved the king."

> "It cannot be!" cried Arthur, starting to his feet, while his frank blue eyes dilated, and his lip quivered with indignation.[38]

It is only fair to add that when Lot's wife, whom this author, too, persists in calling Belisant, comes to Arthur's court with her four sons, this writer does fall into an adaptation of Malory's language and allows that Belisant, loved beyond measure by Arthur, bore him a son, Mordred. He is clearly influenced by Tennyson, not Malory, when he has Guinevere say, "Arthur and the good, the noble! . . . my lord commands my highest esteem, profoundest veneration—I cannot give my love. . . . The king is too spotless pure—too high above me."[39] This free adaptation of Malory's narrative (with assists from Tennyson's), more than most of the works considered in this essay, shows the author's moral concerns as much through addition as through omission.

Sidney Lanier's *The Boy's King Arthur*, published in 1880, was enormously popular, its title announcing the intended audience. While Lanier does not say what previous edition(s) of Malory he used, it is unimportant, since Lanier's version of Malory is selective, modernized, expurgated, and in part inaccurate.

Lanier does call the *Morte d'Arthur* a "beautiful old book," describing its author as "our own simple, valorous, wise, tender . . . Malory."[40] He mentions the "intrinsic faults and beauties" of the work but does not go on to discuss any faults. Rather, he cites Lancelot's splendid behavior throughout and his "majestic manhood," especially as seen in his patient enduring of Gawain's taunts throughout the two sieges. Lanier closes his introduction by passing on to his "young readers" Caxton's "farewell to his maturer audience," quoting the passage in which Caxton says "all is wryton for our doctryne" and admonishes us to "take the good and honest actes in . . . remembraunce, and . . . folowe the same."[41]

Of his unidentified text, Lanier says: "Every word in the book, except those . . . in brackets, is Malory's unchanged, except that the spelling is modernized."[42] In brackets, he explains, will appear editorial "connective clauses . . . convenient to preserve the thread of a story which could not be given entire." One set of brackets contains the following explanation of the events described above, which precede Lancelot's madness: "It happened that Queen Guenever was angered with Sir Launcelot, yet truly for no fault of his, but only because a certain enchantress had wrought that Sir Launcelot seemed to have shamed his knighthood."[43] This hardly mirrors accurately Lancelot's being lured a second

156

time to Elaine's bed and then talking in his sleep about his love of Guinevere.

Lanier's abridged version simply skips a number of episodes presumably thought dangerous to boys. It skips Morgause's coming to court and thus the begetting of Mordred; it skips Gawain's behavior with Ettard, Gaheris' killing of his mother, and the begetting of Galahad and brackets Lancelot's ripping out the window bars and leaving blood on Guinevere's bed—"And then while they abode in that castle Sir Meliagrance appealed the queen of treason."[44]

Lanier's intended audience was boys; Ernest Rhys' abridged edition of *Malory's History of King Arthur and the Quest of the Holy Grail* was intended for the common man, who "reads for the sake of life and not for the sake of letters."[45] Published in 1886, this work introduced the Camelot Series. In it, Rhys returns to the justifications of earlier abridgers and expurgators to explain his considerable omissions and alterations to Wright's text of Stansby. As his title suggests, Rhys omitted much of Malory's material, reserving the bulk of Lancelot's adventures, those of Beaumains and Tristram, and the Grail adventures of Bors for a proposed companion volume to be published later. Noting that "awkward confusions and repetitions abound" in Malory, Rhys intended through his extensive cutting "to throw the Arthurian history proper into clearer and more coherent form."[46] In addition, he modernized the spelling and substituted modern equivalents for difficult, older words. The purpose of his revisions was to "facilitate the reading of the book with pleasure," and to that end, he "slightly altered" certain "phrases which the squeamishness of these days might object to."[47]

This modernizing, abridging, clarifying, and expurgating had the well-meant but inevitably condescending aim of making classic literature accessible to the common man. In a typical passage, Rhys expresses the hope that these policies of the Camelot Series would "help a little in making the higher literature really responsive to everyday life and its needs."[48] Rhys notes, however, that, in Malory's account, Arthur "is not immaculate; he errs and sins and suffers, is defeated and shamed often, and for that reason appeals more closely to the human heart" (than what or whom he does not say).[49] Thus, perhaps because Arthur's sins are seen as making him more appealing to the everyday reader, Arthur in this version is allowed to "set his love greatly" upon Lyonors, who bore a son by him. Since 1858, only Strachey's edition had included this information.

Rhys' expurgations are much like Strachey's. Arthur did not "desire to lie by" Morgause, nor did he "beget upon her Mordred"; but he did "cast great love unto her, and in this wise was Mordred begotten."[50] The begetting of Galahad, too, is treated much in Strachey's manner. In fact, Rhys' version is franker than Strachey's in at least one aspect. After Lancelot wrests the bars from Guinevere's window and gets into her bedchamber, Strachey has the queen warn Lancelot to be quiet because of the wounded knights lying nearby. In Strachey, the next sentence makes Lancelot aware that he can tarry no longer. Rhys, however, keeps Malory's line which allows Lancelot to take "his pleasure and his liking until it was in the dawning of the day" before realizing that he must not tarry.[51] It is pleasing to know that Ernest Rhys continued the work of making literature accessible, becoming general editor of the Everyman Series in 1906 and that the Malory edition used for the series was a modernized but not expurgated text of Caxton.

Oskar Sommer's scholarly edition of Caxton, published in 1889, was the first complete, unexpurgated Caxton since 1817. It was followed by several complete, unexpurgated popular editions with modernized spelling—those of Simmons (with Beardsley's illustrations), Gollancz, and Pollard—in the decade up to 1900. Nevertheless, expurgated and abridged versions continued to appear. Thomas Wright's edition of 1858, reissued in a series of Sir John Lubbock's Hundred Books in 1893, was bowdlerized for this appearance.[52] Two years earlier, a "modernized version of the 'Morte d'Arthur,'" by Charles Morris, was published in a three-volume edition.[53] Morris does not specify a text, but, as with other versions examined, it hardly matters, as his rendition is not only abridged and modernized (in both spelling and wording), but almost unrecognizably altered through expurgation and substitutions of his own devising.

Morris regarded Malory himself as a gifted editor and expurgator: "Malory did a work of high value in editing the confused mass of earlier fiction, lopping off its excrescences and redundancies, reducing its coarseness of speech, and producing from its many stories and episodes a coherent and continuous narrative."[54] Without giving examples of either matter or romances, Morris added that "there is repulsive matter in the old romances, which [Malory] freely cuts out." In Malory's hands, the "coarse and crude material with which he had to deal" gained a "degree of poetic fervor."[55] The book, however, is not without its own defects, such as confusing chronology, monotony, and obsolete language.[56] To make it "easier reading," Morris says, "we shall leave it as we find it," except for a few changes which include abridging the narrative, reducing the "confusion," and putting what is left into modern English.

Morris apparently aimed at an adult audience. Toward the end of his introduction he expresses the hope that "some . . . may turn with pleasure from the most philosophical of modern novels to wander awhile through this primitive domain of thought." It is surprising, then, but an indication of what is to come, that the first words of his text are "Once upon a time."[57] Morris skips from Uther's reign to Uther's death without mentioning Igraine, although he has her say later: "After the death of my lord . . . King Uther married me, and I bore him a son."[58] He skips Morgause's visit to Arthur's court and has Merlin warn Arthur—"your sister shall bear a son who will destroy you and all the knights of your land"—without mentioning that the son is also Arthur's.[59] He has Lancelot, under Pelles' enchantment, make Elaine "his wife . . . fancying that it was Guenever whom he had wedded" but does not mention the fathering of Galahad. After Lancelot has arrived at the castle of Meliagraunce to rescue Guinevere and has, by her intercession, been restrained from dealing with the abductor,

Morris—like others ignoring the window bars, the bleeding hand, and the bed—says simply and misleadingly: "All went peacefully that night at the castle, but the next morning there was new trouble." One of the castle maidens, not Meliagraunce, found "what seemed to be the print of a bloody hand on the coverings of the queen's bed," not the sheets, and Meliagraunce's accusation of treason proceeds from that.

One of the most amusing treatments of this incident came somewhat earlier, in 1884, in another "modified" version of Malory.[60] In this version—illustrated by F. A. Fraser and written by Henry Frith as a "volume for the young," accompanying the Meliagraunce story—is a picture of Lancelot, on a ladder, in the moonlight, pulling at the bars of a window. It is as if Frith had somehow to fit his narrative to the pictures provided by an illustrator who had failed to consider the problems of expurgators. Since Frith apparently cannot just skip that part, he modifies it in two ways. First, he entitles the chapter "Sir Launcelot to the Rescue" and places an even more specific caption beneath the picture: "Sir Launcelot to the Rescue of the Queen." Second, he transposes incidents. Lancelot, upon his arrival at the castle, Frith says, found it all locked up but knocked down the porter, found a ladder, pulled out the iron window bars, and "entered to the Queen and the ten wounded knights."[61] Only then is Meliagraunce advised of Lancelot's arrival, whereupon he seeks out the queen, begging mercy.[62] After Lancelot is appeased, we are told, Meliagraunce, this time on no given grounds, sends a letter to the king, accusing the queen of unspecified treason, and then traps the unsuspecting Lancelot in a cave under the castle.

In his preface, Frith is straightforward in arguing the necessity of expunging and altering, " 'toning down' motives and conduct, which if painted in their true colours would offend."[63] He will not, however, "particularly specify the places where such alterations have been made," since, as he points out, those familiar with the story will recognize them and those who are not will not miss them.[64] Although Frith does not admit it, he is surely safeguarding against providing a

160

Sir Lancelot to the Rescue of the Queen. *Illustration by F. A. Fraser. In Henry Frith*, King Arthur and His Knights of the Round Table *(London: George Routledge, 1884).*

sort of key to the spicier passages in a complete Malory, should his young readers come into the possession of one. "We will not apologize for our alterations and omissions," he added, as "writing for boys, we have preserved all the vigour and valour of the action . . . with a due regard for good taste and their improvement."[65] Malory's Arthur, Frith says, was a "pure-minded and self-denying King," and there is nothing in Frith's edition of Malory to contradict this assertion.[66]

With such an expurgator/expunger, as with others discussed in this essay, one is bound to wonder: If so much of the matter is objectionable, why did these editors want to publish at all? The same question might occur regarding almost any of the numerous expurgations of those works written in (and for) periods preceding the nineteenth century, with its refined sensibilities and moral progressiveness. Expurgated *Gulliver* and expurgated *Shakespeare* certainly arise from the same impulse as does expurgated Malory. Also, like a Shakespeare or a Swift, Malory had shaped and inspired the imaginative consciousness of the age, particularly in its compelling fascination with the medieval, the idea of the Gothic—from Scott through Tennyson and Morris and beyond.

Roger Ascham's denunciation of Malory's "bold bawdrie" served as much as anything else to call attention to the book's popularity at court, and a similar phenomenon is evident in the mixed response to Malory common through much of the nineteenth century and illustrated in part by the survey in this essay. The fact that Malory's *Morte d'Arthur* was published with such frequency, particularly from the 1860s until 1900, suggests that beneath the various attempts to improve Malory—to rescue him from the flaws of his narrative method, to make him fit for youthful or general readers—lay a defensive appreciation of his enormous appeal.

Tennyson's Camelot Revisited: An Augustinian Approach to the *Idylls*

DAVID L. BOYD

In a short preface to the *Idylls*, Hallam Tennyson, recording the medieval sources on which his father's work is founded, notes that the poem was based

> on Malory, on Layamon's *Brut,* on Lady Charlotte Guest's translation of the *Mabinogion,* on the old Chronicles, on old French Romance, on Celtic folklore, and largely on his own imagination.[1]

Ever since Hallam enumerated these sources, scholars have so taken for granted the medieval foundation of the *Idylls* that ironically they have failed to investigate the extent to which the Middle Ages shaped this work. Recently, David Staines, in *Tennyson's Camelot: The "Idylls of the King" and Its Medieval Sources,* demonstrated that Malory—and, to a lesser extent, certain works from the Old French Vulgate Cycle and the *Mabinogion*—provided the poet only with such elements as setting, character names, plot, and story line. Tennyson's intent in composing his epic was not merely to create another Arthurian poem but to use the ancient Arthurian milieu as a starting point for a medieval work that would "articulate his own mature vision."[2] This being the case, it is to other non-Arthurian medieval sources that we must turn to better un-

163

derstand the *Idylls,* sources that likely would have fed the poet laureate's imagination throughout his life.

One source that seems to have had a major influence on Tennyson's imagination was the thought of Saint Augustine. As the son of an Anglican priest whose sermons reflect Augustinian concerns, Tennyson grew up in a household that not only encouraged the poet to read the Greek and Latin classics but that would have stressed the importance of the early Church Fathers as well.[3] As a student at Cambridge, the poet could hardly have escaped exposure to the writings of the saint, especially since, as a member of the Apostles, he would have spent much time fostering theological debates.[4] As an adult, Tennyson possessed intellectual and religious concerns that would have included Augustine; not only have some of the poet's ideas about evolution been viewed as essentially Augustinian, but it is also known that an important issue in the nineteenth-century Anglican church was Augustinian theology.[5] In addition, Augustine's works evidently were important in the poet's household; in her journal, Lady Tennyson documents her own reading of the *Confessions.*[6] And Tennyson makes allusions to Augustine's writings and theology in his *In Memoriam* and "The Gardener's Daughter."[7] Further, there are explicit references to *The City of God* in "Columbus":

> The great Augustine wrote that none
> could breathe
> Within the zone of heat; so might
> there be
> Two Adams, two mankinds, and that
> was clean
> Against God's word.
>
> (ll. 51–54)

Not only would Tennyson have been exposed to Augustinian ideas throughout his life but the saint's theology influenced his poetry as well.

It is to the *Idylls* themselves, however, that we must turn in order to see the extent to which Augustinian theology influenced the poet. There are certain pressing theological aspects of the *Idylls* not found in the poet's medieval belletristic sources. Critical are those aspects dealing with the antithetical natures of the kingdom of Camelot and the other Kingdoms of Britain; the use of the imagery of ontological light in the conquest of Britain; the characterization of the guilt-laden Lancelot; and, of course, the problematical fall of Arthur's realm. In the thought of Saint Augustine, however, we can find the source of these theological ideas presented in Tennyson's epic. Although the important similarities between Augustine's thought and that of Tennyson have gone unnoticed, they merit attention, for they bring into sharper focus the theological dimensions of the *Idylls of the King*.

The division of humanity into two kingdoms, the City of God and the City of Man, is central to Augustine's theology. The members of the spiritual City of God practice charity, or *caritas*, worshiping God and directing their will *(voluntas)* toward the higher good, the *bonum in communis*. The rulers of this city are in perfect harmony with its citizens; they do not govern for their own selfish interests but instead for the benefit of all. Those who reside in the City of Man, however, do not practice charity, but selfishness *(cupiditas);* they respect only themselves and direct their wills toward egocentric concerns. By the same token, their rulers govern out of selfish motives and must compel their subjects to obey. As opposing spiritual states, these two cities form Augustine's world.

In the *Idylls*, the City of God is represented by the city of Arthur, Camelot. As with the citizens of Augustine's celestial city, Arthur's knights initially practice *caritas*, forsaking selfish concerns and submitting their wills to the higher purpose of their king. Having been "Bound . . . by so strait vows" (*Coming*, l. 261) to Arthur, the knights at his coronation shout, "Be thou the king, and we will work thy will / Who love thee" (*Coming*, ll. 258–59). At the marriage of Arthur and Guinevere, the holy priest, Dubric, reinforces this idea of selflessness and amity:

Reign ye, and live and love, and make the world

> Other, and may thy Queen be one with thee,
> And all this Order of thy Table Round
> Fulfil the boundless purpose of their king.
>
> *(Coming,* ll. 471–74)

Thus, Arthur directs the will of his retinue toward the creation of a peaceful realm for all. Battling beasts, heathens, and fierce lords, he draws "All . . . petty princedoms under him, / Their king and head, and [makes] a realm, and [reigns]" (*Coming,* ll. 18–19). This Camelot is indeed "celestial," for, like its Augustinian counterpart, it is a city where all wills combine in the harmony of *caritas.*

Whereas Arthur's realm interacts through charity in its early stages, the realms of the Earl of Doorm and of the Red Knight—Tennyson's "City of Man"—wallow in *cupiditas.*[8] In the lands of the Earl of Doorm, a "realm of lawless turbulence," no one manifests love or charity. After the wounded Geraint falls from his horse, none of Doorm's vassals will help either him or his wife, the forlorn Enid, for there "A woman weeping for her murdered mate / Was cared as much for as a summer shower." In fact, no one dares "to waste a perilous pity on him" (*Geraint and Enid,* ll. 521–25). The same principle of selfishness abounds in the realm of the Red Knight, who boasts that he has

> . . . founded my Round Table in the North,
> And whatsoever [Arthur's] own knights have sworn
> My knights have sworn the counter to it.
>
> *(Last Tournament,* ll. 78–80)[9]

The message is clear: Whereas Arthur and his knights have sacrificed their own selfish interests, the Red Knight and his retinue have forfeited the *bonum in communis* for egocentric concerns. Arthur's knights have taken vows of peace; those of the Red Knight, vows of violence. Arthur's knights espouse chastity; the Red Knight's vow lasciviousness. Arthur's purpose is to create a realm of harmony; the Red Knight's is to spread violence and discord throughout the land. Like Au-

166

gustine, Tennyson has created two cities—one in which "the princes and the subjects serve one another in love" *(in hac seruiunt inuicem in caritate et praepositi consulendo et subditi obtemperando);* and another in which the princes are "ruled by the love of ruling" *(Illi in principibus eius uel in ies quas subiugat nationibus dominandi libido dominatur).*[10]

Not only does Tennyson seem to draw upon Augustine's concept of the two cities in this section of the *Idylls*, in "The Coming of Arthur," he makes free use of the saint's theory of ontological light as well. For Augustine, one factor that separates man from brute is his potential for illumination—the contemplation of eternal truth. Just as the sun illuminates physical objects, so does the light of God illuminate the mind and soul of man, driving away darkness and evil. Whereas the mind receives intellectual illumination, though, the will receives *moral* instruction. Thus, God's light pervades the darkness of moral turpitude and uncertainty; those who wish to walk in that light direct their wills toward Him. His light will brighten man's path and point out the true way, for "All who know the truth know this Light, and all who know this Light know eternity" *(qui nouit ueritatem, nouit eam, et qui nouit eam, nouit aeternitatem).*[11]

Tennyson seems to have made conscious use of this concept in *The Coming of Arthur*. Before the reign of Arthur, Cameliard and the whole of Britain exist in a state of darkness, moral turpitude, and *cupiditas*. Darkened with tangled forests that admit little light, the land is replete with wild animals and heathen who "[redden] the sun with smoke" (*Coming*, l. 37). Coming to the rescue of the territory, Arthur drives away "The heathen; after, [slays] the beast, and [fells] / The forest, *letting in the sun*" (*Coming*, ll. 59–60 [emphasis mine]). Afterward, he takes Guinevere as his bride so they may reign together and "Have power on this dark land to lighten it" (*Coming*, l. 92). It is with his knights that the process of moral illumination begins.

As the light that illuminates a land of darkness, Arthur must transfer this light to the members of the Round Table, illuminating them spiritually and transforming them in his

167

own image. During his coronation, many of his knights are "pale as at the passing of a ghost, / Some flushed, and others dazed, as one who wakes / Half-blinded at the coming of a light" (*Coming*, ll. 263–65). As he speaks to them with "divine words," Arthur also "lets in" another type of sun, for the light of his soul, like the light of the son of God, falls upon his retinue:

> From eye to eye through all their Order flash[es]
> A momentary likeness of the King
> And ere it [leaves] their faces, *through the
>   cross*
> And those around it and the Crucified,
> Down from the casement over Arthur, smote
> Flame-colour, vert and azure.
>   (*Coming*, ll. 269–74 [emphasis mine])

This light, in the likeness of Arthur, comes into the dark realms of man's moral nature. Destroying the darkness, not only within man but within an entire civilization, Arthur guides the individual will toward a higher good—peace and unity—and illuminates a new direction for moral activity. This king, on whom the "Sun of May descend[s]" (*Coming*, l. 461), is the light that all must follow.[12] *Qui nouit veritatem, nouit eam, nouit aeternitatem.*

Because certain metaphors (the two cities) and certain images (light and darkness) appear to have been prompted by Augustine's writings, it is tempting to look for the same pattern of influences in other aspects of the *Idylls*. Augustine's description of his own battle with lust in the *Confessions*, for instance, closely parallels Lancelot's struggles in Tennyson's grail episode. To a certain degree, Lancelot is the typical courtly lover. Tennyson, however, seems to have drawn many aspects of this character not from Malory or the *Queste del Saint Grail* but from Augustine's expressions of his love of God in the *Confessions*.[13] As a young man, Augustine wrote, he kept a mistress and "created of [himself] a barren waste" (*factus sum mihi regio egestatis* [*Conf.*, II, x, 18]). Realizing the error of his ways, he wished to convert to Christianity but could not rid himself of one sin—lust. Frustrated, the "hope of honour and wealth . . . no longer, as before, a spur to [his] ambition" *(non iam inflammantibus cupiditatibus, ut solebant, spe honoris et pecuniae ad tolerandam illam seruitutem tam grauem),* he was nonetheless "held firm in the bonds of woman's love" *(sed adhuc tenaciter conligabar ex femina [Conf., VIII, i, 2]).* Thus, torn between the desire to satisfy his lusts and the desire to live for God, Augustine recalled that "these two wills within me, one old, one new, one the servant of the flesh, the other of the spirit, were in conflict between them that tore my soul apart" *(duae voluntates meae, una uetus, alia noua, illa carnalis, illa spiritalis, confligebant inter se atque discordando dissipabant animam meam [Conf., VIII, v, 101]).* Indeed, "the impulses of nature and the impulses of the spirit are at war with one another" *(caro concupisc[it] adversus spiritum et spiritus aduersus carnem [Conf., VIII, v, 11]).* At first, he followed the will of the flesh, but at the next struggle—after talking to the holy man Ponticianus—Augustine, beside himself with "madness that would bring [him] sanity" *(tantum insaniebam salubriter [Conf., VIII, viii, 19]),* confronted his inner nature. Recalling the veritable sea of emotions welling up inside his youthful self that left him half-drowned in a "whirlpool of sin" *(mersabat gurgite flagitiorum [Conf., II, ii, 2]),* he laments that a "great storm broke within" him *(oborta est procella ingens [Conf., VIII, xii, 28]).*

Lancelot's struggles with his own sins contain the same imagery found in Augustine. In his illicit affair with Guinevere, which indirectly leads him into "waste fields far away" *(Holy Grail, l. 785),* Lancelot, too, struggles to free himself from the sin of lust. He acknowledges his error and longs to reunite himself with his king. Like Augustine, he no longer cares for his position or his honor: "What profits me my name / Of greatest knight?" *(Lancelot and Elaine, ll. 1402–03).* He, too, longs to "break / These bonds that so defame [him]" *(Lancelot and Elaine, l. 1410).* In *The Holy Grail,* the knight describes the nature of his sin:

> So strange . . . that all of pure,

> Noble, and knightly in me twined and clung
> Round that one sin, until the wholesome flower
> And poisonous grow together, each as each,
> Not to be plucked asunder.
>
> (ll. 470–74)

These two flowers, like Augustine's two wills, strive against one another. On one hand, Lancelot must love Guinevere; on the other, Arthur. Here, classically, is "Sense at war with Soul."[14] Then, just as Augustine searches for truth in Christianity to relieve himself of the burden of his sins, so Lancelot, advised by a holy hermit, embarks on his quest for the Grail to expiate his sin of adultery. "Madness [comes] upon [him] as of old" (*Holy Grail*, ll. 784). His sea breaks into a storm; the boat he is to use is "Half-swallowed" by the waves (*Holy Grail*, ll. 792–800). Just as Augustine is "swept away" by the tides (*sequens impetum fluxus mei* [*Conf.*, II, ii, 4]), Lancelot is driven "along the weary deep" (*Holy Grail*, l. 805). This correspondence is too close to be merely coincidental.

Besides the characterization of Lancelot, another aspect of the *Idylls* that seems to have been influenced by Augustine's writings is the fall of Camelot. Unlike Tennyson's medieval sources, the collapse of Arthur's civilization mirrors Augustine's conception of the Fall of Man, in which man falls not through concupiscence but pride.[15] Although adultery, Guinevere's "shameful sin with Lancelot" (*Guinevere*, l. 484), is widely viewed as the destroyer of Arthur's civilization, it is strange that even this "blackest of sins" should bear full responsibility.[16] As Stanley J. Solomon points out, "it is hardly conceivable that even much weaker kingdoms than Camelot would collapse over a matter so personal as adultery."[17] Indeed, there is reason to think it does not.

The summit of God's creation, the Garden of Eden, existed in a state of harmony and perfection so long as the human wills of its inhabitants remained subordinated to the will of their Maker. According to Augustine's conception of the creation, God made a world from "a primal, formless state" (*inchoata et informia* [*Conf.*, XIII, ii, 2]) and then brought forth

Adam and Eve from the dust of this earth. Formed in God's image, these two were to live in perfect bliss, enjoying the gift of intimate communion with their Maker so long as their unselfish love of Him *(caritas)* bound their wills to His. In fact, human nature is "so created that submission is advantageous to it, while fulfilment of its own will in preference to the Creator's is destruction" *(ita facta est, ut ei subditam esse sit utile; perniciosum autem suam, non eius a quo creata est facere uoluntatem* [*City of God*, XIV, xii, 14–15]). According to Augustinian theology, the harmony of Eden broke down as soon as Adam and Eve experienced desires at variance with those of God. This errant, self-centered concern, referred to by Augustine as the will of the *animalis homo* (animal-man), refuses to submit to a higher will, following instead the doctrine of "man living according to man" *(id est secundum hominem vivens homo* [*City of God*, XIV, iv, 49–51]). When this bestial will possessed Adam and Eve, they disobeyed God and were expelled from Eden.

Tennyson conceives of Arthur as attempting to re-create an Edenic kingdom in a fallen world.[18] Like God Himself, he succeeds in forming an earthly paradise from a chaotic land, a "realm . . . gone to wrack" *(Coming,* l. 226), but the continuing existence of this new civilization is also dependent on human submission to a higher will. When the young Arthur enters Leodogran's dominion, he encounters a place of chaos in which wild dogs, wolves, and bears rule, a territory in which "there grew great tracts of wilderness, / Wherein the beast was ever more and more / But man was less and less" *(Coming,* ll. 10–12). Arthur enters this wilderness, establishes his realm, and—God-like—forms the inhabitants of his Eden after his own image. Lancelot, Guinevere, and the Round Table are to be lifted "from the dust" *(Coming,* l. 490) through their love of the king. Like Adam and Eve, Camelot's inhabitants can exist in a state of peace and harmony and live in perfect contentment only as long as they bind their wills to that of its creator and evince an unselfish love for him. Lancelot and the king swear "on the field of death a deathless love" *(Coming,* l. 131) to one another; Guinevere pledges, "Let chance what will, I love thee to the death" (*Coming*, 1. 467); and Queen Bellicent, describing how Arthur lifts his knights of the Round Table from the dust, notes that he binds them by "straight vows to his own self" (*Coming*, 1. 261), while they cry: "Be thou the king, and we will work thy will / Who love thee" (*Coming*, ll. 258–59). As in Eden, there are at first no selfish desires in Arthur's Camelot.

Like Eden, however, Camelot breaks down as soon as Lancelot and Guinevere give free rein to the bestial will and ignore their vows to Arthur. Although sworn to love their king to the death and to sacrifice their personal interests to his, both turn disloyal. In their adultery, each becomes Augustine's *animalis homo;* living only according to themselves, they set off a chain reaction which, according to Edward Engelberg, releases the beast in all members of Camelot's society and entails the breaking of vows and a preference for selfish, passionate concerns.[19] To emphasize this idea, Tennyson fills the *Idylls* with bestial imagery. Thus Balan, overhearing Lancelot and Guinevere's courtly love conversation, is "blind and deaf to all / Save that chained rage, which ever yelpt within" (*Balin and Balan*, ll. 313–14); Vivien, desiring a magic formula from Merlin, is said to have "Writhed toward him, slided up his knee / . . . . / curved an arm about his neck, / Clung like a snake" (*Merlin and Vivien*, ll. 237–40)[20]; and the Red Knight is reduced to a beast who draws "his claws athwart the face" of one of Arthur's churls (*Last Tournament*, l. 63). Arthur's knights themselves, slaying the Red Knight, behave like a pack of unruly animals, for they "shouted and leapt down upon the fallen; / There trampled out his face from being known, / . . . and slimed themselves" (*Last Tournament*, ll. 468–70). Like Adam and Eve, Lancelot and Guinevere pay heed only to their own wills; their actions result in the destruction of an entire Edenic world.

The ultimate source of their bestial, errant will is not adultery, but pride. In Augustine's analysis of the Fall of Eden, it was *superbia*, not Eve's succumbing to the Satanic temptation, that resulted in a state of *cupiditas*. As Augustine writes: "What is the origin of our evil will but pride? For 'pride is the beginning of sin'" (*Porro malae voluntatis intium quae potuit esse nisi superbia? Initium enim omnis peccati superbia est* [*City of God*, XIV, xiii, 3–5]). Both Adam and Eve allowed their wills to fall away from that of God because they were already corrupt through *superbia*. They preferred their own desires over those of their Creator. As Augustine explains, "the soul abandons Him to whom it ought to cleave as its end, and becomes a kind of end to itself" (*Peruersa enim est celsitudo deserto eo, cui debet animus inhaerere, principio sibi quodam modo fieri atque esse principium* [*City of God*, XIV, xiii, 6–8]). It was this pride that engendered Adam and Eve's selfish passions.

In the *Idylls*, Tennyson goes a step further than the medieval Arthurian writers. It is pride—not Guinevere's adultery with Lancelot—that engenders the selfishness that destroys Arthur's Edenic kingdom.[21] After Arthur leaves her at the Almesbury nunnery and rides away to contend with Modred, the queen laments her "false, voluptuous pride, that took / Full easily all impressions from below" (*Guinevere*, ll. 636–37).[22] The word *pride* is employed nineteen times in the *Idylls* but only thirty-five times in all the rest of Tennyson's works combined.[23] Its repetition seems to make manifest Tennyson's debt to an Augustinian conception behind the fall of Camelot, as Guinevere's pride spreads to infect that entire civilization. In *The Marriage of Geraint*, Geraint pursues the villainous Sparrowhawk in order to "break his pride" (l. 221); in *Gareth and Lynnette*, Lynnette claims that the knights holding her sister's castle under siege resemble old knights-errant who do but what they will and who are beastlike and "Proud in their fantasy" (l. 618). Indeed, all the subjects of Arthur's kingdom "place their pride in Lancelot and the Queen" (*Merlin and Vivien*, l. 25).

Thus the pride of Lancelot and Guinevere causes the eventual destruction of Camelot. It is the pride to which Tennyson refers when he speaks of the queen's "shameful sin" (*Guinevere*, l. 484). As with Eve's temptation, Guinevere's adultery is merely a reflection of the false egocentrism that corrupts her will. Camelot remains Edenic only so long as individual wills remain subjugated to that of Arthur; but the "bestial nature"—Augustine's *homo animalis*—takes over, and self-centered deeds proliferate. Thus, just as Adam and Eve must die exiled from Eden, their grossly flawed natures awaiting redemption from an original sin of pride, the denizens of Camelot lose their glory, "Reel back into the beast" (*Last Tournament*, l. 125), and must place their hope in a "new sun . . . bringing in the new year" (*Passing of Arthur*, l. 469).

Such parallels as these suggest that certain fundamental ideas in Augustine's thought were a shaping influence on the *Idylls of the King*. Whereas the *Idylls*, as H. Tennyson noted, was founded largely on Tennyson's imagination, the poet laureate's ideas were to some extent at least based on the thought and writings of Saint Augustine. Although the belletristic medieval sources—namely, Malory, the *Mabinogion*, and certain Old French Romances—are concerned in part with theological issues, they lack the same Augustinian concerns and emphases that Tennyson employs in his epic. These were most likely supplied from Augustine, whose concepts of *caritas* and *cupiditas* seem not only to have intrigued the human imagination and triggered poetic inspiration but also to have illuminated both the rise and fall of a great civilization and the struggles of the human soul.

Arthurian Myth Devalued in Walker Percy's *Lancelot*

JOHN BUGGE

Walker Percy's one-word title, *Lancelot,* may seem a simple, bold stroke announcing a straightforward use of Arthurian myth; but those who persevere through his narrator's shocking and vertiginous account of adultery and murderous revenge learn otherwise. The title is ironic, and so is Percy's use of the material throughout. He employs the Arthuriad only to devalue it against standards established in his own existential philosophy of cognition.

In a way, the narrative is rather too vehemently Arthurian, a pretty good hint that Percy has something ingenious planned. Made aware of the novel's Arthurian pretensions even before we turn to the first page, we must endure Lance the narrator's ostentatious lecturing of his interlocutor, Harry Percival, on the significance of their names, plus much else that is supererogatory.[1] Yet part of the appeal of the mythographic method here is that its effects are hidden and submerged, not, as we first suspect, all floating conspicuously on the surface of Lance's narrative consciousness. Not even this sometimes maniacally perceptive observer realizes how deeply his own thoughts and actions are anchored in the Arthurian myth—and this is basic to Percy's plan. For example, Lance is sure his father named him for the Arthurian hero. He prefers to believe that the middle name "Andrewes"

175

was merely a dodge, "tacked on by him to give it Episcopal sanction." Here is a hint that it is Lance who dodges association with the morally stringent Anglican divine in favor of one with Lancelot du Lac (p. 116). Further, although Lance is relatively knowledgeable about his chosen namesake, his awareness of such mythic identification is far from complete: Percy inserts details designed to work as a kind of dramatic irony, permitting the reader to see deeper into Lance's "received" character than he himself can. His surname "Lamar," for example, is "the pool" *(la mare)* in French, strikingly close to "du Lac," to be sure, yet with connotations of comparative shallowness and inconsequence. Again, Malory's Lancelot goes through a period of madness after his rejection by Guinevere until he is cured by being brought into the presence of "the holy vessell of the Sankgreall."[2] Correspondingly, although Lance is a patient in a mental hospital, his narrative convinces us he is sane, that he only gives himself "license to talk crazy" (p. 160). This means, of course, that he is fully responsible for the murders he has committed. As we shall see, Lance's blindness to these and other similar discrepancies between the myth and his own experience suggests that, though he may conceive of himself as Lancelot *redivivus*, we are everywhere encouraged to see his actions as a dangerous case of what Percy decries as "impersonation."

Only two other characters have names directly from the tradition: Harry Percival and Bob Merlin. Thus the three are marked as the only survivors from that grand age of heroic myth. Percy is fond of survivors among the ruins, out of place in their time and alienated from their surroundings (cf. *Love in the Ruins*); the world these three inhabit is far removed from the mythic Golden Age of Arthur. Lance's father once had shown him the nighttime sky and pointed out "how far away Arcturus was," a dim star, thirty light-years away, too remote to serve as a beacon or cast its influence on the degenerate world of 1976 (pp. 56–57). Each of the survivors has lost his bearings in the modern age. Lance is a pseudo-heroic Lancelot adrift in a world that no longer provides opportunities for heroic action, whether in deeds of arms or love. Harry

176

Percival, reflex of the tradition's pure and sensitive God-bitten ascetic, is someone whose Christian commitment has been more foppish aestheticism than substance. Bob Merlin, contemporary version of the tradition's mighty thaumaturge and seer, is reduced to the level of a filmmaker whose only magic is the disreputable and shallow illusionism of the silver screen. All are debased, failed versions of their mythic originals; their fundamentally illusory lives in the here and now illustrate Percy's favorite theme: lack of existential authenticity.

Perhaps this is clearest in Lance's relationship with Bob Merlin, who has cuckolded him and fathered the child Lance had thought his own. His discovery of his wife Margot's past adultery with Merlin propels the narrative. Merlin is now in residence at Belle Isle, Lance's estate, to oversee the making of a film; and Lance can express only well-founded contempt for the specious profundities of its scenario as mouthed by the people involved in making it. Still, he finds himself strangely drawn to Merlin. Lance feels that he, of all the eccentric movie people, is the most sensible and intelligent and, despite Merlin's offense against him, the one he finds most sympathetic (p. 47). Unwittingly, Lance draws closer to Merlin, imitating his ideas, his speech patterns, even—most telling of all—his moviemaking. Thus, an important key to Lance's predicament is his "impersonation" of Merlin; despite his boast that all the actions prompted by his catastrophic discovery of the adultery proceed from a newfound self-possession, we actually hear in the contours of his speech and thought that he has surrendered title over his own being to this modern magus. Lance's unconscious alliance with Merlin helps to certify Lance's failure to achieve authenticity.[3]

Such prominence given to the movies in the novel, together with Percy's own epistemological speculation on how "moviegoing" prevents access to being, seems to invite us to draw a moral antithesis between the specious modern world of merely celluloid reality, represented by Merlin, and the ancient verities of a worthier age, as handed down through the Arthurian tradition.[4] Our own reverence for that tradition,

177

perhaps in some way justified by the strong pull of Tenny-sonian pieties that have come to inform it, naturally inclines us to believe that Percy must think the Arthurian myth has value for those dwelling in alienation in the twentieth century. The author's neatest trick in *Lancelot,* however, is both to play on these sympathies for all they're worth and, at the same time, to vitiate our most fundamental assumptions about the value of myth as a way of structuring reality.[5] If we prize Percy's finesse in scattering through the text so many subtle correspondences between Lance Lamar and his medieval counterpart—Lance resides along the "English Coast" of the Mississippi (Logres), separated from the "French" aristocracy of New Orleans by the river (the English Channel), in a landscape of chaste, incorrupt chapels (that of medieval romance) (pp. 14, 46, 116), and so on—we risk falling into the same trap as does the narrator, who records these parallels without consciously remarking on them. That is, we fall enthusiastically into Lance's mythographic way of seeing and thinking, only to be brought up short when we discover that Percy is using the Arthurian myth with neither sympathy nor admiration, but portraying it as a distinctly negative force and equating it with the movies as a source of illusion. Like the movies, myth, too, prevents access to true being.

The central issue of the novel, a constant theme in Percy's writings on epistemology, is the difficult one of ascertaining one's own identity.[6] Lance remarks of the movie people that they didn't seem to know who they were but were "like puffballs," blown "in and out of their roles" (p. 112). He complains about Margot, of *nouveau* oil-*riche* Texas origins, and her determination to take on the identity of the *chatelaine* of Belle Isle (p. 88). Of himself, Lance says that before the discovery he did not know who he was; it is a revelation forcibly brought home by the odd circumstance of his momentary failure to recognize his own reflection in a mirror (pp. 63–64). Purportedly, of course, he "finds himself" when he makes his discovery; but that sense of identity—the self he discovers, indeed, appropriates—comes mainly from the Arthurian myth. Just as the role Merlin's movie actor Troy Dana plays

178

lends him an aura of authenticity while the klieg lights burn (pp. 146–48), Lance Lamar *is* someone only—and just as iron-ically—when he is impersonating Lancelot du Lac and attempting to find the meaning of his existence in the golden vagaries of the myth.

Lance's disposition to approach reality through the filter of the Arthurian myth is as feckless as Merlin's own obsession with a mystique of blood and roses all too obviously that of Ernest Hemingway's tight-lipped macho heroes (for example, pp. 201–205). Neither character takes reality straight. In Lance's case, his possession by the Arthurian myth of a heroic past prevents him from seeing the reality of his own existence in the present.[7] Here, Percy's own comments about true seeing are as relevant to Lance as to Merlin. In writing about a sightseer's first view of the Grand Canyon, Percy describes how such a person in fact fails to see the canyon as it is, to make noetic contact with its reality, because his act of knowing is inhibited by a pre-formed "symbolic complex" already present in his mind (through postcards, travel folders, and so on). This intervenes and prevents objective reality from being known on its own terms. The situation demonstrates what Percy, following Whitehead, would call the fallacy of misplaced concreteness: we mistakenly regard the symbol as more real than the actual concrete reality it signifies.[8] The Arthurian myth fits the definition of just such a pre-formed symbolic complex.

It is important to see that the entire myth takes possession of Lance—not just one character in the tradition. Lance cannot rest content being only Lancelot du Lac. In his moments of wildest vaticination, he plays the role of Merlin himself, of prophet and seer. In his plan to establish a new American social order in Virginia, Lance would be a reincarnation of Arthur as well, returned from a purgatorial city of the dead to reestablish the Round Table amid the American moral wilderness. In what turns out to be his most salutary role, he plays Fisher King to his old friend Percival's Percival. Shifting as he does between these various avatars, however, Lance most consistently plays Lancelot, the Great Lover of the tradition and, in consequence, the most important failure in the quest of the Holy Grail.

As Lance remembers his Malory, the number of knights who have had a glimpse of the Grail is only two, Lancelot and Percival (p. 116); now their namesakes are once again united, sharing their consternation at not having achieved the goal.[9] Lance introduces the Grail theme with typically hyperbolic, brazen posturing: "Do you know what I was? The Knight of the Unholy Grail. . . . Sexual sin was the unholy grail I sought" (pp. 138, 140). Lance's tone whenever he refers to himself in this vein threatens to drown out the quieter echoes of the Grail-quest myth with which Percy has invested the narrative, and which are so essential to his point in the novel. Nevertheless, dozens of significant details override Lance's own hollow self-mockery, suggesting that the Grail-quester correspondence is far stronger (and more in possession of his consciousness) than he himself realizes. For example, he seems not even to realize the abbreviated form of his name is a pun connected to the phallic and vaginal symbolism of the grail articles (lance and cup). In its full form ("lance a lot"), it helps illuminate the spiritual aridity of his definition of "lancing" as the meaning of life (pp. 11–12, 168–69), as well as pointing up his own peculiar manic obsessiveness about sex (as seen, for example, in his weird sexual theory of history [pp. 35–36, 176–80]). His wife Margot is the holy vessel Lance seeks to be united with, specifically a "sanctuary guarded by the heavy gold columns of her thighs," where, in blasphemous mimicry of the Eucharist, he reports to Percival: "That was my communion, Father—no offense intended" (p. 171). Having discovered her infidelity and embarked on his search for absolute ocular proof of her adultery—a "vision" of this unholy grail—Lance becomes the medieval knight setting out on his quest. He becomes ascetic: beginning a new life, he discovers that he "didn't need a drink. It became possible to . . . watch and wait" (p. 63). He practices mortification of the flesh, involving tests of his physical strength (p. 65). Preparatory to his quest, he bathes carefully and ritually purifies himself (p. 66). He spends a night in vigil peering through a window of stained glass as if at devotions in a medieval chapel (p. 86). Finally, in drug-induced hallucination, he imagines he receives a sword from a woman who resembles the Lady of the Lake; it is his ritual "charge" to carry out the quest. He comes to his senses holding not a sword but a Bowie knife (pp. 225–26).

The setting, too, contributes to the theme of grail quest. Several times, Lance's antebellum home, Belle Isle, is likened to a boat or ship, the equivalent of the mysterious vessels that carry Malory's Grail knights to their destination. The belvedere atop the house is a captain's deck; during the hurricane "it rattled and rocked like the *Tennessee Belle*," a river steamer (p. 174); and from its height the river is "like the sea" (p. 171). When the storm worsens, Lance can hear the house creak as if it were "laboring through heavy seas" (p. 230; cf. p. 228). When the scene shifts to the interior of the darkened house, the imagery becomes liturgical. Lance can hear the "organ sounds" made by the wind in the loft of the house (p. 227). In the blackness he finds his way by feeling with his hand for a "cathedral chair" (p. 230). In the master bedroom he finds what he is searching for in an ornate "Gothic bed" also "like a cathedral," whose posts taper to "spires and gargoyles," and whose headboard is likened to an "altar screen" (p. 237). The bed is a perverse Grail chapel. Finally, in the explosive climax of Lance's quest, the murder of Margot's lover accomplished, he strikes a match in the house now filled with methane. "All was light and air and color and movement. . . ." Belle Isle blows up, but Lance is blown free: "When I came to myself," he says, "the fire was hot against my cheek" (p. 246). Lance's account recalls his namesake's experience in the presence of the Grail, when, in Malory, Lancelot "saw the chambir dore opyn, and there cam oute a grete clerenesse, that the house was as bryght as all the tourcheis of the worlde had bene there." Though warned not to enter the chamber, Lancelot does so anyway, attempting to come close to the Grail itself: "and whan he cam nyghe hit he felte a

181

breeth that hym thought hit was entromedled with fyre, which smote hym so sore in the vysayge that hym thought hit brente hys vysayge" (*Works*, pp. 1015–16).

All these detailed correspondences provide more than a mere deepening mythic dimension to the action, however undeniably attractive such resonance may be. In Percy's scheme, the primary function of the correspondences is to work a colossal irony upon the "hero," who tells us all this by way of demonstrating, the seductive correspondences notwithstanding, how impossibly at variance with the true quest of the Grail is Lance's action of murderous revenge and how it must be judged when seen from any perspective other than his own solipsistic one. As Lance uses the Grail-quest theme as a source of overheated metaphor, Percy shows him in the grip of "automythography"—finding meaning in one's existence by apprehending it in mythic terms. This is no way to live a life. To engage in such misplaced concreteness is to act without authenticity.

Everyone in Percy's existentialism is capable of "the search," a concept Percy takes from Kierkegaard. To engage in it, however, one must first be aware of one's predicament, and such knowledge is not easy to acquire; for, as Kierkegaard writes (in *Sickness unto Death*, used by Percy as the epigraph to *The Moviegoer*), "the specific character of despair is precisely this: it is unaware of being despair." Nevertheless, once one has been forcibly made aware of one's own predicament through the sort of catastrophic discovery Lance makes, the search must proceed honestly and not, as it were, vicariously, seeking reality through symbolization, as in the movies. As Binx Bolling remarks in *The Moviegoer*, "The movies are onto the search, but they screw it up. The search always ends in despair."[10] Just as the movies offer no satisfaction to one alienated and in despair, however, neither does myth. The proof lies in Lance's final confession to Percival when his account of the terrible night at Belle Isle is over. He "felt nothing at all. Nothing good, nothing bad, not even a sense of discovery. . . . I feel nothing now except a certain coldness" (p. 253). He seems to end where he began—in despair.

The other search, or quest, in the novel is that of Harry Percival.[11] It too is told in terms of the traditional Arthurian quest of the Grail but only because Lance is telling it, seeing it through the same mythographic filter he uses for his own experience. Lance remarks expansively that in youth Harry was called "Parsifal, who found the Grail and brought life to a dead land" (p. 10). Once again, however, although we are perhaps even more tempted here to think of such mythic correspondences as *reinforcing* the meaning of Percival's quest, it is absolutely necessary that we (and Percival) reject them if we are to see how the search can be successful. Lance's sketchy, elliptical account of Percival's youth reveals him to have been a "melancholy and abstracted" sort (p. 15), given to putting on "acts." Suddenly converted to Catholicism, Harry had gone "from unbeliever to priest" and had set out idealistically for Biafra to change the world. Now apparently painfully disillusioned, he has returned empty, having reached Lance's same low point of despair. Lance asks him if he has lost his faith—"or is it a woman?" (p. 61). In a way it turns out to be both.

In the mythic terms Lance prefers (but does not fully appreciate here), the entire novel comprises a single episode in the traditional account of the Grail quest—the visit of Percival to Corbenic, the castle of Malory's "Maymed Kynge." Modern America is the land mysteriously laid waste, New Orleans is "the city of the dead" (p. 254), the *uscio dei morti* of the novel's epigraph from the *Purgatorio*. Seeming to preside over everything is Lance as the Fisher King, immured and immobilized in his upper-story cell of the mental asylum, from which he looks down on the blasted cityscape below. In actuality, Lance's passive role as Fisher King is more important to us than his overt impersonation of Lancelot du Lac; but it is one of the book's central ironies that he does not realize he is playing the former role. Many details he supplies incidentally, however, support the association. For example, Lance is a "drinker," even to the point of incipient alcoholism. Perhaps we are to see his excessive thirst as implying a need to relieve the spiritual dessication that has overtaken his life. Lance confesses that he hadn't even seen the river for years (p. 56); he's had no contact, not even visual, with the water that flows by Belle Isle (because literally, of course, it is obscured by the levee). At another point, Lance unwittingly lets slip a crucial indication of his mythical status. Like King Pellam in Malory (*Works*, pp. 84–87), rendered sexually impotent by the Dolorous Stroke, Lance has been "like a man favoring a secret wound. . . . It was that lately I had trouble making love to Margot" (p. 66).

Lance's role as Fisher King clarifies the mythic one played by Anna, the young woman in the next room, victim of a brutal sexual assault. She seems a thoroughly modern avatar of the female Grail bearer, the unidentified, almost faceless woman who carries the Grail articles silently and mysteriously before the quester. Like that figure, Anna resides "with" the wounded king, fulfilling her part in a highly enigmatic relationship that also involves the questing knight—in this case, Harry Percival himself—and which contains the promise of spiritual fulfillment. Thus it should not be surprising to the reader (though it is to Lance), when Harry announces on the last page of the novel that he knows Anna well enough to predict that she will, after all, join Lance's future in Virginia (p. 257).[12] The triangular relationship among the three principals suggests the potential for grace and renewal that exists in the similar triangle of the grail myth, involving quester, bearer, and wounded king.

In some versions of the grail myth (for example, Chrétien's *Conte del Graal*), Percival fails in his quest through his unaccountable silence when the Grail is made manifest to him.[13] True, the vocations of this Percival (he is both priest and psychiatrist) make him a professional listener less inclined to talk than listen. But it only *seems* that he shares the taciturnity of his namesake; in fact, he is full of probing questions, to which the apparent monologue that is the narrative comprises the answers. The point is crucial, of course, for it says

184

Percival's quest will succeed. Also in Percival's favor is that, being both priest and physician, two kinds of healer, he is the only figure in the novel who seems capable of restorative action. By the end of his long and problematical interview with Lance, the questions Percival has not failed to ask appear to have revitalized him spiritually. Although we are forced to view it through the obscurantism of Lance's relentless egotism, Percival undergoes a regeneration in the encounter— "You know, something has changed in you" (p. 254)—as shown by the string of Yes's that are his only words of spoken dialogue. They are words of purest affirmation, in response now to questions from Lance (perhaps a hopeful symptom of the latter's eventual escape from the prison of the self). However tantalizing and enigmatic they may be, they are counterpoint to the hopeless negativity, the "nothingness" that has afflicted Lance's existence.

Percival is Lance's opposite in another way. As if to prove that Percival does *not* suffer from the delusion of modeling his own experience after the career of a mythic prototype, Percy's more sympathetic character does not—like Malory's Percival, for instance (*Works*, pp. 1035–36)—exchange the world of action for one of cloistered contemplation of the mystery he has been privy to. Instead, he will go back into the world, to Alabama, where he will "preach the gospel, turn bread into flesh, forgive the sins of Buick dealers" (p. 256). What could be more drab and humdrum—and less mythic? Such is precisely the author's point, however. If we feel a pang of disappointment that Percival's new (and obviously genuinely spiritual) quest is no longer fitted out in Arthurian dress, then we too have been taken in by the fallacy of misplaced concreteness; we will have assumed that Percival should somehow play out the role Lance has created for him. Truly to find himself, though, to create his own self in action, Percival must impersonate no one.[14]

Perhaps the strategic triumph of the novel is that Percy puts the reader squarely in Percival's situation (which is also the author's—"Percy" being Percival for short). Both Percival and the reader listen to Lance and pose unstated questions. They find him an immensely engaging storyteller; they suspect his sanity at first but, to their horror, gradually realize that he is perfectly sane. Deprived of sympathy for Lance's mythographic sensibility by the violence and shocking nihilism of his account, the reader gets the same salutary "vision" Percival receives at the end of the novel and goes away from the book feeling that he, like Percival, has acquired a crucial insight that Lance has not yet achieved. Specifically, although he introduces it early (p. 4) and brings up the subject again at the end of his narrative (p. 250), Lance never comes to realize what a half-obscured sign located around a corner outside his window really says. He has been looking at it for a year, yet can still make out only

Free &

Ma

B

"Notice that it is impossible to see more than that," says Lance (p. 4). For him, yes; for he does not realize even now (though he may in time) that, all along, the sign has said just what he has been reading and no more, that one is "Free and Ma(y) B(e)"—but only if one can learn to see the reality there in front of one's eyes.

Lancelot is an astonishingly creative exploitation of the Arthurian myth: both a narratorial tour de force of artful correspondences that illustrates all too well the seductiveness of myth as a way of escaping reality; and a cool-handed demolition of the epistemological underpinnings of such a mythographic approach. Our admiration for the ingenuity of Percy the novelist in reshaping the Arthurian myth into so engaging a modern likeness must not allow us to forget that for Percy the philosopher, all myth is a species of illusion, in the final analysis as devastating to "the search" as films or any other type of pre-formed symbolic complex that prevents access to true being. *Lancelot* is, finally, about "impersonation" and the title character's chameleon-like quality of facile adaptability.[15] In the course of his story we observe how Lance is drawn into playing a number of roles, but his main impersonation is of the legendary figure whose name he bears. As long as Lance remains "Lancelot" in self-perception as well as in name, he will never take title to his own existence, never have a name to call his own.

"Yet Some Men Say . . . that Kynge Arthure Ys Nat Ded"

CHARLES MOORMAN

. . . but that he is alive and well in contemporary America. Laying aside the almost frenetic activities of Arthurian scholars of the past half-century—the archaeological discoveries, the attempts to discover the identity of the historical Arthur, the reappraisals of Malory—it is surely a testimony to the continuing existence of this quondam king that we have in the past decade witnessed live Arthurian tournaments in New Jersey, sword-in-the-stone paperweights in airport gift shops, Richard Burton touring in *Camelot, The Once and Future King* on the paperback "Classics" shelf in mall bookstores, Disney's cartoon and John Boorman's epic and Monty Python, bless his heart, on prime-time TV, and at least a half-dozen new King Arthur novels, one by a Nobel laureate. The influence of the Arthur story has everywhere infiltrated the pop culture of our time; Luke Skywalker obviously owes much to the Arthurian knight-errant, as does Obie Ben Kenobi to Merlin.

Nor is our own age alone in re-doing the Arthur legend. E. A. Robinson delved into the psychology of both Merlin and Miniver Cheevy, and Tennyson cast Albert as Arthur and Victoria as Guinevere, though he never seemed quite clear as to the identity of Lancelot. Keats and Shelley flirted on and off with the splendors of knighthood, and going back even further, Milton almost chose the Arthur story as the subject of his projected epic. (It is, of course, a mercy that he did not!) It seems remarkable that, except for a few years in the early eighteenth century, Malory's *Morte Darthur* has been continuously in print ever since Caxton first printed it in 1485, a fact that suggests more about the English Enlightenment than it does about Malory.

Who was this King Arthur, then, that he should so endure? After all, the French do not, every fifty years or so, resurrect Charlemagne or the Germans Frederick Barbarosa. One answer would seem to lie perhaps in the peculiarly English nature of the legend and its theme. Despite the great variety of its sources—English chronicles, French romances, Welsh legends—it is from Malory's English compilation that with a few exceptions all succeeding treatments of the Arthur story descend. From Malory, too, they inherit the central, tragic, universal concept that has made the Arthur story worth redoing in every generation—the idea that though by the practice, to quote from the oath Arthur's knights must take yearly, by the practice of "courage . . . , mercy, humility, graciousness, and good faith," man can raise himself from barbarism and create a society based on justice and virtue. Yet, in the end, man is only man; the old, primitive, barbaric standards and values continue to reassert themselves; and even the most nobly conceived society cannot survive the failings of human nature. Despite Arthur's efforts, Gawain will in the end be Gawain. Even the noble Lancelot is trapped by the confusion of love versus duty inherent in the chivalric code. Thus, from the start, chivalry at its best is doomed to failure; the Round Table, shot through with immorality and civil strife, eventually must crumble.

It is, of course, a peculiarly British theme, this worship of the glorious failure. For who, in fact, are the great English heroes? Robert Falcon Scott died in the Antarctic, having failed to reach the South Pole because, like a gentleman, he would not eat his sled dogs. Mallory (George this time, not Thomas) was photographed in a Norfolk jacket at 16,000 on Everest and died in a final foolish assault on the summit. Surely the most glorious of them was Admiral Lord Horatio

Nelson, four-foot-ten-inch military genius, blatant adulterer, vain as a peacock, having lost an arm and an eye in combat, striding the bridge of the *Victory* at Trafalgar, arrayed in full admiral's uniform and wearing all his medals and on being warned of snipers on the enemy ships, proudly turning his blind eye to the French fleet, and saying "I see no snipers!" No wonder the British say that Arthur will return. For Arthur is the embodiment of the Englishman's image of himself: idealist; a man of vision; a creator of a stable and beneficent government; in times of adversity stalwart, patient, enduring; a man created by destiny to rule yet doomed to destruction by the passions of those who do not share his vision or understand the nature of his creation.

There may be another reason for the endurance of the Arthur legend, one lying in the circumstances of the legend's origin and growth. Like most heroic literature, it developed in a purely oral tradition a long time—nearly four hundred years—before it was written down in any form. It is thus a mixture of history, legend, and myth. As in most such literature, the tale itself and the theme it embodies come to be more important that any single telling of it. C. S. Lewis, in fact, compares the Arthur story to a great cathedral to which the builders of many centuries contributed.[1] Therefore, if I may delay for yet a few more paragraphs any discussion of specific modern versions of the story, I should like to deal with the legend as a means of indexing the literary qualities, genres, and values that contributed to its early growth.

For example, the variations of the developing legend indicate a great deal about style, about the changing nature of the legend and its degree of appropriateness. Let us look briefly at a sampling of medieval Arthurian works that generally are said to possess artistic and/or historical value, at what purports to be a history: the chronicle of Geoffrey of Monmouth, the first writer to set down the Arthur story in a skeleton form; a French romance, *Lancelot*, by the first and best of the romance writers, Chrétien de Troyes; and Malory's *Morte Darthur*.

The first thing that comes to mind is that, whereas Geof-

190

frey's work claims to be a history and Chrétien's a *roman*, a work of fiction, the distinction between their author's, and hence their audience's, view of genre and hence of actuality is considerably more blurred than ours. The semi-fictitious Arthur in Geoffrey is presented side by side with what we would consider "true" historical personages; verifiable Romans throughout the book rub shoulders with legendary Britons. What is true in particular of Geoffrey is true generally of the medieval view of history; the famous Nine Worthies include not only Caesar and Godfrey of Bouillon but Hector and Arthur as well, and the custom of beginning histories of Britain with the legendary Brutus extended into Elizabethan times.

Similarly, although they are clearly *romans*—stories rather than chronicles, histories, their aim being to tell a series of adventures rather than relate an entire history—the romances of Chrétien are presented as true adventures having taken place in historical times. To be sure, they contain marvels—giants, sorceresses, magical fountains—but so do the histories, and their characters, their Arthurs and Lancelots, are the heroes of chronicles as well as romances.

I do not mean to imply that the fourteenth-century reader believed in the wars of Arthur or the quests of Gawain in much the same way that he believed in the Hundred Years War, though it probably never would have occurred to Froissart to make such a distinction. But he did not, I am convinced, make the same kind of clear separation between romance and history that we routinely do today. The important thing about a medieval narrative was not its objective truth but its fidelity to its sources. The historian-romancer might clarify (but not basically change) character; he might restructure, but not basically change, incident in terms appropriate to his own age, but he was always careful to include, as Milton said, "that which hath received approbation from so many."[2] True or not true from the modern point of view, this fidelity to one's source was, again, according to Milton, the "due and proper subject of story."

History and *story* tend to merge in other ways during the

191

Middle Ages. History, like romance, still dealt with people; social history, military history, economic history, and political history had not yet arrived to render the past impersonal. As to Emerson and Carlyle, to medieval man history was the "lengthened shadow of a man"; it was the story of what men did, not a record of the forces acting upon them.

In the same way that history and romance shared a common subject matter, they existed in the same time frame as well, in what might be called the "simultaneous present." Some events, of course, happened before others in both romance and chronicle; but all actions, being, in the modern sense, clearly neither historical nor fictional, essentially were contemporaneous. As C. S. Lewis says, for us, "the past is, before all else, a 'costume play.'"[3] It was not so for our ancestors. Trojan warriors wore medieval armor, and there was even a "Sir Orfeo." Malory is thus writing essentially a *Morte* for his own time, the mid-fifteenth century, a work both romance and history, which he and his printer, William Caxton, regarded neither as pure fiction nor as pure fact but as a story "that hath approbation from so many," placed somewhere in a past much resembling his own time in attitude and in the conduct of life, a story whose subject matter he inherited, but which by consolidation and alteration he transformed into a statement of the inherent tragedy of chivalry for his own age.

Now then (and I am at last getting to my main point), Malory's technique, it seems to me, points to the reason why in our own age Thomas Berger's *Arthur Rex* is a howling success and John Steinbeck's *Acts of King Arthur* is to some degree a failure, though both were written in the same year. Malory, like the architects of his age, knew that one cannot simply "correct" the works of the past. He can reshape and reconstruct them, but he cannot merely tinker with them as they are. The cathedral architects of Malory's day happily tore out and pointed the round arches of Norman churches, added fan-vaulted ceilings, and supported vast walls of glass with external buttressing, thus modernizing them. In much the same way, Malory changes the mystical emphasis of the Grail quest by greatly reducing the prophecies of Merlin, leaving

out the final tragedy of Tristram and Iseult, and almost eliminating the courtly love psychologizing of the Lancelot and
Guenevere affair to fit his concept of the total story and to suit
the tastes of his age.

Also in the same way (and this is the main point), those
writers whose treatments of the Arthur story in our own time
are most successfully realized are those that have essentially
abandoned the medieval models in style and emphasis,
though not in "that which hath received approbation from so
many," just as Malory abandoned the style and emphasis of
his sources. Thomas Berger has used Malory only as one
might use a plot outline. T. H. White has used him only sug-
gestively, and Mary Stewart and Parke Godwin have abandoned him almost entirely. For Berger, Stewart, Godwin, and
White, and a great many others—E. A. Robinson, John Heath-
Stubbs, Charles Williams, the list goes on and on—have realized, whether through study or instinct I do not know, that
there has been a revolution since Malory's time in our attitude toward history and romance, that they have in fact
been separated, that we now "believe" in history as we "believe" in mathematics or in empirical science as an accurate
record of "true" events. On the other hand, fiction, no matter
how "realistically" conceived, we do not believe in, as in matu-
rity we do not believe in the playfellows of our childhood
imaginations.

The same principle applies, I think, to the making of films.
Simply to transfer an old book such as Malory's from page to
screen is to invite disaster. Aside from the fact that strict
translation from a verbal to a visual idiom is in itself an im-
possibility, the attempt to present a medieval story in anything like its own terms is bound to result in incomprehensi-
bility, no matter what the motives or the skill involved. I recall a lamentable Arthurian screen epic starring Robert Taylor a couple of dozen years ago which, out of a kind of pious
regard for the respected Arthur story, attempted to film Malory "straight" and which resulted in a futile meandering back
and forth from long-winded court scenes to meaningless combats which made it unsuited even for revival on late-night TV,

the traditional burial ground of cinema turkeys. Equally dolorous was Eric Rohmer's *Perceval*, filmed during the 1970s, which willfully attempted to picture Chrétien's story of the first Grail knight as a medieval audience might have envisioned it, all fanciful and highly stylized papier-mâché forests and turrets. The most successful Arthurian films, like the most successful Arthurian novels, have been those that have reworked the old stories—Boorman's *Excalibur* with its exploitation of full screen and color and its thoroughly cinematic treatment of Mordred, his face covered by a gold mask, and its identification of Morgan as the captor of Merlin; or, better still, *Monty Python and the Holy Grail*, which counterposes the muddy, dismal, superstitious world in which the historical Arthur doubtless lived with the tinseled romanticism that later writers imposed on it, and thus comes up with such wonderful incongruities as King Arthur and his ridiculous crew riding stick horses through real mud, the heavenly vision of a pop-art and shifty-eyed God, and a bunny rabbit with Satanic power which is destroyed by a grenade kept in a reliquary.

I should like to present by way of a very crude demonstration parallel presentations of the same episode, the conception of Arthur, as it appears in Geoffrey, Malory, Mary Stewart's *The Crystal Cave*, Steinbeck's *Acts of King Arthur*, and Berger's *Arthur Rex*. I could have chosen random passages in each book that would have made my point more solidly, but I think the reader will agree that the choice of parallel passages is a clearer, more honest policy.

First, Geoffrey of Monmouth in Lewis Thorpe's translation:

> The King agreed and listened carefully to what he had to do. In the end he handed the siege over to his subordinates, took Merlin's drugs, and was changed into the likeness of Gorlois. Ulfin was changed into Jordan and Merlin into a man called Britaelis, so that no one could tell what they had previously looked like. They then set off for Tintagel and came to the Castle in the twilight. The moment the guard was told that his leader was approaching, he opened the gates and the men were

let in. Who, indeed, could possibly have suspected anything, once it was thought that Gorlois himself had come? The King spent that night with Ygerna and satisfied his desire by making love with her. He had deceived her by the disguise which he had taken. He had deceived her, too, by the lying things that he said to her, things which he planned with great skill. He said that he had come out secretly from his besieged encampment so that he might make sure that all was well with her, whom he loved so dearly, and with his castle, too. She naturally believed all that he said and refused him nothing that he asked. That night she conceived Arthur, the most famous of men, who subsequently won great renown by his outstanding bravery.[4]

Now for an immediate comparison, Malory writing, remember, not chronicle but fiction and some 300 years later at the very end, past the end really, of the romance tradition:

So after the deth of the duke kyng Uther lay with Igrayne, more than thre houres after his deth, and begat on her that nygh(t) Arthur; and or day cam, Merlyn cam to the kyng and bad hym make hym redy, and so he kist the lady Igrayne and departed in all hast. But whan the lady herd telle of the duke her husband, and by all record he was dede or ever kynge Uther came to her, thenne she merveilled who that myghte be that laye with her in lykenes of her lord. So she mourned pryvely and held hir pees.[5]

I have, for the sake of space, quoted only the actual seduction scene. I might add, however, that Geoffrey's account is prefaced by an account of Uther's meeting with Igraine that is fuller, that is, more detailed, than Malory, including a detailed description of the banquet at which the king "kept ordering plates of food to be passed and to her, too, kept sending his own personal attendants with gold goblets of wine" and kept "smiling at her in spritely conversation." Geoffrey, again unlike Malory, reports that when Gorlois' messengers came to report their leader's death, they "blushed red with astonishment to see that the man whom they had left behind dead in the siege had in effect arrived there safely before them." Whereupon, Geoffrey says, "the King put his arms around the Duchess and laughed aloud."

Malory, as I say, having cut away even what little extra detail remained from Geoffrey in his French source, would have none of this; he simply states that "the Kyng lyked and loved the lady well." And the reason for this is obvious. His interest is not in the least in the seduction but in the chronology and his theme. Even so, one is struck by the very reverse of what one would have expected. The ostensible writer of fiction is sparser, more matter-of-fact than is the chronicler. It is Geoffrey who seemingly luxuriates in the particulars, Malory, despite his use of direct discourse, who provides us with a mere plot skeleton.

By this comparison, I do not wish to imply that Geoffrey is too fanciful a historian or Malory too prosaic a writer of fiction. I do think, however, that, on the basis of these and a great many similar passages, it is possible to say that the differences in technique (if, indeed, there are any) between medieval chronicle and medieval romance are much less great than are those between medieval romance and modern novel.

Here, for comparison, are some additional modern accounts of the seduction. First, Mary Stewart, writing in the full exuberant glory of the romantic historical tradition of Walter Scott, Rider Haggard, and Anthony Hope Hawkins:

> Suddenly, at the head of the second flight of steps, a door opened wide, and there, full in the blaze of light, stood Ygraine. She was in white, as I had seen her before; but not this time in a night-robe. The long gown shimmered like lake water. Over one arm and shoulder, Roman fashion, she wore a mantle of soft dark blue. Her hair was dressed with jewels. She stretched out both her hands, and the blue robe and the white fell away from wrists where red gold glimmered.
> "Welcome, my lord!" Her voice, high and clear, brought both guards round to face her. Uther took the last half dozen steps to the landing in two leaps, then was past them, his cloak brushing the sword-blades, past Ralf's blazing torch, and starting quickly up the second flight of steps. . . .
> Uther had reached the head of the stairway. He took her hands, and there in front of the lighted door, with his enemies' swords catching the torchlight below him, the King bent his

head and kissed Ygraine. The scarlet cloak swung round both of them, engulfing the white. Beyond them I saw the shadow of the old woman, Marcia, holding the door.

Then the King said: "Come," and with the great cloak still covering them both, he led her into the firelight, and the door shut behind them.

So we took Tintagel.[6]

Compare Stewart's rhapsodic romanticism with Steinbeck's small beer, small because he has tried, by his own admission, for the most part simply to "redo" and "correct" Malory, not to write his own book as Stewart and Berger obviously have:

When Uther and Merlin and Sir Ulfius rode through the starlit darkness toward the sea, the fog moved restlessly over the moors like wispy ghosts in floating clothes. Half-formed mist people crept with them and the forms of riders grew changeable like figures of cloud. When they came to the guarded gates of Tintagel on its high sharp rock above the whispering sea, the sentries saluted the recognized forms of the duke, and Sir Brastias and Sir Jordanus, two of his trusted men. And in the dim passages of the castle the Lady Igraine welcomed her husband and dutifully led him to her chamber. Then King Uther lay with Igraine and that night she conceived a child.

When daylight came, Merlin appeared as he had promised. And in the misty light Uther kissed the lady Igraine and hastily departed. The sleepy sentries opened the gates to their supposed lord and his retainers and the three rode away into the mist of morning.[7]

Now let us look at Thomas Berger—more contemporary in style than Mary Stewart though at times deliberately archaic, slightly sardonic, slightly removed from the subject, his tone consciously ironic, his language perfectly suited to attitude and theme:

But recognizing her husband's mean figure she did corrupt her beauty with a grimace and say in ill-humor, "Gorlois! How in heaven's name—" But seeing him begin to divest himself of

his clothing she left off the expression of disagreeable amaze-
ment at his return alive, and she hastened to inform him of the
sickness that had claimed her on his departure this fortnight,
which surely was the pestilence, association with which would
kill him quickly as it was killing her by degrees. . . .

But if the king heard these exceptions to his purpose he gave
no answer, being occupied, damnably, with the to him foreign
fastenings of the duke's garb, which did defy his fingers, and
soon in frenzy he abandoned all restraint and tore himself altogether naked, dropping the tatters where they fell, and then
he vaulted onto the bed, . . . and then he closed with her ala-
baster body as a ram doth address an ewe.

Now the fire had dwindled to powdery ash before Uther Pendragon did unjoin himself, . . . and then, thrusting his tongue
into the cavern of his cheek, he spake as follows.

"My dear Ygraine, I confess to thee that I am greatly relieved
to find that thou hast been faithful to me—for no appetite that
had been fed within the last fortnight could yet be so keen as
thine."

"Methinks," said the fair Ygraine, "that absence hath also
done thee a world of good, my dear Gorlois."[8]

There are, I suppose, a dozen bases of comparison and a
dozen generalizations that could be made from these passages; but I shall content myself with the obvious—that the
modern novelist (I am discounting Steinbeck, who here suffers not from lack of knowledge of the genre but from confusion of intent and failure) rejoices in the freedom of his
fiction, in the license to exploit a scene, to report not only the
occasion as do Geoffrey and Malory, but to ring upon it all its
changes, to wreath round that "which hath approbation from
so many" with purely fictive garlands in an extravagant, exuberant way that the medieval writer, whose view of Arthurian
fiction was tempered by his belief in its historicity, could not.
To Malory, a castle is only a castle and a forest is at best deep
or dark. In modern fiction, though, the sense of place, of being
in the castle or the forest, often is more important than the
events that occur there. This is why E. M. Forster, at the outset of examining the qualities of the novel at great length,

.

remarks in a deliberately off-handed way: "Oh, yes, the novel tells a story."[9]

I have, I realize, been wandering about in one of Logres' deep forests; but I have done so to make a simple—though, I would hope, valid point—that the best Arthurian literature is that which is contemporaneous with its own age in technique, style, and theme. Mary Stewart, for example, in *The Crystal Cave* takes from Geoffrey the story of the early Merlin, and Thomas Berger places Arthur in the historical milieu of Saxon and Celt. The works of both writers, however, are patently modern novels exhibiting patently modern techniques and themes. They are not rewritings of medieval books but re-creations of a medieval story. That is the only way, as they and Malory before them well knew, by which that "which hath received approbation from so many" *quondam,* "once upon a time," may continue to do so *futurus,* "for ages to come."

NOTES

Introduction *(Mary Flowers Braswell and John Bugge)*

1. See esp. Roger Sherman Loomis, ed., *Arthurian Literature in the Middle Ages: A Collaborative History* (Oxford: Clarendon, 1959); see also Douglas D. R. Owen, ed., *Arthurian Romance: Seven Essays* (Edinburgh: Scottish Academic, 1970); Kurt Wais, ed., *Der arthurische Roman* (Darmstadt: Wissenschaftliche Buchgesell-schaft, 1970); P. B. Grout et al., eds., *The Legend of Arthur in the Middle Ages: Studies Presented to A. H. Diverres by Colleagues, Pupils, and Friends* (Cambridge: D. S. Brewer, 1984).

2. Kenneth Varty, ed., *An Arthurian Tapestry: Essays in Memory of Lewis Thorpe* (Glasgow: French Department of the University, 1981); Varty concentrates on Chrétien de Troyes; Rupert T. Pickens, ed., *The Sower and the Seed: Essays on Chrétien de Troyes* (Lexington, Ky.: French Forum, 1983); James W. Spisak, ed., *Studies in Malory* (Kalamazoo, Mich.: Medieval Institute Publications, 1985); Robert J. Blanch, ed., *Sir Gawain and Pearl: Critical Essays* (Bloomington: Indiana University Press, 1966); Donald Howard and Christian Zacher, eds., *Critical Studies of "Sir Gawain and the Green Knight"* (Notre Dame, Ind.: Notre Dame University Press, 1970); Karl H. Göller, ed., *The Alliterative Morte Arthure: A Reassessment of the Poem* (Cambridge: D. S. Brewer, 1981).

3. Geoffrey Ashe, ed., *The Quest for Arthur's Britain* (London: Pall Mall Press, 1968); Jean-Charles Payen, ed., *La Légende Arthurienne et la Normandie* (Condé-Sur-Noireau: Éditions Charles Corlet, 1983).

The Convergence of Arthurian Studies *(Geoffrey Ashe)*

1. E. K. Chambers, *Arthur of Britain* (1927; repr. New York: Barnes and Noble, 1964, and London: Sidgwick & Jackson, 1966).

2. See, for example, Ashe (as editor and co-author), *The Quest for Arthur's Britain* (London: Pall Mall Press, 1968); and Ashe (as sole author), *Avalonian Quest* (London: Methuen, 1982).

3. The person in question is the High King of the Britons in the mid-fifth century, known by the title, or honorific, "Riothamus." See Ashe, "A Certain Very Ancient Book," *Speculum* 56 (1981): 301–23;

and Ashe, *The Discovery of King Arthur* (New York: Doubleday, 1985), pp. 53 and passim.

4. Ashe, *Discovery of King Arthur*, pp. 20–21, 24–25.

Boethian Themes and Tragic Structure in Geoffrey of Monmouth's *Historia Regum Britanniae (Maureen Fries)*

1. Whereas no medieval Arthurian work calls itself a tragedy, the connection between chronicle history and tragedy was well established long before Shakespeare. Samuel C. Chew, "Time and Fortune," *English Literary History* 6 (1939): 83–113, points to the cumulative imagery of many centuries linking human nature, time, and fortune. See also, G. Giovanni, "The Connection between Tragedy and History in Ancient Criticism," *Philological Quarterly* 22 (1943): 308–14.

2. J. S. P. Tatlock, *The Legendary History of Britain* (Berkeley: University of California Press, 1950), p. 392; William Matthews, *The Tragedy of Arthur: A Study of the Alliterative "Morte Arthure"* (Berkeley: University of California Press, 1960), esp. pp. 95–150; Russell Peck, "Willfulness and Wonders: Boethian Tragedy in the Alliterative *Morte Arthure*," in *The Alliterative Tradition in the Fourteenth Century*, ed. Bernard S. Levy and Paul E. Szarmach (Kent, Ohio: Kent State University Press, 1981), pp. 153–82; Richard A. Wertime, "The Theme and Structure of the Stanzaic *Morte Arthur*," *PMLA* 87 (1972): 1075–82; Robert M. Lumiansky, ed., *Malory's Originality: A Critical Study of "Le Morte Darthur"* (Baltimore: Johns Hopkins University Press, 1964), passim; Charles Moorman, *The Book of King Arthur* (Lexington: University Press of Kentucky, 1965), passim; Eugène Vinaver, ed., *The Works of Sir Thomas Malory*, 2nd ed., 3 vols. (Oxford: Clarendon Press, 1967), Intro. and "Commentary," passim (quotation in text, Vinaver, 3:1621).

3. Matthews, *Tragedy of Arthur*, pp. 105–12 passim; and Peck, "Wilfulness and Wonders," passim, examine the *Alliterative Morte* as Boethian without Galfridian references.

4. See Wilhelm Cloetta, *Komödie und Tragödie im Mittelalter*, in *Beiträge zur Literaturgeschichte des Mittelalters und der Renaissance* (Halle: Niemeyer, 1890–92), vol. 1; and Willard Farnham, *The Medieval Heritage of Elizabethan Tragedy* (Berkeley: University of California Press, 1936).

5. Gilbert Highet, *The Classical Tradition: Greek and Roman Influ-*

ences on Western Literature (Oxford: Clarendon Press, 1949), p. 571. For vernacular translations see A. van de Vyver, "Les traductions du *De Consolatione Philosophiae* de Boèce en Littérature Comparée," *Humanisme et Renaissance* 6 (1939): 247–73. For general studies consult Howard R. Patch, *The Tradition of Boethius: A Study of His Importance in Medieval Culture* (New York: Oxford University Press, 1935); and Pierre Courcelle, *La Consolation de Philosophie dans la tradition littéraire: antécédents et postérité de Boèce* (Paris: Études augustinennes, 1967).

6. Howard R. Patch, *The Goddess Fortuna in Medieval Literature* (1927; repr. New York: Octagon Books, 1967), p. 151 and passim.

7. "Fortune, Fate, and Chance," in *Dictionary of the History of Ideas*, ed. Phillip P. Wiener, 5 vols. (New York: Scribner's, 1973), vol. 2, p. 231.

8. Patch, *Goddess Fortuna*, p. 165.

9. Ibid., pp. 152ff. Patch's distinction as to Fortune's turning or being turned upon her wheel has no relevance for my own argument. Honorius' *Speculum ecclesiae* was "the most popular handbook of sermons in the Middle Ages," according to Henry Osborn Taylor, *The Mediaeval Mind*, 2 vols. (London: Macmillan, 1914), vol. 2, p. 76.

10. Taylor, *Mediaeval Mind*, vol. 2, pp. 161, 162.

11. For a full discussion see Robert W. Hanning, *The Vision of History in Early Britain: From Gildas to Geoffrey of Monmouth* (New York: Columbia University Press, 1966), pp. 23–32.

12. Ibid., pp. 33, 37–42.

13. "Fortune, Fate, and Chance," p. 230.

14. Hanning, *Vision of History*, p. 121; see also p. 176, where Hanning says that Geoffrey's *Historia* is even "subversive of . . . Christian assumptions" in earlier fall-of-Britain texts.

15. Ibid., p. 120.

16. For a detailed analysis of Alfred's extensive changes, see F. Anne Payne, *King Alfred and Boethius: An Analysis of the Old English Version of The Consolation of Philosophy* (Madison: University of Wisconsin Press, 1968).

17. A. M. S. Boethius, *The Consolation of Philosophy*, with the English trans. of "I.T." (1609), rev. H. F. Stewart, Loeb Classical Library (Cambridge: Harvard University Press, 1918), I, *pr.* III. Subsequent references appear in the text by book and *prosa* or *metrum* number.

18. I am indebted to Hanning for this analysis as the core of fall-of-Britain texts. He distinguishes Geoffrey from his predecessors Gildas, Bede, and Nennius because of his "removal from history of

the idea of eschatological fulfillment, in both its national and personal manifestations," p. 171. I concur.

19. For a detailed discussion of this pattern in Geoffrey before Arthur, see Hanning's discussion in *Vision of History*, pp. 121–72.

20. Edmond Faral, *La Légende Arthurienne: Études et Documents; Première Partie: Les Plus Anciens Textes*, 3: *Documents* (Paris: H. Champion, 1929), p. 229. Subsequent references are from this volume and appear in the text by chapter and page number.

21. This ambivalent archetype begins with the Cuchulainn-Conchobar relationship in the Old Irish Ulster saga. It apparently was so popular that Roland was turned from an unimportant vassal into Charlemagne's nephew in *La chanson de Roland*. See Raymond Thompson, "Gawain against Arthur: The Impact of a Mythological Pattern upon Arthurian Tradition in Accounts of the Birth of Gawain," *Folklore* 85 (1974): 113–21; and Thomas A. Garbáty, "The Uncle-Nephew Motif: New Light into Its Origins and Development," *Folklore* 88 (1977): 221–35.

22. Monica E. McAlpine, *The Genre of Troilus and Criseyde* (Ithaca: Cornell University Press, 1978).

23. *The Death of King Arthur*, trans. James Cable (Baltimore: Penguin Books, 1971), p. 222.

24. Farnham, *Medieval Heritage*, p. 80.

25. Maureen Fries, "Tragic Pattern in Malory's *Morte Darthur:* Medieval Narrative as Literary Myth," ACTA 5: 1978: 81–99.

A Possible Source of Geoffrey's Roman War?
(Mary L. H. Thompson)

1. IX, xi–xii, 446–55. Reference here, as subsequently, is to *The Historia Regum Britanniae of Geoffrey of Monmouth*, ed. Acton Griscom (London: Longmans, Green, 1929). Roman numerals indicate book and chapter divisions, Arabic numbers the pagination of the modern edition.

2. Geoffrey Ashe, "'A Certain Very Ancient Book': Traces of an Arthurian Source in Geoffrey of Monmouth's *Historia*," *Speculum* 56 (1981): 301–23.

3. Lewis Thorpe, introduction to Geoffrey of Monmouth, *The History of the Kings of Britain* (London: Penguin, 1966), p. 18.

4. J. S. P. Tatlock, *The Legendary History of Britain: Geoffrey of Monmouth's "Historia Regum Britanniae" and Its Early Vernacular*

Versions (Berkeley and Los Angeles: University of California Press, 1950), pp. 119–20; Hans Keller, "Two Toponymical Problems in Geoffrey of Monmouth and Wace: *Estrusia* and *Siesia*," *Speculum* 49 (1974): 694.

5. Edmond Faral, *La Légende Arthurienne: Études et Documents*, Première Partie, *Les Plus Anciens Textes*, 2 vols. (Paris: H. Champion, 1929), vol. 2, pp. 291–92.

6. Reference, as subsequently in the text, is to book and chapter divisions in *C. Iuli Caesaris Commentarii de bello Gallico*, ed. T. Rice Holmes (Oxford: Clarendon, 1914).

7. Mary H. L. Thompson, "'Geoffrey Did Not Invent It': The Roman War in the *Historia Regum Britanniae*," *Actes du 14ᵉ Congrès International Arthurien* (Rennes: Presses Universitaires, 1985), vol. 2, pp. 627–34. Specific points covered are: the relative size of the two opposing forces—about 70,000 Romans versus about 250,000 Celts in each work; the location of main battles (Geoffrey's skirmish near the Aube and the Battle of Siesia occur in the same area as do Caesar's movements in the last part of Book VI of the *Commentary*); and certain coincidences of place names (for example, a nineteenth-century map drawn by military engineers under Napoleon III shows a stream called "Badin" in the area of a Gallic attack on the Romans south of Langres).

8. Translations throughout this essay are from Julius Caesar, *The Battle for Gaul*, trans. Anne and Peter Wiseman (Boston: David Godine, 1980).

9. Pierre Malvezin, *Dictionnaire des Racines Celtique*, 2nd ed. (Paris: Chez l'auteur, 1923), s.v.

10. Ibid.

Transformations of a Theme: The Depoliticization of the Arthurian World in the *Roman de Brut* (Jean Blacker-Knight)

1. Charles Muscatine, *Chaucer and the French Tradition: A Study in Style and Meaning* (Berkeley: University of California Press, 1957), pp. 12–30.

2. Hans Ulrich Gumbrecht, "Literary Translation and Its Social Conditioning in the Middle Ages: Four Spanish Romance Texts of the 13th Century," *Yale French Studies* 51 (1974): 205–22, 219–20.

3. C. S. Lewis, *The Discarded Image: An Introduction to Medieval*

and Renaissance Literature (Cambridge: Cambridge University Press, 1964), p. 209.

4. *The Historia Regum Britanniae of Geoffrey of Monmouth,* ed. Acton Griscom (London: Longmans, Green, 1929).

5. For discussions of the early vernacular versions of the *Historia,* see J. S. P. Tatlock, *The Legendary History of Britain: Geoffrey of Monmouth's "Historia Regum Britanniae" and Its Early Vernacular Versions* (Berkeley: University of California Press, 1950), pp. 451–531; R. W. Leckie, Jr., *The Passage of Dominion: Geoffrey of Monmouth and the Periodization of Insular History in the Twelfth Century* (Toronto, University of Toronto Press, 1981), pp. 102–19; Alexander Bell, ed., *An Anglo-Norman "Brut,"* Anglo-Norman Text Society 21–22, Oxford, 1969: xv–xix.

6. *Le Roman de Brut de Wace,* ed. Ivor Arnold, Société des Anciens Textes Français, 2 vols. (Paris: Garnier, 1938). It is believed, too, that Gaimar wrote an *Estoire des Bretuns* (pre-1130) which may have contained Arthurian material; see Alexander Bell, "The *Munich Brut* and the *Estoire des Bretuns,*" *Modern Language Review* 34 (1939): 321–54.

7. Because the emphasis in this essay is ideological and not formalistic, changes that could have resulted from turning prose into verse are not an issue. Robert Caldwell has shown that, although Wace used the Variant Version of the *Historia* in preparing the *Roman de Brut,* mainly he relied on the Vulgate Version—referred to in this essay simply as the *Historia*—for his Arthurian portion. For the interrelationships between Wace's text and these two versions of Geoffrey's, see Caldwell, "Wace's *Roman de Brut* and the *Variant Version* of Geoffrey of Monmouth's *Historia Regum Britanniae,*" *Speculum* 31 (1956): 675–82; Hans-Erich Keller, "Wace et Geoffrey de Monmouth: Problème de la chronologie des sources," *Romania* 98 (1977): 1–14, and Geoffrey of Monmouth, *"Historia Regum Britanniae": A Variant Version Edited from Manuscripts,* ed. Jacob Hammer (Cambridge, Mass.: The Mediaeval Academy of America, 1951).

8. The Bern manuscript—according to Griscom (33–34), one of the earliest and best of the *Historia*—contains an epilogue in which Geoffrey warns William of Malmesbury and Henry of Huntingdon against writing about the history of the British kings, since he is the only one (so he alleges) in possession of the "true" source of the material: "Reges vero saxonum Willelmo Malmesberiensi et Henrico Huntendonensi quos de regibus Britonum tacere iubeo cum non habeant librum istum Britannici sermonis quem Gualterus Oxenefor-

densis archidiaconus ex Britannia advexit quem de historia eorum veraciter editum in honore predictorum principum hoc modo in Latinum sermonem transferre curavi" (XII, xx, 535–36). (The kings of the Saxons I leave to William of Malmesbury and Henry of Huntingdon. Concerning the kings of the Britons, I bid them to remain silent since they do not have that book which Walter, archdeacon of Oxford, brought with him from Brittany, the book containing the true story in the honor of the above-named princes, which I have taken care to translate into the Latin tongue.)

9. For historiographical and stylistic analyses of historical poems by Gaimar, Wace, and Benoît de Sainte-Maure, see Jean Blacker-Knight, "From *Historia* to *Estoire:* Literary Form and Social Function of the Twelfth-Century Old French Verse and Latin Prose Chronicle of the Anglo-Norman *Regnum*" (Ph.D. diss., University of California at Berkeley, 1984).

10. When Wace uses the term *romanz,* he refers to the Old French language, not to the nascent genre of narrative fiction that later bore its name.

11. Wace, *La Vie de Sainte Marguerite,* ed. E. A. Francis, Classiques Français du Moyen Âge (Paris, 1932).

12. Translations from the Old French are my own.

13. Wace, *La Vie de Sainte Marguerite,* p. xiv.

14. Wace, *The Life of Saint Nicholas,* ed. Mary S. Crawford (Ph.D. diss., University of Pennsylvania, 1923).

15. Crawford, ed., *Life of Saint Nicholas,* p. 33.

16. Crawford speculates that "Robert le fiz tiout" was the son of Louis Thibault (Louis VI of France), but the attribution appears tenuous at best. Ibid., pp. 21–24 n. 4.

17. Caldwell, "Wace's *Roman de Brut,*" p. 680.

18. Roger Sherman Loomis, *The Development of Arthurian Romance* (London: Hutchinson, 1963), p. 40, characterized Wace's contribution to the Arthurian corpus as follows: "This French version, of course, extended the knowledge of Geoffrey's book to the courtly classes, and much of its interest lies in the methods Wace used to adapt the narrative to this new audience by toning down the barbarities, adding picturesque detail, and giving costumes, customs, and combats a very up-to-date air." For similar views, see Robert H. Fletcher, *The Arthurian Material in the Chronicles,* Harvard Studies and Notes in Philology and Literature no. 10 (Cambridge, Mass., 1906; repr. New York: Burt Franklin, 1966), pp. 127–43; Margaret Houk, "Sources of the *Roman de Brut* of Wace," *University of Califor-*

nia Publications in English 5:2 (1944): 161–356; Margaret Pelan, *L'Influence du 'Brut' de Wace sur les romanciers français de son temps* (Paris: E. Droz, 1931), pp. 147–66; Peter Rickard, *Britain in Medieval French Literature, 1100–1500* (Cambridge: Cambridge University Press, 1956), pp. 71–89. For another perspective, see Norris Lacy on larger narrative patterns ("doubling technique") and modes of characterization, in "The Form of the *Brut's* Arthurian Sequence," in *Jean Misrahi Memorial Volume: Studies in Medieval Literature,* ed. Hans R. Runte, Henri Niedzielski, and William L. Hendrickson (Columbia, S.C.: French Literature Publications, 1977), pp. 150–58.

19. See Blacker-Knight, "From *Historia* to *Estoire,*" pp. 144–63, for a detailed discussion of the theme of internecine warfare as developed in the *Historia Regum Britanniae.*

20. See Richard W. Southern, *Medieval Humanism* (New York: Harper & Row, 1970), pp. 204–33, on the reign of Henry I, and R. H. C. Davis, *King Stephen, 1135–1154* (Berkeley: University of California Press, 1967) on the extended civil war that marked Stephen's reign.

21. Griscom, ed., *Historia Regum,* p. 74.

22. Leckie, *Passage of Dominion,* p. 19.

23. Geoffrey's chronology gives the year A.D. 689 for the fall of the Britons (XII, xviii–xix, 534–35).

24. Translations from the Latin are my own.

25. Layamon's remark that Wace gave the *Roman de Brut* to Eleanor has been accepted without question; see Layamon, *Brut,* ed. G. L. Brook and R. F. Leslie, 3 vols., Early English Text Society 250 (London: Oxford University Press, 1963), vol. 1, p. 2. Although there is no reason to doubt automatically the word of the English poet who wrote nearly fifty years after Wace, there is equally no evidence that would preclude Wace's having written the poem for both king *and* queen, as he did the *Roman de Rou* (c. 1160–74), which he dedicated to the royal couple but aimed primarily at Henry; see *Le Roman de Rou de Wace,* 3 vols., ed. A. J. Holden, Société des Anciens Textes Français (Paris, 1970), vol. I, Chronique ascendante, ll. 17–20. On Wace's patrons and audience, see Charles H. Haskins, "Henry II as a Patron of Literature," in *Essays in Medieval History Presented to Thomas Frederick Tout,* ed. A. G. Little and F. M. Powicke (S.N.) (Manchester, 1925), pp. 71–77; Walter F. Schirmer and Ulrich Broich, *Studien zum literarischen Patronat im England des 12. Jahrhunderts,* Wissenschaftliche Abhandlungen der Arbeitsgemeinschaft für Forschung des Landes Nordrhein-Westfalen 23 (Köln: West-

deutscher Verlag, 1962), pp. 67–93; and Diana B. Tyson, "Patronage of French Vernacular History Writers in the Twelfth and Thirteenth Centuries," *Romania* 100, 2 (1979): 180–222.

26. Merlin's prophecies may have circulated separately as well, and usually were considered by contemporaries an indispensable part of the Arthurian story. See Marjorie Chibnall, ed. and tr., *The Ecclesiastical History of Orderic Vitalis*, 6 vols. (Oxford: Oxford University Press, 1969–80), vol. 6, pp. xviii, 381–82 n5.

27. Orderic Vitalis, who included a portion of the Prophecies in Book XII of his *Historia Ecclesiastica*, interpreted some of them as referring to twelfth-century events; in a way not untypical of Geoffrey's contemporary readers, he read, for example, references to "the lion of justice" as meaning Henry I, "at whose roar the towers of Gaul shall shake and the island dragons shall tremble" (Chibnall, 6: xii, 386–88). Ralph Diceto, an administrative historian active toward the end of Henry's reign (1154–89), was among readers of the Prophecies who viewed current events as fulfillment of what was contained in Merlin's "text"; see Antonia Gransden, *Historical Writing in England c. 550–c. 1307* (Ithaca, N.Y.: Cornell University Press, 1974), p. 235 n129.

28. G. Paris and J. Ulrich, *Merlin: Roman en prose du XIIIe siècle*, 2 vols., Société des Anciens Textes Français (Paris: Firmin Didot et cie, 1886). See also Paul Zumthor, *Merlin le prophète: un thème de la littérature polémique de l'historiographie et des romans* (Geneva: Librairie Payot, 1943), pp. 215–31, on the characterization of Merlin as magician in Old French literature.

29. Wace's concern for accuracy is reflected in many passages, where he seems to regret a lack of information or explanation in his sources: "Altres baruns i out assez / Dunt jo n'ai pas les nuns trovez" (11,117–18) (There were many other barons / Whose names I did not find); "La reïne rout ses servanz / Ne vus sai dire quels ne quanz" (10,483–84) (The queen had her servants / I do not know to tell you which ones or when); "Ne puis tut ne ne sai numer / Ne les richesces acunter" (10,491–92) (I do not know nor can I name all of them / Nor tell of the riches). Some protests could be conventional versions of the "inexpressibility topos"; their frequency, however, more likely indicates a genuine concern for recounting the "truest" version of events.

30. See Wilfred L. Warren, *Henry II* (Berkeley: University of California Press, 1973), pp. 399–555, on Henry's troubled relationship with the church.

31. Five fragments are extant in addition to the nineteen complete manuscripts (Arnold, xii–xiv). Brian Woledge and Ian Short recently concluded that one of the fragments (Bodleian Lib., Rawl. D. 913) dates from as early as the late twelfth century ["Liste provisoire de manuscrits de XIIe siècle contenant des textes en langue française," *Romania* 102, no. 1 (1980): 1–16]. Wace does not say when he received this gift. He could have received the prebend in payment for the *Brut* after the fact, or for the *Rou* which he eventually abandoned c. 1174. For the two sides of the issue, see Broich, *Literarische Patronat*, p. 67, in Schirmer and Broich, *Studien zum literarischen Patronat im England des 12. Jahrhunderts*. For the dating of the *Brut*, see ll. 14,863–66. For the dating of the *Rou*, see *Rou*, Chronique ascendante, ll. 1–4.

32. For the extent of literacy (Latin, Old French, and Anglo-Saxon) in the twelfth century, see James W. Thompson, *The Literacy of the Laity in the Middle Ages* (University of California Press Publications 9, 1939; repr. New York: Burt Franklin, 1960), pp. 116–95; R. M. Wilson, "English and French in Ireland: 1100–1300," *History* 28 (1943): 37–60; W. Rothwell, "The Teaching of French in Medieval England," *Modern Language Review* 63 (1968): 37–46; M. T. Clanchy, *From Memory to Written Record: England 1066–1307* (Cambridge, Mass.: Harvard University Press, 1979); and Ian Short, "On Bilingualism in Anglo-Norman England," *Romance Philology* 3 (1980): 467–79.

33. The resultant amount of relatively free adaptation of materials practiced by contemporary vernacular historians and storytellers strongly suggests that twelfth-century audiences were, in general, less concerned with the exact sources of what they heard and read than with the relevance of the stories and histories to their own lives.

A Jungian Interpretation of Sexually Ambiguous Imagery in Chrétien's *Erec et Enide (Jan A. Nelson)*

1. All citations of the text of *Erec et Enide* have been taken from *Les Romans de Chrétien de Troyes*, 1: *Erec et Enide*, ed. Mario Roques (Paris: H. Champion, 1955). The translations are my own.

2. For recent discussions of conjointure, see Douglas F. Kelly, *Sens and Conjointure in the Chevalier de la Charrette* (The Hague: Mouton, 1966); Douglas F. Kelly, "The Source and Meaning of Conjointure in Chrétien's *Erec* 14," *Viator* 1 (1970): 179–200; and Michelle A. Free-

man, *The Poetics of Translatio Studii and Conjointure: Chrétien de Troyes's Cligés* (Lexington, Ky.: French Forum, 1979). See also Douglas F. Kelly, *Chrétien de Troyes: An Analytic Bibliography* (London: Grant & Cutler, 1976).

3. In doing this study of the animal imagery in Chrétien's *Erec et Enide*, I have in general adopted the method of critical analysis discussed and illustrated by A. C. Spearing: "This approach to literature is based on the assumption, whether or not this is stated, that the distinctive qualities of a complete literary work will be present and detectable locally in its verbal detail, so that this detail can be used to support more general statements about the work." Spearing, *Criticism and Medieval Poetry* (London: E. Arnold, 1964), p. 1.

4. For a discussion of this device as a means of amplifying the style or texture of a literary composition, see Edmond Faral, *Les Arts poétiques du XIIe et du XIIIe siècle: recherches et documents sur la technique littéraire du moyen âge* (1924; repr. Paris: E. Champion, 1962), pp. 63–67. Tom Peete Cross and William Albert Nitze discuss *expolitio* as the organizing principle in Chrétien's work in *Lancelot and Guenevere: A Study in the Origins of Courtly Love* (Chicago: University of Chicago Press, 1930), pp. 63–65.

5. The male sparrow hawk is called a "musket." See Edward B. Michell, *The Art and Practice of Hawking* (1900; repr. Boston: C. T. Branford, 1960), p. 160. The term occurs in *Dels auzels cassadors,* ed. Alexander H. Schutz (Columbus: Ohio State University Press, 1945), l. 759, as *mosquet.* The French form is *muchet.* See Gunnar Tilander, *Glanures lexicographiques* (Lund: C. W. K. Gleerup, 1932), p. 175.

6. I cite the text as Chrétien would have known it from the *Biblia Sacra,* Vulgatae Editionis.

7. François Villon, *Oeuvres,* ed. André Mary (Paris: Garnier, 1962), p. 127.

8. The male goat, or *boc,* occurs in Chrétien's *Der Percevalroman (Li Contes del Graal),* ed. Alfons Hilka (Halle: M. Niemeyer, 1932), l. 4630, which is then repeated among the variants for l. 6988.

9. *Isidori Hispalensis episcopi Etymologiarum sive originum,* ed. W. M. Lindsay, 2 vols. (Oxford: Clarendon Press, 1962), XII, 2, 11.

10. Erec's treatment of Enide in the second part of the romance has long been the subject of debate. I am in complete agreement with Stefan Hofer's views as expressed in "Die Problemstellung im Erec," *Zeitschrift für Romanische Philologie* 48 (1928): 123–28, with regard to the probable medieval premises for Erec's actions. Fur-

thermore, I find that Hofer's views are compatible with the Jungian interpretation of animal imagery presented here.

11. *Isidori Hispalensis episcopi Etymologiarum sive originum,* XII, 1, 15.

12. "Prologue," *Les Lais de Marie de France,* ed. Jeanne Lods (Paris, H. Champion, 1959), ll. 11–20. Marie's comments in the prologue to the *Lais* frequently have been cited in an effort to understand the relationship between the medieval writer and his source; they are, of course, equally valid when the medieval text itself becomes the source.

13. See C. G. Jung, *Psychological Types: Or the Psychology of Individualization,* trans. H. G. Baynes (New York: Harcourt, Brace, 1926), esp. chap. 11, secs. 48 and 49; also, Jung, "The Relations between the Ego and the Unconscious," in *Two Essays on Analytical Psychology,* trans. R. F. C. Hull, Bollingen Series no. 20 (New York: Pantheon, 1953), esp. part 2, chap. 2; and Emma Jung, *Animus and Anima,* trans. C. F. Baynes and Hildegard Nagel (1957; repr. New York: Spring Publications, 1969; Zurich, 1974).

14. The *anima* figure often has a father who facilitates her emergence into consciousness: "perhaps another motif which has not yet been mentioned deserves consideration; namely, the fact that these elemental beings quite often possess a (more or less hidden) father. The Valkyries are Odin's maidens and Odin is a god of wind and spirit. In the tale of the huntsman and the swan maiden, who has to be released from the glass mountain, her father is with her and is released at the same time. The Welsh nixie's father gives her in marriage to the man, and Undine, too, is sent by the sea-king, her father, to live among men in order to gain a soul" (Emma Jung, *Animus and Anima,* pp. 79–80). Clearly, the vavasor motif merits more attention.

15. When Erec first sees Maboagrins, he is described as towering above the trees: "A tant ez vos un chevalier, sor les arbres, par le vergier" [Behold a knight, above the trees, in the garden (ll. 5847–48)].

16. See Emma Jung, *Animus and Anima,* pp. 12–13, for a discussion of possession by the *animus* in women. For instance, "I would conclude from the presence of a powerful animus figure—a so-called 'possession by the animus'—that the person in question gives too little attention to her own masculine-intellectual logos tendency, and has either developed and applied it insufficiently or not in the right way. Perhaps this sounds paradoxical because, seen from the

outside, it appears as if it were the feminine principle which is not taken sufficiently into account."

17. The fact that Erec himself is an *animus* figure becomes clear at the close of the romance, where he is provided with a robe on which are depicted the arts of the quadrivium, that is, the mathematical sciences (ll. 6671–6730). "With the *animus*, the emphasis does not lie on mere perception—which as was said has always been woman's gift—but true to the nature of the logos, the stress is on knowledge, and especially on understanding. It is the function of the *animus* to give the meaning rather than the image" (Emma Jung, *Animus and Anima*, p. 26).

18. Ibid., p. 23.

"Now I Se and Undirstonde": The Grail Quest and the Education of Malory's Reader *(Stephen C. B. Atkinson)*

1. Vinaver calls it a "confused and almost pointless story" [*Malory* (Oxford: Oxford University Press, 1929), p. 84] and "an attempt to secularize the Grail theme" [*The Works of Sir Thomas Malory*, 2nd ed. (Oxford: Clarendon Press, 1967), p. 1535; cited hereafter as *Works*]. Alfred Kellogg, "Malory and Color Symbolism: Notes on His Translation of the *Queste del Saint Graal*," in *Arthur, Langland, Chaucer*, ed. Alfred Kellogg (New Brunswick, N.J.: Rutgers University Press, 1972), p. 18, believes it has "scraped the surface off a quite delicate artifact." Mark Lambert, *Malory: Style and Vision in Le Morte Darthur* (New Haven, Conn.: Yale University Press, 1975), p. 107, feels it has lost the "sense of inner reality" found in the French.

2. See, for instance, Vida Scudder, *Le Morte Darthur of Sir Thomas Malory and Its Sources* (New York: E. P. Dutton, 1921), pp. 266–68.

3. My approach in this essay is closest perhaps to the early work of Stanley Fish. See esp. his *Self-Consuming Artifacts: The Experience of Seventeenth-Century Literature* (Berkeley: University of California Press, 1972), pp. 383–427.

4. I am not suggesting that readers of the French *Queste* were not also readers of the *Mort Artu*, but clearly there is a closer connection between Malory's last three tales than between separate branches of the Vulgate cycle. The one-volume, synoptic character of Malory's work has been convincingly established by Larry D. Benson, *Malory's Morte Darthur* (Cambridge, Mass.: Harvard University Press, 1976), esp. pp. 3–16.

5. All quotations and citations follow *Works*. Page and line numbers are given in parentheses.

6. Differences between "The Tale of the Sankgreall" and its French source play no part in the experience of Malory's readers. On occasion, however, Malory's aims with regard to the reader can be clarified by such comparisons. For instance, at this point in the French version, the monk carefully explains that the killing of the seven knights deprived them of the opportunity for repentance [*La Queste del Saint Graal*, ed. Albert Pauphilet (Paris: E. Champion, 1923), p. 54; cited hereafter as *Queste*]. Although he frequently summarizes such explanations, Malory rarely omits them entirely. He does so here, I suspect, because to offer a rationale for the monk's unexpected rebuke would soften its impact. At this early stage in the tale, Malory is concerned more with undercutting the reader's expectation than with instructing him—concerned more, we might say, with educating the reader than the Christian.

7. I have put into words here an inference that many readers no doubt leave unarticulated. An unspoken sense of how the operations of the Grail world differ from those of the world of chivalric adventure will serve Malory's reader (if not the critic) as well as such an overt formulation as mine.

8. The white bulls are Malory's own addition to the recluse's speech, as Vinaver notes (*Works*, p. 1543). Clearly, they are an anticipation of Gawain's dream, designed to introduce the black-white pattern as early as possible.

9. Kellogg discusses, though in disparaging terms, the way in which Malory's version of the dream differs from the French; see his "Malory and Color Symbolism," pp. 12–14. In fact, all of Malory's changes serve to sharpen the dream's black-white symbolism: the French bulls, which were spotted with sin, have become black; and Bors—described confusingly in the *Queste* as "ne bien tachiez ne bien sanz tache," to suggest his repentant condition—has, like the other Grail knights, become white, but with one black spot. Compare *Works*, 942.3–8 and *Queste*, p. 149. Once again, Malory is concerned more with conditioning the reader's response than with explicating subtleties of doctrine.

10. Vinaver attributes the confusing reference to "the grete birde" in 963.31–32 to Malory's mistranslation of the French; see *Works*, p. 1566. It seems possible, though, that Malory's version is intentional, part of a plan—reflected in other confusing sentences in the balance of the passage—to make this fraudulent interpretation less

coherent, and hence more clearly suspect, than it is in the *Queste*.

11. At this point, Malory deliberately, and significantly, departs from his source. Lancelot's soliloquy is unrelated to the vague self-reproaches of the French account (compare *Queste*, pp. 61–62), and the sentence quoted above condenses a far longer French passage in such a way as to change entirely its meaning:

> Et quant il ot ceste parole, si est tant dolenz qu'il ne set que il doit fere. Si se part maintenant d'iluec sospirant dou cuer et lermoiant des eulz, si maudit l'ore quil fu nez, car ce set il bien qu'il est venuz au point qu'il n'avra ja mes honor, puis qu'il a failli a savoir la verite del Saint Graal. Mes les trois paroles dont il a este apelez n'a il pas oubliees ne n'oubliera ja mes tant come il vive, ne se sera granment aeise devant que il sache por quoi il fu einsi apelez.   (*Queste*, p. 61)

By juxtaposing only two clauses of the original, Malory has altered the whole emphasis of the speech; in place of helpless lamentation, we have intellectual initiative of the same sort Malory requires of the reader.

12. See, for example, the reactions of Stephen J. Miko, "Malory and the Chivalric Order," *Medium Ævum* 35 (1966): 223; Lambert, *Malory: Style and Vision*, pp. 176–80; Benson, *Malory's Morte Darthure*, p. 161.

13. My reading of this episode is offered in greater detail in Stephen C. B. Atkinson, "Malory's 'Healing of Sir Urry': Lancelot, the Earthly Fellowship, and the World of the Grail," *Studies in Philology* 78 (1981): 341–52.

14. Scudder, *Le Morte Darthur*, p. 268.

Prophecy and Nostalgia: Arthurian Symbolism at the Close of the English Middle Ages *(Caroline D. Eckhardt)*

1. See Flora Alexander, "Late Medieval Scottish Attitudes to the Figure of King Arthur: A Reassessment," *Anglia* 93 (1975): 17–34; Sidney Anglo, "The *British History* in Early Tudor Propaganda," *Bulletin of the John Rylands Library* 44 (1961–62): 17–48; Laura Keeler, *Geoffrey of Monmouth and the Late Latin Chroniclers, 1300–1500* (Berkeley: University of California Press, 1946); T. D. Kendrick, *Brit-*

ish Antiquity (London: Methuen, 1950); Gordon Kipling, *The Triumph of Honor: The Burgundian Origins of the Elizabethan Renaissance* (The Hague: Leiden University Press, 1977); Roger Sherman Loomis, "Edward I, Arthurian Enthusiast," *Speculum* 28 (1953): 114–27; May McKisack, "Edward III and the Historians," *History* 45 (1960): 1–15, esp. pp. 5, 7; James D. Merriman, *The Flower of Kings: A Study of the Arthurian Legend in England between 1485 and 1835* (Lawrence: University Press of Kansas, 1973); and Charles Bowie Millican, *Spenser and the Table Round: A Study in the Contemporaneous Background for Spenser's Use of the Arthurian Legend* (Cambridge, Mass.: Harvard University Press, 1932). In the fifteenth century, however, doubts were raised about the veracity of the Arthurian story. See John E. Housman, "Higden, Trevisa, Caxton, and the Beginnings of Arthurian Criticism," *Review of English Studies* 23 (1947): 209–17; as well as Kendrick, *British Antiquity*, pp. 11–14 and chaps. 6–7.

2. Caroline D. Eckhardt, ed., *The Prophetia Merlini of Geoffrey of Monmouth: A Fifteenth-Century English Commentary* (Cambridge, Mass.: Medieval Academy, 1982), p. 58. Brutus is given brief mention as well in the literary tradition—for example, at the beginning of *Sir Gawain and the Green Knight* and in Chaucer's "Complaint to His Purse," which addresses Henry IV as "conqueror of Brutes Albioun"—but the poets do not tend to dwell on his story.

3. Millican, *Spenser and the Table Round*, p. 18, citing from Bernard André (tutor of Prince Arthur).

4. Ibid., pp. 27–28.

5. See plate XIb in Kendrick, *British Antiquity*, and pp. 35–36; on the Round Table at Winchester, see Philip Howard, "Likely Date of 1336 for 'Round Table,'" *The [London] Times* (21 December 1976): 1–2; and P. J. C. Field, "The Winchester Round Table," *Notes & Queries*, n.s. 25 (1978): 204.

6. On Arthur Plantagenet, see *Dictionary of National Biography* (s.v. Plantagenet) and Cokayne, *Complete Peerage* (s.v. Lisle).

7. On Humphrey's son, see *Dictionary of National Biography* (s.v. Humphrey). Charles L. Kingsford, *English Historical Literature in the Fifteenth Century* (Oxford: Clarendon Press, 1913; repr. New York: Burt Franklin, 1962), pp. 364–65, gives a list of "the names of the Duke of Glowcetteris maynye [including 'Arteys'] that were taken at Bery, and sent in to dyuerse places to preson." *Gregory's Chronicle*, in *The Historical Collections of a Citizen of London in the Fifteenth Century*, ed. James Gairdner (Camden Society, 1876; repr. New York:

215

Johnson Reprint Co., 1965), p. 188, provides a description of Arthur's arrest.

8. *Gregory's Chronicle, Historical Collections of a Citizen of London,* p. 188.

9. The Beauforts were descended from John of Gaunt and his third wife, Catherine Swynford; the children of this union had been born out of wedlock but subsequently were legitimated; see *Dictionary of National Biography.* There were many other instances of legitimacy belatedly made, unmade, or questioned in this period. The Yorkists, for example, claimed that Prince Edward, heir of Henry VI until the prince's death at Tewkesbury in 1471, was not really Henry VI's son; see James H. Ramsay, *Lancaster and York: A Century of English History (A.D. 1399–1485)* (Oxford: Clarendon Press, 1892), p. 2:166.

10. Henry IV's second wife was Joanna of Navarre, widow of John Duke of Burgundy; the second son of Joanna and John, named Arthur, was active on the French side in the Hundred Years War. See, for example, the index entries in Ramsay, *Lancaster and York,* vol. 2.

11. The child died in infancy; see *Complete Peerage.* Alexander, "Late Medieval Scottish Attitudes," describes the chronicles that regard Mordred as the legitimate heir and Arthur as a usurper.

12. Vol. 13 of the *Complete Peerage* includes an appendix on the frequency of personal names, from which the comment on the name Arthur is cited (p. 630). Kingsford refers to an incident involving one "Arthur the squire" (*English Historical Literature,* p. 26), and there must have been other examples outside the royal family; but the name seems to have been quite uncommon. Gairdner's list of the mayors and sheriffs of London, 1199–1470, includes many instances of John, Henry, William, and so on, but none of Arthur (*Historical Collections of a Citizen of London,* pp. 241–58). Similarly, a list of the aldermen of London, 1400–1500, includes numerous instances of John, Henry, William, Thomas, Richard, and Robert but none of an alderman named Arthur. See Alfred B. Beaven, *The Aldermen of the City of London, temp. Henry III,* vol. 2 (London: Eden Fisher, 1908), pp. 2:2–19.

13. Merlin's prophecies (uttered to King Vortigern) constitute Book VII of the *Historia;* see *The Historia Regum Britanniae of Geoffrey of Monmouth,* ed. Acton Griscom (New York: Longmans, Green, 1929), pp. 383–97. Here, Merlin aids Uther Pendragon, Arthur's father.

14. In the *Historia* there are two separate prophecies on a Celtic restoration: Merlin's prophecy to Vortigern (see note 13 above); and

an angel's prophecy to Cadwalader at the end of the work, saying that Cadwalader himself will not regain Britain but that the Britons will reign again at the time which Merlin has identified (Book XII, p. 533, in Griscom's edition). On the later medieval development of the Merlin prophecies, see Eckhardt, *Prophetia Merlini*, pp. 3–15.

15. *Chronica Regum Angliae per Thomam Otterbourne*, ed. Thomas Hearne, in *Duo rerum Anglicarum scriptores veteres* (Oxford, 1732), p. 1:210; John Webb, "Translation of a French Metrical History of the Deposition of King Richard the Second," *Archaelogia* 20 (1824): 168–69; *Chronicon Adae de Usk*, ed. Edward M. Thompson (London: J. Murray, 1876), pp. 24, 132–33; Froissart, cited by Webb, "Translation of a French Metrical History," pp. 259–63.

16. Anglo, "*British History* in Early Tudor Propaganda," discusses these genealogies (pp. 21–24) and provides an appendix (pp. 41–48) describing the genealogical rolls and similar documents for Henry VI, Edward IV, Henry VII, and Henry VIII.

17. Although this manuscript is only indirectly genealogical, given its claim of Edward's British descent, it shares the assumptions of the genealogies (see note 16 above). On the manuscript, see Eckhardt, *Prophetia Merlini*, pp. 58–59.

18. "The Battle of Barnet (1471)," in *Historical Poems of the XIVth and XVth Centuries*, ed. Rossell Hope Robbins (New York: Columbia University Press, 1959), pp. 226–27, ll. 21–22. If it were not for this poem's pointed references to contemporary events, the political value of the comparison between Edward and Arthur would be slight, since there are many such comparisons in which the name of Arthur has no political or prophetic force but simply represents a nostalgic general idea (as in some of the literary texts, discussed below). John Paston III, for example, describing the court of Charles, Duke of Burgundy, in 1468 (Paston accompanied Margaret of York, sister of Edward IV, to her marriage with the Duke), remarks: "asfor the Dwkys coort, as of lordys, ladys, and gentylwomen, knytys, sqwyirs, and gentyllmen, I knew neuer of non lyek to it saue Kyng Artourys cort"—*Paston Letters and Papers of the Fifteenth Century*, ed. Norman Davis, part 1 (Oxford: Clarendon Press, 1971), p. 539. On continental references to the name of Arthur used in this way, see Diana B. Tyson, "King Arthur as a Literary Device in French Vernacular History Writing of the Fourteenth Century," *Bulletin bibliographique de la Société internationale arthurienne* 33 (1981): 237–57, esp. pp. 250–52. The comparison of Henry IV with Arthur and with Alexander in the Christmas tournament of 1400 suggests the Nine

Worthies tradition; see below, and note 24. On the tournament's Arthurian reference, see Larry D. Benson, "The Date of the *Alliterative Morte Arthure*," in *Medieval Studies in Honor of Lillian Herlands Hornstein*, ed. Jess B. Bessinger, Jr., and Robert R. Raymo (New York: New York University Press, 1976), p. 36 and note 49. The widespread Arthurian references and comparisons with various kings suggest that we should regard with caution Richard R. Griffith's viewpoint that Sir Thomas Malory's readers "would have been predisposed to identify Arthur with his Yorkist descendant [Edward IV] and only specific disclaimers . . . would have prevented this"; see "The Political Bias of Malory's *Morte Darthur*," *Viator* 5 (1974): 365–86, esp. p. 381.

19. On the banner and its symbol, see Anglo, "*British History* in Early Tudor Propaganda," pp. 35–40.

20. "Aspects of the European Tradition of Historical Writing," *Transactions of the Royal Historical Society*, 5th series, 20 (1972): 173–96. An excellent discussion of the biblical basis of this view is given by Erich Auerbach, "Figura," trans. Ralph Manheim, in *Scenes from the Drama of European Literature: Six Essays* (New York: Meridian, 1959), pp. 11–76. See also Robert W. Hanning's survey, "The Formation of the Early Medieval Historical Imagination," in his *Vision of History in Early Britain: From Gildas to Geoffrey of Monmouth* (New York: Columbia University Press, 1966), pp. 1–43; and Norman Cohn, *The Pursuit of the Millennium*, rev. and expanded ed. (New York: Oxford University Press, 1970).

21. See Eckhardt, *Prophetia Merlini*, p. 85, l. 488.

22. A convenient overview of the English Arthurian romances is provided by Helaine Newstead, "Arthurian Legends," in *A Manual of the Writings in Middle English, 1050–1500: Fascicule 1, Romances*, ed. J. Burke Severs (New Haven, Conn.: Connecticut Academy of Arts and Sciences, 1967), pp. 38–79, 224–56. Although the *Alliterative Morte Arthure* is there dated c. 1360, more recent work suggests that it belongs to the beginning of the fifteenth century; see Benson, "Date of the *Alliterative Morte Arthure*," pp. 19–40.

23. Ed. Ernst Sieper, *Lydgate's Reson and Sensuallyté*, Early English Text Society, Extra Series 84 (London: Kegan Paul, Trench, Trübner, 1901–03): pp. 1: 83–84 (lines 3139–48, 3167–73). Punctuation slightly modified.

24. Roger Sherman Loomis, "Verses on the 'Nine Worthies,'" *Modern Philology* 15 (1917–18): 211–19; citation from p. 218. On Arthur

in the Nine Worthies tradition, see Tyson, "King Arthur as a Literary Device," pp. 240–47, and the references given there.

25. *The Floure and the Leafe; and, The Assembly of Ladies*, ed. D. A. Pearsall (Manchester, Eng.: Manchester University Press, 1980), p. 99 (lines 502–503); the Round Table is named a few lines later, at l. 515.

26. On the declining ages of the world and related apocalyptic concepts, see Marjorie Reeves, *The Influence of Prophecy in the Later Middle Ages: A Study in Joachimism* (Oxford: Clarendon Press, 1969); Benoit Lacroix, *L'Historien au Moyen Âge* (Montréal: Institut d'Études Médiévales, 1971), esp. pp. 90–95; Valerie M. Lagorio, "The Apocalyptic Mode in the Vulgate Cycle of Arthurian Romances," *Philological Quarterly* 57 (1978): 1–22; and James Dean, "The World Grown Old and Genesis in Middle English Historical Writings," *Speculum* 57 (1982): 548–68.

27. *The Works of Sir Thomas Malory*, 2nd edition, ed. Eugène Vinaver (Oxford: Clarendon Press, 1967; reprinted with corrections, 1973), 3:1119–20. On Malory's chivalric and political interpretations of the Arthurian ideal, see Elizabeth T. Pochoda, *Arthurian Propaganda: Le Morte Darthur as an Historical Ideal of Life* (Chapel Hill: University of North Carolina Press, 1971); chap. 2 of this work, "Medieval Political Theory and the Arthurian Legend," pp. 23–60, provides a useful discussion of previous criticism.

28. Robert E. Lerner, "The Black Death and Western European Eschatological Mentalities," *American Historical Review* 86 (1981): 533–52.

29. McKisack, "Edward III and the Historians," p. 5. Such assessments of the late medieval period as one of perceived pessimism or disillusionment are not uncommon. Compare Morton W. Bloomfield's analysis of heroism in literary texts, which associates a postulated decline of the heroic with "the rising sadness of the later Middle Ages" and the "strong suspicion of earthly achievement," and concludes that "the decline of the hero in the later Middle Ages must reflect this spirit of denial and the suspicion of worldly success." Bloomfield, "The Problem of the Hero in the Later Medieval World," in *Concepts of the Hero in the Middle Ages and the Renaissance*, ed. Norman T. Burns and Christopher Reagan (Albany, N.Y.: State University of New York Press, 1975), pp. 27–48, esp. 39, 42.

30. "On the Times, 1388," in *Political Poems and Songs Relating to English History*, ed. Thomas Wright, Rolls Series 14 (London: Long-

man, Green, Longman, Roberts, 1859), 1:270 (ll. 30–38).

31. *Works*, ed. Vinaver, 3:1229.

32. *The Works of Geoffrey Chaucer*, 2nd ed., ed. F. N. Robinson (Boston: Houghton Mifflin, 1957), p. 84 (*Canterbury Tales*, III: 857–63); emphasis added.

33. Prologue to *Polychronicon*, in *Selections from William Caxton*, ed. N. F. Blake (Oxford: Clarendon Press, 1973), p. 1.

34. Cited by Anglo, "*British History* in Early Tudor Propaganda," pp. 28–29.

35. Thus the assessments of McKisack and Bloomfield, as well as similar statements, should be understood as applying to only *one* aspect of late medieval thought. It is not difficult to cite expressions of pessimism; but, insofar as history was perceived in prophetic or typological terms, it also invited optimistic interpretations. Compare the conclusion to Reeves' study of Joachimism: "The outstanding impression which remains . . . is the significance of the motif of optimism about history. This unites the medieval and Renaissance periods in an unexpected way" (*Influence of Prophecy*, p. 507). Lerner points out as well that chiliastic thinking can "encourage perseverance in the face of persecution and bring hope in the face of trials" (p. 538). The viewpoint that the late medieval period was characterized by predominant pessimism owes a great deal to Huizinga's concept of the "waning" of the Middle Ages; for a critique see Maurice Keen, "Huizinga, Kilgour, and the Decline of Chivalry," *Medievalia et Humanistica*, New Series 8 (1977): 1–20.

"An ancient idea of Chivalric greatness": The Arthurian Revival and Victorian History Painting *(Debra N. Mancoff)*

1. William Dyce to Charles Locke Eastlake, 20 July 1848, in James Stirling Dyce, "Life Correspondence of William Dyce, R.A., 1806–1864, Painter, Musician and Scholar, by his son," Aberdeen Art Gallery, vol. 3, XXVII, letter 49.

2. As early as 1742, Batty Langley published a treatise on national architecture entitled *Gothic Architecture Improved by Rules and Proportions in many Grand Designs of Columns, Doors, Windows, Chimneypieces, Arcades, Colonnades, Porticos, Umbrellos, Temples and Pavillions, & c., with plans, elevations and profiles, geometrically explained.* Other publications included Francis Grose's *Treatise on Ancient Armour and Weapons* (London: S. Hooper, 1785) and John Carter's *Specimens of Ancient Sculpture and Painting* (London: n.p.,

1780). Joseph Strutt made a substantial contribution with studies of ecclesiastical vestment in 1773, a study of arms and manners in 1774 and, between 1794 and 1799, his magnum opus, *A Complete View of the Dress and Habits of the People of England* (London: J. Nichols, 1769–99). For a full discussion of the archaeological compendia of the eighteenth century, see Roy Strong, *Recreating the Past: British History and the Victorian Painter* (London: Thames and Hudson, 1978), pp. 47–66.

3. Richard Hurd, *Letters on Chivalry and Romance,* ed. Edith J. Morley (London: Henry Froude, 1911), p. 118 (letter VIII).

4. "Thomas Percy," *The Dictionary National Biography,* ed. Sir Leslie Stephen and Sir Sidney Lee, 22 vols. (London: Oxford University Press, 1917–), p. 15:883.

5. The term "George-Ellis-specimens" can be traced to Mrs. Amelia Heber, *The Life of Reginald Heber, D. D., Lord Bishop of Calcutta,* 2 vols. (New York: Protestant Episcopal Press, 1830), p. 1:323. See James D. Merriman, *The Flower of Kings: A Study of the Arthurian Legend in England between 1485 and 1835* (Lawrence: University Press of Kansas, 1973), p. 128.

6. These editions were the compact Wilks and the Walker and Edwards. Concerning abandoned projects and the eventual re-publication of *Le Morte Darthur,* see J. Phillip Egger, *King Arthur's Laureate: A Study of Tennyson's "Idylls of the King"* (New York: New York University Press, 1971), pp. 218–20; and Merriman, *Flower of Kings,* pp. 129–31.

7. Strong, *Recreating the Past,* pp. 15–16.

8. Ibid., p. 81. West invested long hours in research at the arms and weapons collections at the Tower of London and in careful study of the recently published works of Strutt, particularly *Horda Angelcynnan, or A compleat View of the Manners, Customs, Arms, Habits, etc. of the Inhabitants of England (1774–76),* and *Regal and Ecclesiastical Antiquities* (1773).

9. The one exception to the neglect of Arthurian subjects affirms the "archaeological dependency" of the British historical artist of the eighteenth century. John Hamilton Mortimer's *The Discovery of Prince Arthur's Tomb by the inscription on the leaden cross* (1768) celebrates an archaeological event, however, apocryphal it might be. The painting, unlocated, is known only through preliminary drawings and an engraving after the painting by J. Ogborne, published in 1797. See John Sunderland, "Mortimer, Pine and Some Political Aspects of English History Painting," *Burlington Magazine* 116 (June 1974): 317–26.

10. A sound discourse on the theory of Félibien is found in A. Fontaine's *Les doctrines d'Arte en France; peintures, amateurs, critiques de Poussin à Diderot* (Paris: Renouard, H. Laurens, 1909), pp. 56–57.

11. On the French Philosophes, see James A. Leith, *The Idea of Art as Propaganda in France, 1750–1799: A Study in the History of Ideas* (Toronto: University of Toronto Press, 1965), pp. 8–16. The declaration of La Font de Saint-Yenne is from *Réflexions sur quelques causes de l'état présent de la peinture en France* (The Hague, 1747), as quoted in Wend Graf Kalnein and Michael Levey, *Art and Architecture of the Eighteenth Century in France* (Harmondsworth, Middlesex: Penguin Books, 1972), p. 108.

12. On the School of Virtue, see Leith, *Idea of Art*, pp. 36–39. The quotation is from Diderot's *Pensées detachées sur la peinture* (1776–81), as quoted in Lorenz Eitner, ed., *Neoclassicism and Romanticism, 1750–1850: Sources and Documents*, 2 vols. (Englewood Cliffs, N.J.: Prentice-Hall, 1970), p. 1:66.

13. On the reading of Roman history in French schools, and on Corneille's tragedy as a partial source of David's painting, see L. D. Ettlinger, "Jacques Louis David and Roman Virtue," *Journal of the Royal Society of Arts* 115 (January 1967): 105–23.

14. See Keith Andrews, *The Nazarenes: A Brotherhood of German Painters in Rome* (Oxford: Clarendon Press, 1964); and Herbert Schindler, *Nazarener: Romantischer Geist und christliche Kunst im 19. Jahrhunderts* (Regensburg: Friedrich Pustet, 1982).

15. See Inken Nowald, *Die Nibelungenfresken von Julius Schorr von Carolsfeld im Königsbau der Münchner Residenz, 1827–1867* (Kiel: Keinsthalle, 1978).

16. Sir Joshua Reynolds, *Discourses on Art*, ed. Robert R. Wark (New Haven, Conn.: Yale University Press, 1981), pp. 42, 57, 70.

17. James Barry, *An Inquiry into the real and imaginary Obstructions to the Acquisition of the Arts in England* (London: T. Becket, 1775), pp. 132–33.

18. James Barry, *A Letter to the Dilettanti Society* . . . (London: J. Walker, 1798), p. 26.

19. To explain his allegory, Barry published two pamphlets for distribution to his viewers. The contemporary writer Edward Edwards mused: "This was a very proper precaution, for several of the portraits could not have been understood to represent what he meant to express, without such elucidation." *Anecdotes of Painters who have resided or been born in England with critical remarks on their productions* (London: Leigh and Sotheby, 1808), p. 302.

20. Sir Walter Scott, *Ivanhoe*, 2 vols. (Boston and New York: Houghton Mifflin, 1913), p. 2:95.

21. The popularity of Digby's now almost unreadable treatise is evident in writings throughout the nineteenth century. Charles Whibley called it "the breviary of Young England" in *Lord John Manners and His Friends*, 2 vols. (Edinburgh and London: Blackwood, 1925), p. 1:33; and Edward Burne-Jones reportedly kept the books on his night-stand to the end of his life. See Georgiana M. Burne-Jones, *Memorials of Edward Burne-Jones* (London: Macmillan, 1904), p. 1:56.

22. For a highly amusing account of the Eglinton Tournament, see Ian Anstruther, *The Knight and the Umbrella: An Account of the Eglinton Tournament* (London: G. Bles, 1963).

23. Charles Dickens, "The Spirit of Chivalry" (August 1845), as quoted in *A Memoir of Daniel Maclise, R.A.*, ed. W. Justin O'Driscoll (London: Longmans, Green, 1871), pp. 90–92.

24. J. S. Dyce, Aberdeen MS, vol. 3, XXVI, p. 992.

25. "Varieties," *Art Union* 3 (1 December 1844): 360.

26. Dyce, Aberdeen MS, vol. 3, XXVII, letter 49; Thomas John Gullick, "Dyce's Frescoes in the Queen's Robing-Room of the Westminster Palace," *The Art-Journal* 27 (1865): 333.

27. William Dyce to Charles Locke Eastlake, 20 July 1848, Dyce, Aberdeen MS, vol. 3, XXVII, letter 49.

28. According to a letter from Charles Locke Eastlake to William Dyce, 22 July 1848, Dyce, Aberdeen MS, vol. 3, XXVII.

29. T. J. Gullick, *Descriptive Handbook for the National Pictures in the Westminster Palace* (London: Bradbury, Evans and Company, 1865), p. 333.

30. *The Works of Sir Thomas Malory*, ed. Eugène Vinaver, 2nd ed., 3 vols. (Oxford: Clarendon Press, 1967), p. 3:1192.

31. Charles Locke Eastlake to H. R. H. Prince Albert, 15 October 1852, Dyce, Aberdeen MS, vol. 3, XXIX; and Gullick, *Descriptive Handbook*, p. 25.

Malory's Expurgators *(Marylyn Jackson Parins)*

1. For example, see Larry D. Benson, "Sir Thomas Malory's *Le Morte Darthur*," in *Critical Approaches to Six Major English Works*, ed. Robert M. Lumiansky and Herschel Baker (Philadelphia: University of Pennsylvania Press, 1968), pp. 81–85. Benson notes several stric-

tures from the nineteenth century but distinguishes between critical appreciation and popularity, allowing that Malory was widely read. As a more recent instance, Laila Z. Gross sums up: "In the nineteenth century, though read and reworked, Malory was not really appreciated." *The Romance of Arthur*, ed. James J. Wilhelm and Laila Z. Gross (New York: Garland, 1984), p. 243.

2. A useful, entertaining discussion of expurgated books in the nineteenth century and later is provided by Noel Perrin, *Dr. Bowdler's Legacy* (New York: Atheneum, 1969). Most of the abridgements and adaptations of Malory are listed by Page West Life in her *Sir Thomas Malory and the Morte Darthur* (Charlottesville: University Press of Virginia, 1980), pp. 60–69; and several were noted by H. Oskar Sommer in volume 2 of his edition of Malory (London: David Nutt, 1889–91). Several of the popular editions examined in this essay are discussed by David Staines, who emphasizes the influence of Tennyson's treatment on these publications and provides publication information showing the large number of editions and reprints most of these works went through. See his "King Arthur in Victorian Fiction," in *The Worlds of Victorian Fiction*, ed. Jerome H. Buckley, Harvard English Studies 6 (Cambridge, Mass.: Harvard University Press, 1975), pp. 288–92. Strachey's edition of Malory has been treated in detail by Yuri Fuwa, "The Globe Edition of Malory as a Bowdlerized Text in the Victorian Age," *Studies in English Literature* (Tokyo), English Number (1984): 3–17.

3. *English Works of Roger Ascham*, ed. William Aldis Wright (1904; reissued Cambridge: Cambridge University Press, 1970), p. 231.

4. "Preface or Advertisement to the Reader," reprinted in *La Mort d'Arthure: The History of King Arthur and of the Knights of the Round Table*, ed. Thomas Wright, 3rd ed., 3 vols. (London: Reeves and Turner, 1889), vol. 1, p. xxv.

5. O. F. Christie, *The Transition from Aristocracy, 1832–1867: An Account of the Passing of the Reform Bill, . . .* (London: Seeley, Service, and Co., 1927), p. 79.

6. Eliot, "The.Voice of His Time: T. S. Eliot on Tennyson's *In Memoriam*," *The Listener* (February 12, 1942), pp. 211–12; quoted by Christopher Ricks, *Tennyson* (New York: Collier Books, 1972), p. 273.

7. Walter E. Houghton, *The Victorian Frame of Mind, 1830–70* (New Haven, Conn.: Yale University Press, 1957), p. 372.

8. F. J. Furnivall, ed., *La Queste del Saint Graal* (London: J. B. Nichols and Sons, 1864), p. vi.

9. Ibid., pp. v–vi.

10. The paper was published the following year; see William Blake Odgers, *King Arthur and the Arthurian Romances* (London: Longmans, Green, 1872). Subsequent reference is to this edition.

11. Ibid., p. 60.

12. William Minto, *Characteristics of English Poets from Chaucer to Shirley* (Edinburgh and London: William Blackwood and Sons, 1874), p. 110. Subsequent references are to this edition.

13. Ibid.

14. Frederic Harrison, *The Choice of Books and Other Literary Pieces* (1886; repr. London: Macmillan, 1906), pp. 80, 80–81n2.

15. Kathleen Tillotson, *Novels of the Eighteen-Forties* (Oxford: Clarendon Press, 1954; repr. 1971), pp. 57–58.

16. Ibid., pp. 54ff.; and Houghton, *Victorian Frame of Mind*, p. 357n45.

17. James T. Knowles, *The Story of King Arthur and His Knights of the Round Table* (London: Griffith and Farran, 1862), pp. ii–iii. Subsequent page references are to this edition.

18. Ibid., p. iii.

19. Ibid., p. 13.

20. Ibid.

21. Ibid., p. 292.

22. Conybeare, *La Morte d'Arthur: The History of King Arthur* (London: Edward Moxon, 1868), p. iii. Subsequent references are to this edition.

23. Ibid., p. iv.

24. Ibid., p. v.

25. Ibid., pp. 1–2.

26. Ibid., pp. 367, 308.

27. Ibid., p. 226.

28. Ibid., p. 352.

29. Edward Strachey, *Morte Darthur: Sir Thomas Malory's Book of King Arthur and His Noble Knights of the Round Table*, Globe edition (London: Macmillan, 1868), p. xvii. Subsequent references are to this edition.

30. Ibid., p. xviii.

31. Ibid., p. xiii.

32. Ibid., p. xviii.

33. These alterations regarding Mordred have been pointed out by Fuwa, "Globe Edition of Malory," p. 10.

34. B. Montgomerie Ranking, *La Mort D'Arthur: The Story of King Arthur and His Knights of the Round Table* (London: Chatto and

Windus, 1871), p. 7. Subsequent references are to this edition.

35. Ibid., p. 10.

36. Ibid., p. 8.

37. *Life and Exploits of King Arthur and His Knights of the Round Table* (London: Milner and Company, 1871), p. 12. Subsequent references are to this edition.

38. Ibid., pp. 44–45.

39. Ibid., p. 202.

40. Lanier, *The Boy's King Arthur: Being Sir Thomas Malory's History of King Arthur and His Knights of the Round Table* (New York: Charles Scribner's Sons, 1880), pp. iii and xvi. Subsequent references are to this edition. Although Lanier did not find it necessary to expurgate, his high evaluation of Malory at least made publication thinkable. Other authors did not stand so well with him; referring to the works of Sterne, Fielding, Smollett, and Swift, Lanier said: "If I had my way with these classic books, I would blot them from the face of the earth." *The English Novel and the Principle of Its Development* (New York: Charles Scribner's Sons, 1883), p. 180; quoted by Perrin, *Dr. Bowdler's Legacy*, p. 6.

41. Lanier, *Boy's King Arthur*, pp. xxii–xxiii.

42. Ibid., p. xxii.

43. Ibid., p. 79.

44. Ibid., p. 349.

45. Ernest Rhys, ed., *Malory's History of King Arthur and the Quest of the Holy Grail* (London: Walter Scott, 1886), p. xi. Subsequent references are to this edition.

46. Ibid., pp. xvi, 326.

47. Ibid., p. 326.

48. Ibid., p. xxviii.

49. Ibid., p. xxxi.

50. Ibid., p. 27.

51. Ibid., p. 262.

52. Noted by Fuwa, "Globe Edition of Malory," p. 7n1, who adds that this 1893 edition is "no less bowdlerized than the Globe edition."

53. Charles Morris, *King Arthur and the Knights of the Round Table* (London: W. W. Gibbings, 1892). Subsequent references are to this edition.

54. Ibid., vol. 1, p. 8.

55. Ibid., pp. 8–9.

56. Ibid., p. 11.

57. Ibid., pp. 15, 17.

58. Ibid., p. 38.

59. Ibid., p. 360.

60. Henry Frith, *King Arthur and His Knights of the Round Table* (London: George Routledge, 1884). Subsequent references are to a later, quite similar edition (Philadelphia: David McKay, 1912).

61. Ibid., p. 372.

62. There are, of course, other ways to explain the illustration. One is that Fraser, in complete innocence, illustrated the episode as Frith had described it. Another is that Fraser, aware of Frith's alterations, chose, in a tongue-in-cheek manner, to illustrate this particular moment in the story.

63. Frith, *King Arthur,* p. iv.

64. Ibid., p. iii.

65. Ibid., p. iv.

66. Ibid., p. v.

Tennyson's Camelot Revisited: An Augustinian Approach to the *Idylls (David L. Boyd)*

1. Quoted in *The Poems of Tennyson,* ed. Christopher Ricks (London: Longmans, Green, 1969), p. 1460. Subsequent references to Tennyson's works are from this edition and are cited in the text.

2. David Staines, *Tennyson's Camelot: The "Idylls of the King" and Its Medieval Sources* (Waterloo, Ontario: Wilfred Laurier University Press, 1982), p. i.

3. The Reverend Tennyson's sermons seem to have contained several "Augustinian" views. In an unpublished treatise on the nature of sin, he writes of the struggles between the spirit and the flesh. I am indebted to Susan Gates of the Tennyson Research Center for supplying me with this sermon, dated February 5(?), 1824. Reverend Tennyson's sermon is uncalendared and untitled. For Alfred Tennyson's reading of the classics and Dr. Tennyson's collection of theological writings, see Susan Shatto, "Tennyson's Library," *The Book Collector* 27 (1978): 494–513.

4. At Cambridge, "The Apostles" were prominent in the advancement of theology as a field of study and frequently debated theological questions. See G. M. Trevelyan, *Trinity College: An Historical Sketch* (Cambridge: Cambridge University Press, 1943); and Martha

M. Garland, *Cambridge before Darwin: The Ideal of a Liberal Education, 1800–1860* (Cambridge: Cambridge University Press, 1980), pp. 83–84.

5. See Charles F. G. Masterman, *Tennyson as a Religious Teacher* (Methuen, 1900; repr. New York: Octagon, 1977), pp. 114–15, 171; Stephen W. Sykes, *The Integrity of Anglicanism* (New York: Seabury Press, 1978), p. 77.

6. James O. Hoge, ed., *Lady Tennyson's Journal* (Charlottesville: University Press of Virginia, 1981), p. 219.

7. For *In Memoriam*, see Jerome H. Buckley, *Tennyson: The Growth of a Poet* (Cambridge, Mass.: Harvard University Press, 1967), pp. 122–23; for "The Gardener's Daughter," see Robert Pattison, *Tennyson and Tradition* (Cambridge, Mass.: Harvard University Press, 1979), pp. 75–76. For other allusions to Augustinian thought in Tennyson's works, see John R. Reed, *Perception and Design in Tennyson's "Idylls of the King"* (Athens: Ohio University Press, 1970), pp. 3–4; Howard W. Fulweiler, "The Argument of 'The Ancient Sage': Tennyson and the Christian Intellectual Tradition," *Victorian Poetry* 21 (1983): 203–16. Neither, however, suggests the direct influence of Augustine's writings on the *Idylls*.

8. Such a pointed contrast between the city of Arthur and the cities of his enemies is not found in Malory's *Morte Darthur*. Only in Tennyson's epic do we find this city in which the knights are so thoroughly subjugated to their ruler. As Staines (p. 47) points out, "Malory has the oath emphasize the obligations of the knights to the outside world," while Tennyson's oath emphasizes the submission of the knights' will to that of the king.

9. Such a "Table Round," with knights who have sworn to act in opposition to Arthur's knights, is another Tennysonian addition to the epic. Compare Malory, *Tale of Sir Gareth*, VII, xvii, where the Red Knight fights only to fulfill an obligation to a fair damsel whose brothers were slain by one of Arthur's men.

10. Augustine, *De civitate Dei*, XIV, xxviii, 7–10. Corpus Christianorum Series Latina, 47–48 (1955). Subsequent references appear in the text. Translations throughout are from *The City of God: The Works of Aurelius Augustine, Bishop of Hippo*, trans. Marcus Dods et al., 2 vols. (Edinburgh: Clark, 1871). Subsequent references appear in the text.

11. Augustine, *Confessionum, libri XIII*, VII, x, 16, ed. L. Verheijen, Corpus Christianorum, Series Latina, 27 (1981). Translations throughout are from R. S. Pine-Coffin, *Saint Augustine: Confessions*

(Baltimore: Penguin Books, 1961). Other discussions of ontological light can be found in Augustine's *Tractatus de Joannis Evangelium* and *De libero arbitrio*.

12. Malory does not employ such light and dark imagery in his short account of the coming of Arthur:

> And than kynge Arthure, kynge Ban and kynge Bors departed with hir felyship, a twenty thousand, and cam within seven dayes into the contrey of Camylarde; and there rescowed kynge Lodegraunce, and slew there muche people of kynge Ryons, unto the numbir of ten thousand, and putte hem to flyght. And than had thes thre kynges grete chere of kynge Lodegraunce, and he thanked them of theire grete goodnes that they wolde revenge hym of his enemyes. (*Merlin*, I, xviii)

From *The Works of Sir Thomas Malory*, ed. Eugène Vinaver (London: Oxford University Press, 1954), p. 31.

13. Although both of Tennyson's sources for the grail story, *Morte Darthur* and *Queste del Saint Graal*, are heavily theological, Tennyson alters the meaning of the legend to fit the lack of spiritual optimism in the nineteenth century. See Celia Morris, "From Malory to Tennyson: Spiritual Triumph to Spiritual Defeat," *Mosaic* 7.3 (1974): 87–98. Tennyson's treatment of Lancelot differs significantly from the earlier works. In the medieval versions of the Grail Quest, the character of Lancelot is "primarily the type . . . of the good Knight" and is not a "fully realised character," as he is in Tennyson's portrayal. See Derek Brewer, "The Presentation of the Character of Lancelot: Chrétien to Malory," in *Arthurian Literature III*, ed. Richard Barber (Cambridge: D. S. Brewer, 1984), p. 26. Further, Malory and the author of the *Queste* are concerned with Lancelot's lament, confession, and repentance of his adulterous sin with Guinevere. In the *Idylls*, however, Tennyson deals with Lancelot's bitter inner struggles between his lust for Guinevere and love for Arthur.

14. "To the Queen," l. 37, in the epilogue to the *Idylls*.

15. In Malory and in the Vulgate Cycle, sexual sins—especially Arthur's incest with his sister and Lancelot's adultery with Guinevere—not pride, are the cause of the fall of Arthur's realm. See Larry D. Benson, *Malory's Morte Darthur* (Cambridge, Mass.: Harvard University Press, 1976), pp. 205–209; and T. Grove, "Sexual Intemperance and the Fall of the Round Table," *Explorations* 5 (1978): 11–21.

16. See, for example, Buckley, *Tennyson* (1967), p. 178; Stanley J. Solomon, "Tennyson's Paradoxical King," *Victorian Poetry* 1 (1963): 258–71; and Staines, *Tennyson's Camelot*, p. 48. Walter E. Houghton, *The Victorian Frame of Mind, 1830–70* (New Haven, Conn.: Yale University Press, 1957), p. 356.

17. Solomon, "Tennyson's Paradoxical King," p. 263.

18. Compare Malory, *Merlin*, I, viii, in which Arthur simply establishes all of the "countries" around London and conquers most of his enemies through the prowess of the Round Table.

19. See Edward Engelberg, "The Beast Image in Tennyson's *Idylls of the King*," *English Literary History* 22 (1955): 287–92. Engelberg, however, is concerned with image patterns and not with the will.

20. It is significant that here, as throughout the *Idylls*, Tennyson adds this beast imagery to the medieval account. Compare the medieval French *Romance of Merlin* printed in the introduction to Southey's edition of Malory (1817):

> When Vivian heard this, for her great treason, and the better to delude and deceive him, she put her arms round his neck, and began to kiss him, saying, that he might well be hers, seeing she was his: You well know, said she, that the great love which I have in you, has made me leave father and mother that I may have you in my arms day and night. (Quoted in Staines, p. 27.)

21. Both Buckley and Reed note in passing that pride plays a part in Guinevere's sins but fail to recognize the Augustinian source of this pride. See Buckley, *Tennyson*, p. 190; and Reed, *Perception and Design*, p. 114.

22. Significantly, this emphasis on pride as the destroyer of Arthur's realm—and, in fact, the entire Guinevere idyll—is Tennyson's creation. Compare Malory, *Le Morte Darthur*, XXI, vii:

> And whan quene Gwenyver undirstood that kynge Arthure was dede and all the noble knyghtes, sir Mordred and all the remanaunte, than she stale away with fyve ladyes with her, and so she wente to Amysbyry. And there she lete make herselff a nunne, and wered whyght clothys and blak, and grete penaunce she toke uppon her, as ever ded synfull woman in thys londe. And never creature coude make her myry, but ever she lyved in fastynge, prayers, and almesdedis, that all maner of people mervayled how vertuously she was chaunged.   (p. 873).

23. Arthur E. Baker, *A Concordance to the Poetical and Dramatic Works of Alfred Lord Tennyson* (New York: Barnes & Noble, 1967), p. 551.

Arthurian Myth Devalued in Walker Percy's *Lancelot* *(John Bugge)*

1. Walker Percy, *Lancelot* (New York: Farrar, Straus, & Giroux, 1977), pp. 9–10. Further citations from this edition appear in the text in parentheses.

2. *The Works of Sir Thomas Malory,* ed. Eugène Vinaver, 2nd ed., 3 vols. (Oxford: Clarendon Press, 1967), pp. 805–24. Further citations from this edition appear in the text in parentheses.

3. John Bugge, "Merlin and the Movies in Walker Percy's *Lancelot,*" *Studies in Medievalism* 2, no. 4 (1985): 39–55.

4. On the movies as preventing access to reality, instead providing only transcendent pseudo-religious experience, see Lewis A. Lawson, "Walker Percy's Indirect Communications," *Texas Studies in Language and Literature* 11 (1969): 867–900.

5. The ambivalence toward the Arthurian story besetting the reader here recalls a similar strategy (if that is what it is) in Twain's *Connecticut Yankee,* where the narrator, Hank Morgan, also falls victim to a kind of myth-madness that precipitates his role in a final apocalyptic dissolution.

6. See, most recently, Walker Percy, *Lost in the Cosmos: The Last Self-Help Book* (New York: Farrar, Straus & Giroux, 1983).

7. The Arthurian past is paired and conflated with the myth of the Old South, linked in Lance's mind, as in his father's before him, with the past of his Confederate ancestors (pp. 115–16). Both seem to have been times of great deeds—of heroic enterprise, storied valor, austere integrity. In the course of the narrative, however, at least the myth of the Old South is effectively deflated, and in "Questions They Never Asked Me," a "self-interview" in *Esquire* 88 (December 1977), Percy undermines the idea of a special Southern literary mystique based on "sense of identity, tragic dimension, community, history and so forth. . . . I was never quite sure," writes Percy, "what it meant" (p. 172).

8. Walker Percy, "The Loss of the Creature," in *The Message in the Bottle* (New York: Farrar, Straus & Giroux, 1975), pp. 46–63.

9. The novel's Galahad figure, Lance's unnamed son, has never set out. Unlike Lancelot's son by Elayne, Lance's son by his first wife Lucy avoids the Sege Perelous by refusing to fight in Vietnam and, in a perverse burlesque of Galahad's ethereal chastity, shuns the company of women and becomes a "mild homosexual" (pp. 17, 177).

10. Walker Percy, *The Moviegoer* (New York: Knopf, 1961; repr. 1975), p. 13.

11. On Percival's role as quester, see Robert D. Daniel, "Walker Percy's *Lancelot:* Secular Raving and Religious Silence," *Southern Review* 14 (1978): 186–94; Corinne Dale, "*Lancelot* and the Medieval Quests of Sir Lancelot and Dante," *Southern Quarterly* 18, no. 3 (1980): 99–106; and Lewis A. Lawson, "Walker Percy's Silent Character," *Mississippi Quarterly* 33 (1980): 123–40.

12. It is significant that Anna is named for the mother of the Virgin, in that role a "bearer" of the gift of salvation. For a similar reason, Lance's wife is named "Mary Margaret" (after the Virgin, and with the connotations of the pearl's purity), and not after Guinevere ("Gwen"?), who is less relevant—indeed, antithetical—to the Grail myth. Margot's more important mythic function is hinted at when Lance says she seemed strangely like Anna (a true Grail bearer) in her last moment alive at Belle Isle (pp. 245–46).

13. See also, Jessie L. Weston, *From Ritual to Romance* (first published, 1920; repr. Garden City, N.Y.: Doubleday, 1957), pp. 12–24.

14. To her credit, neither does Anna subscribe to Lance's myth-making. For example, she rejects as the arrant nonsense it is Lance's "great secret of life . . . the ignominious joy of rape and being raped" (p. 252).

15. See Lewis J. Taylor, "Walker Percy and the Self," *Commonweal* 100, no. 10 (10 May 1974): 234.

"Yet Some Men Say . . . that Kynge Arthure Ys Nat Ded" *(Charles Moorman)*

1. "The English Prose *Morte*," in *Essays on Malory*, ed. J. A. W. Bennett (Oxford: Clarendon Press, 1963), pp. 25ff.

2. Quoted by C. S. Lewis in *The Discarded Image: An Introduction to Medieval and Renaissance Literature* (Cambridge: Cambridge University Press, 1964), p. 180.

3. Ibid., p. 182.

4. Lewis Thorpe, trans., *History of the Kings of Britain* (London: The Folio Society, 1969), p. 8.

5. *The Works of Sir Thomas Malory,* ed. Eugène Vinaver, 3 vols. (Oxford: Clarendon Press, 1967), vol. 1, p. 9.

6. Mary Stewart, *The Crystal Cave* (Greenwich, Conn.: Fawcett, 1971), pp. 160–61.

7. John Steinbeck, *The Acts of King Arthur and His Noble Knights* (New York: Farrar, Straus & Giroux, 1976), p. 13.

8. Thomas Berger, *Arthur Rex* (New York: Delacorte Press, 1978), pp. 10–11.

9. E. M. Forster, *Aspects of the Novel* (New York: Harcourt, Brace, 1927), p. 26.

BIBLIOGRAPHY

Adam of Usk. *Chronicon Adae de Usk*. Ed. Edward M. Thompson. London: J. Murray, 1876.

Alexander, Flora. "Late Medieval Scottish Attitudes to the Figure of King Arthur: A Reassessment." *Anglia* 93 (1975): 17–34.

Andrews, Keith. *The Nazarenes: A Brotherhood of German Painters in Rome*. Oxford: Clarendon Press, 1964.

Anglo, Sidney. "The *British History* in Early Tudor Propaganda." *Bulletin of the John Rylands Library* 44 (1961–62): 17–48.

An Anglo-Norman "Brut." Ed. Alexander Bell. Anglo-Norman Text Society nos. 21–22. Oxford: Basil Blackwell, 1969.

Anstruther, Ian. *The Knight and the Umbrella: An Account of the Eglinton Tournament*. London: G. Bles, 1963.

Ascham, Roger. *English Works of Roger Ascham: Toxophilus, Report of the Affairs and State of Germany*. Ed. William Aldis Wright. 1904; repr. Cambridge: Cambridge University Press, 1970.

Ashe, Geoffrey. *The Discovery of King Arthur*. New York: Doubleday, 1985.

———. *Avalonian Quest*. London: Methuen, 1982.

———. *Camelot and the Vision of Albion*. London: Heinemann, 1971.

———. "'A Certain Very Ancient Book': Traces of an Arthurian Source in Geoffrey of Monmouth's *Historia*." *Speculum* 56 (1981): 301–23.

———, ed. *The Quest for Arthur's Britain*. London: Pall Mall Press, 1968.

Atkinson, Stephen C. B. "Malory's 'Healing of Sir Urry': Lancelot, the Earthly Fellowship, and the World of the Grail." *Studies in Philology* 78 (1981): 341–52.

Auerbach, Erich. "Figura." Trans. Ralph Manheim. In *Scenes from the Drama of European Literature: Six Essays*. New York: Meridian, 1959, pp. 11–76.

Augustine, Saint. *Saint Augustine: Confessions*. Ed. R. S. Pine-Coffin. Baltimore: Penguin Books, 1961.

———. *Confessiorum. Confessionum libri XII*. Corpus Christianorum, Series Latina 27. Turnholt, 1981.

———. *The City of God: The Works of Aurelius Augustine, Bishop of Hippo*. Trans. Marcus Dods et al. 2 vols. Edinburgh: Clark, 1871.

———. *De civitate Dei*. Corpus Christianorum Series Latina 47–48. Turnholt, 1955.

Baker, Arthur E. *A Concordance to the Poetical and Dramatic Works of Alfred Lord Tennyson.* New York: Barnes & Noble, 1967.

Barry, James. *A Letter to the Dilenttanti Society, respecting the obtention of certain matters essentially necessary for the improvement of public taste, and for accomplishing the original views of the Royal Academy of Great-Britain.* London: J. Walker, 1798.

———. *An Inquiry into the real and imaginary Obstructions to the Acquisition of the Arts in England.* London: T. Becket, 1775.

"The Battle of Barnet (1471)." *Historical Poems of the XIVth and XVth Centuries.* Ed. Rossell Hope Robbins. New York: Columbia University Press, 1959, pp. 726–27.

Beaven, Alfred B. *The Aldermen of the City of London, temp. Henry III.* 2 vols. London: Eden Fisher, 1908.

Bell, Alexander, ed. *An Anglo-Norman "Brut."* Anglo-Norman Text Society 21–22. Oxford: Basil Blackwell, 1969.

———. "The *Munich Brut* and the *Estoire des Bretuns.*" *Modern Language Review* 34 (1939): 321–54.

Bennett, J. A. W., ed. *Essays on Malory.* Oxford: Clarendon Press, 1963.

Benson, Larry D. "The Date of the *Alliterative Morte Arthure.*" In *Medieval Studies in Honor of Lillian Herlands Hornstein.* Ed. Jess B. Bessinger, Jr., and Robert R. Raymo. New York: New York University Press, 1976.

———. *Malory's Morte Darthur.* Cambridge, Mass.: Harvard University Press, 1976.

———. "Sir Thomas Malory's *Le Morte Darthur.*" In *Critical Approaches to Six Major English Works: 'Beowulf' through 'Paradise Lost.'* Ed. Robert M. Lumiansky and Herschel Baker. Philadelphia: University of Pennsylvania Press, 1968.

Berger, Thomas. *Arthur Rex.* New York: Delacorte Press, 1978.

Biblia Sacra iuxta Vulgatam Clementinam. 4th ed. Madrid: Biblioteca de Autores Cristianos, 1965.

Blacker-Knight, Jean. "From *Historia* to *Estoire:* Literary Form and Social Function of the Twelfth-Century Old French Verse and Latin Prose Chronicle of the Anglo-Norman *Regnum.*" Ph.D. diss., University of California at Berkeley, 1984.

Blake, N. F., ed. *Selections from William Caxton.* Oxford: Clarendon Press, 1973.

Blanch, Robert J., ed. *Sir Gawain and Pearl: Critical Essays.* Bloomington: Indiana University Press, 1966.

Bloomfield, Morton W. "'The Man of Law's Tale': A Tragedy of Victimization and a Christian Comedy." *PMLA* 87 (1972): 384–90.

――――. "The Problem of the Hero in the Later Medieval World." In *Concepts of the Hero in the Middle Ages and the Renaissance.* Ed. Norman T. Burns and Christopher J. Reagan. Albany, N.Y.: State University of New York Press, 1975, pp. 27–48.

Boccaccio, Giovanni. *De casibus illustrium virorum; A Facsimile Reproduction of the Paris Edition of 1520.* Intro. Louis Brewer Hall. Gainesville: Scholars' Facsimiles and Reprints, 1962.

Boethius. *The Consolation of Philosophy.* Loeb Classical Library. Cambridge: Harvard University Press, 1918.

Braswell, Mary Flowers. *The Medieval Sinner: Confession and Characterization in the Literature of the English Middle Ages.* London and Toronto: Associated University Presses, 1983.

Brewer, Derek. "The Presentation of the Character of Lancelot: Chrétien to Malory." In *Arthurian Literature III.* Ed. Richard Barber. Cambridge: D. S. Brewer, 1984.

Brook, G. L., and R. F. Leslie, eds. Lazamon's *Brut.* 3 vols. Early English Text Society 250. London: Oxford University Press, 1963.

Buckley, Jerome H. *Tennyson: The Growth of a Poet.* Cambridge, Mass.: Harvard University Press, 1967.

Bugge, John. "Merlin and the Movies in Walker Percy's *Lancelot.*" *Studies in Medievalism* 2, no. 4 (1985): 39–55.

Burne-Jones, Georgiana M. *Memorials of Edward Burne-Jones.* 2 vols. London: Macmillan, 1904.

Burns, Norman T., and Christopher Reagan, eds. *Concepts of the Hero in the Middle Ages and the Renaissance.* Albany, N.Y.: State University of New York Press, 1975.

Cable, James, trans. *The Death of Arthur.* Baltimore: Penguin Books, 1971.

Caesar, Julius. *The Battle for Gaul.* Trans. Anne and Peter Wiseman. Boston: David Godine, 1980.

――――. *C. Iuli Caesaris Commentarii de bello Gallico.* Ed. T. Rice Holmes. 7 vols. Oxford: Clarendon Press, 1914.

Caldwell, Robert. "Wace's *Roman de Brut* and the *Variant Version* of Geoffrey of Monmouth's *Historia Regum Britanniae.*" *Speculum* 31 (1956): 675–82.

Carter, John. *Specimens of Ancient Sculpture and Painting.* London: n.p., 1780.

Caxton, Selections from William. Ed. N. F. Blake. Oxford: Clarendon Press, 1973.

Chambers, E. K. *Arthur of Britain.* 1927; repr. New York: Barnes and

Noble, 1964, and London: Sidgwick & Jackson, 1966.

Chaucer, The Works of Geoffrey. 2nd ed. Ed. F. N. Robinson. Boston: Houghton Mifflin, 1957.

Chew, Samuel C. "Time and Fortune." *English Literary History* 6 (1939): 83–113.

Chibnall, Marjorie, ed. and trans. *The Ecclesiastical History of Orderic Vitalis.* 6 vols. Oxford: Oxford University Press, 1968–80.

Chrétien de Troyes. *Erec et Enide.* Ed. Mario Roques. Classiques Français du Moyen Âge, no. 80. Paris: H. Champion, 1955.

———. *Der Percevalroman (Li Contes del Graal).* Ed. Alfons Hilka. Halle: M. Niemeyer, 1932.

Christie, O. F. *The Transition from Aristocracy, 1832–1867: An Account of the Passing of the Reform Bill, the causes which led up to it, and its far-reaching consequences on the life and manners of all grades of society.* London: Seely, Service, and Co., 1927.

Chronica Regum Angliae per Thomam Otterbourne. Ed. Thomas Hearne. In *Duo rerum Anglicarum scriptores veteres.* 2 vols. Oxford, 1732.

Clanchy, M. T. *From Memory to Written Record: England 1066–1307.* Cambridge, Mass.: Harvard University Press, 1979.

Cloetta, Wilhelm. *Komödie and Tragödie im Mittelalter.* Vol. 1: *Beiträge zur Literaturgeschichte des Mittelalters und der Renaissance.* 2 vols. Halle: Niemeyer, 1890–1892.

Cohn, Norman. *The Pursuit of the Millennium.* Rev. and expanded ed. New York: Oxford University Press, 1970.

Cokayne, George E. *Complete Peerage of England, Scotland, Ireland, Great Britain, and the United Kingdom: Extant, Extinct, or Dormant.* 13 vols. 1910–59; repr. New York: St. Martin's Press, 1984.

Conybeare, Edward. *La Morte d'Arthur: The History of King Arthur.* London: Edward Moxon, 1868.

Courcelle, Pierre. *La Consolation de Philosophie dans la tradition littéraire: antécédents et postérité de Boèce.* Paris: Études augustinennes, 1967.

Crawford, Mary S. "The Life of Saint Nicholas." Ph.D. diss., University of Pennsylvania, 1923.

Cross, Tom Peete, and William Albert Nitze. *Lancelot and Guenevere: A Study in the Origins of Courtly Love.* Chicago: University of Chicago Press, 1930.

Curtius, Ernst. *European Literature and the Latin Middle Ages.* Trans. Willard R. Trask. Bollingen Series, no. 36. 1953; repr. Princeton, N.J.: Princeton University Press, 1973.

Dale, Corinne. "*Lancelot* and the Medieval Quests of Sir Lancelot and Dante." *Southern Quarterly* 18, no. 3 (1980): 99–106.

Daniel, Robert D. "Walker Percy's *Lancelot:* Secular Raving and Religious Silence." *Southern Review* 14 (1978): 186–94.

Daude de Pradas, called Dels auzels cassadors, The Romance of. Ed. Alexander H. Schutz. Columbus: Ohio State University Press, 1945.

Davis, Norman, ed. *Paston Letters and Papers of the Fifteenth Century.* Part 1. Oxford: Clarendon Press, 1971.

Davis, R. H. C. *King Stephen, 1135–1154.* Berkeley: University of California Press, 1967.

Dean, James. "The World Grown Old and Genesis in Middle English Historical Writings." *Speculum* 57 (1982): 548–68.

Dickens, Charles. "The Spirit of Chivalry" (August 1845). In *A Memoir of Daniel Maclise, R.A.* Ed. W. Justin O'Driscoll. London: Longmans, Green, 1871.

Dictionary of the History of Ideas. Ed. Philip P. Wiener. 5 vols. New York: Scribner's, 1973.

Dictionary of National Biography, The. Ed. Leslie Stephen and Sidney Lee. 22 vols. London: Oxford University Press, 1917–.

Dyce, James Stirling. "Life Correspondence of William Dyce, R.A., 1806–1864, Painter, Musician and Scholar, by his son." Aberdeen Art Gallery, vol. 3, XXVII, letter 49.

Eckhardt, Caroline D., ed. *The Prophetia Merlini of Geoffrey of Monmouth: A Fifteenth-Century English Commentary.* Cambridge, Mass.: Medieval Academy, 1982.

Edwards, Edward. *Anecdotes of Painters who have resided or been born in England with critical remarks on their productions.* London: Leigh and Sotheby, 1808.

Egger, J. Phillip. *King Arthur's Laureate: A Study of Tennyson's "Idylls of the King."* New York: New York University Press, 1971.

Eitner, Lorenz, ed. *Neoclassicism and Romanticism, 1750–1850: Sources and Documents.* 2 vols. Englewood Cliffs, N.J.: Prentice-Hall, 1970.

Eliot, T. S. "The Voice of His Time: T. S. Eliot on Tennyson's *In Memoriam.*" *The Listener* 27, 683 (February 12, 1942): 211–12.

Engelberg, Edward. "The Beast Image in Tennyson's *Idylls of the King.*" *English Literary History* 22 (1955): 287–92.

Ettlinger, L. D. "Jacques Louis David and Roman Virtue." *Journal of the Royal Society of Arts* 115 (January 1967): 105–23.

Faral, Edmond. *La Légende Arthurienne: Études et Documents;* Première Partie: *Les Plus Anciens Textes*. 3 vols. Bibliothèque de l'École des Hautes Études, nos. 255–57. Paris: H. Champion, 1929.

——. *Les Arts poétiques du XIIe et du XIIIe siècle: recherches et documents sur la technique littéraire du moyen âge*. 1924; repr. Paris: E. Champion, 1962.

Farnham, Willard. *The Medieval Heritage of Elizabethan Tragedy*. Berkeley: University of California Press, 1936.

Field, P. J. C. "The Winchester Round Table." *Notes & Queries*. n.s., 25 (1978): 204.

Fish, Stanley E. *Self-Consuming Artifacts: The Experience of Seventeenth-Century Literature*. Berkeley: University of California Press, 1972.

Fletcher, Robert H. *The Arthurian Material in the Chronicles, Especially Those of Great Britain and France*. Harvard Studies and Notes in Philology and Literature, no. 10. Cambridge, Mass., 1906; repr. New York: Burt Franklin, 1966.

The Floure and the Leafe; and, The Assembly of Ladies. Ed. Derek A. Pearsall. Manchester, England: Manchester University Press, 1980.

Fontaine, A. *Les doctrines d'Art en France; peintres, amateurs, critiques de Poussin à Diderot*. Paris: Renouard, H. Laurens, 1909.

La Font de Saint-Yenne. *Réflexions sur quelques causes de l'état present de la peinture en France*. The Hague, 1747.

Forster, E. M. *Aspects of the Novel*. New York: Harcourt, Brace, 1927.

Francis, E. A., ed. *La Vie de Sainte Marguerite*. Paris: H. Champion, 1932.

Freeman, Michelle A. *The Poetics of Translatio Studii and Conjointure: Chrétien de Troyes's Cligés*. Lexington, Ky.: French Forum, 1979.

Fries, Maureen. "Malory's Tristram as Counter-Hero to the *Morte Darthur*." *Neuphilologische Mitteilungen* 76 (1975): 605–13.

——. "Tragic Pattern in Malory's *Morte Darthur*: Medieval Narrative as Literary Myth." *The Early Renaissance*. ACTA 5 (1978): 81–99.

Frith, Henry. *King Arthur and His Knights of the Round Table*. London: George Routledge, 1884; rev. ed. Philadelphia: David McKay, 1912.

Fulweiler, Howard W. "The Argument of 'The Ancient Sage': Tennyson and the Christian Intellectual Tradition." *Victorian Poetry* 21 (1983): 203–16.

Furnivall, F. J., ed. *La Queste del Saint Graal*. London: J. B. Nichols and Sons, 1864.

Fuwa, Yuri. "The Globe Edition of Malory as a Bowdlerized Text in the Victorian Age." *Studies in English Literature* (Tokyo), English Number (1984): 3–17.

Gairdner, James, ed. *Historical Collections of a Citizen of London in the Fifteenth Century.* Camden Society, 1876; repr. New York: Johnson Reprint Co., 1965.

Garbáty, Thomas A. "The Uncle-Nephew Motif: New Light into Its Origins and Development." *Folkore* 88 (1977): 221–35.

Garland, Martha M. *Cambridge before Darwin: The Ideal of a Liberal Education, 1800–1860.* Cambridge: Cambridge University Press, 1980.

Geoffrey of Monmouth. *The Historia Regum Britanniae.* Ed. Acton Griscom. London: Longmans, Green, 1929.

―――. *Historia Regum Britanniae: A Variant Version Edited from Manuscripts by Jacob Hammer.* Cambridge, Mass.: The Mediaeval Academy of America, 1951.

―――. *The History of the Kings of Britain.* Trans. with an intro. Lewis Thorpe. Harmondsworth: Penguin, 1966.

Giovanni, G. "The Connection between Tragedy and History in Ancient Criticism." *Philological Quarterly* 22 (1943): 308–14.

Göller, Karl H., ed. *The Alliterative Morte Arthure: A Reassessment of the Poem.* Cambridge: D. S. Brewer, 1981.

Gransden, Antonia. *Historical Writing in England c. 550–c. 1307.* Ithaca: Cornell University Press, 1974.

Gregory's Chronicle. In *The Historical Collections of a Citizen of London in the Fifteenth Century.* Ed. James Gairdner. Camden Society, 1876; repr. New York: Johnson Reprint Co., 1965.

Griffith, Richard R. "The Political Bias of Malory's *Morte Darthur.*" *Viator* 5 (1974): 365–86.

Griscom, Acton, ed. *The Historia Regum Britanniae of Geoffrey of Monmouth.* London: Longmans, Green, 1929.

Grose, Francis. *Treatise on Ancient Armour and Weapons.* London: S. Hooper, 1785.

Grout, P. B., et al., eds. *The Legend of Arthur in the Middle Ages: Studies Presented to A. H. Diverres by Colleagues, Pupils, and Friends.* Cambridge: D. S. Brewer, 1984.

Grove, T. "Sexual Intemperance and the Fall of the Round Table." *Explorations* 5 (1978): 11–21.

Gullick, Thomas John. *Descriptive Handbook for the National Pictures in the Westminster Palace.* London: Bradbury, Evans and Company, 1865.

———. "Dyce's Frescoes in the Queen's Robing-Room of the Westminster Palace." *The Art-Journal* 27 (1865): 333–34.

Gumbrecht, Hans Ulrich. "Literary Translation and Its Social Conditioning in the Middle Ages: Four Spanish Romance Texts of the 13th Century." *Yale French Studies* 51 (1974): 205–22.

Hammer, Jacob, ed. *"Historia Regum Brittaniae": A Variant Version Edited from Manuscripts.* Cambridge, Mass.: The Mediaeval Academy of America, 1951.

Hanning, Robert W. *The Vision of History in Early Britain: From Gildas to Geoffrey of Monmouth.* New York: Columbia University Press, 1966.

Harrison, Frederic. *The Choice of Books and Other Literary Pieces.* 1886; repr. London: Macmillan, 1906.

Haskins, Charles. "Henry II as a Patron of Literature." In *Essays in Medieval History Presented to Thomas Frederick Tout.* Ed. A. G. Little and F. M. Powicke. Manchester [S.N.], 1925, pp. 71–77.

Heber, Amelia. *The Life of Reginald Heber, D.D., Lord Bishop of Calcutta.* 2 vols. New York: Protestant Episcopal Press, 1830.

Highet, Gilbert. *The Classical Tradition: Greek and Roman Influences on Western Literature.* Oxford: Clarendon Press, 1949.

The Historia Regum Britanniae of Geoffrey of Monmouth. Ed. Acton Griscom. London: Longmans, Green, 1929.

Hofer, Stefan. "Die Problemstellung im Erec." *Zeitschrift für Romanische Philologie* 48 (1928): 123–28.

Hoge, James O., ed. *Lady Tennyson's Journal.* Charlottesville: University Press of Virginia, 1981.

Holden, A. J., ed. *Le Roman de Rou de Wace.* 3 vols. Société des Anciens Textes Français. Paris: Picard, 1970–73.

Holmes, T. Rice, ed. *C. Iuli Caesaris Commentarii de bello Gallico.* Oxford: Clarendon, 1914.

Houghton, Walter E. *The Victorian Frame of Mind, 1830–70.* New Haven, Conn.: Yale University Press, 1957.

Houk, Margaret. "Sources of the *Roman de Brut* of Wace." *University of California Publications in English* 5:2 (1944): 161–356.

Housman, John E. "Higden, Trevisa, Caxton, and the Beginnings of Arthurian Criticism." *Review of English Studies* 23 (1947): 209–17.

Howard, Donald, and Christian Zacher, eds. *Critical Studies of "Sir Gawain and the Green Knight."* Notre Dame, Ind.: Notre Dame University Press, 1970.

Howard, Philip. "Likely Date of 1336 for 'Round Table.'" *The [London] Times* (21 December 1976):1–2.

Isidore of Seville. *Isidori Hispalensis episcopi Etymologiarum sive Originum libri xx.* Ed. W. M. Lindsay. 2 vols. Oxford: Clarendon Press, 1911; repr. 1962.

Jung, C. G. *Psychological Types: Or the Psychology of Individualization.* Trans. H. G. Baynes. New York: Harcourt, Brace, 1926.

———. "The Relations between the Ego and the Unconscious." In *Two Essays on Analytical Psychology.* Trans. R. F. C. Hull. Bollingen Series, no. 20. New York: Pantheon, 1953.

Jung, Emma. *Animus and Anima.* Trans. C. F. Baynes and Hildegard Nagel. 1957; repr. New York: Spring Publications, 1969; Zürich, 1974.

Kalnein, Wend Graf, and Michael Levey. *Art and Architecture of the Eighteenth Century in France.* Harmondsworth, Middlesex: Penguin Books, 1972.

Kaufmann, Walter. *Tragedy and Philosophy.* Garden City, N.Y.: Doubleday, 1969.

Keeler, Laura. *Geoffrey of Monmouth and the Late Latin Chroniclers, 1300–1500.* Berkeley: University of California Press, 1946.

Keen, Maurice. "Huizinga, Kilgour, and the Decline of Chivalry." *Medievalia et Humanistica,* New Series 8 (1977): 1–20.

Keller, Hans-Erich. "Two Toponymical Problems in Geoffrey of Monmouth and Wace: *Estrusia* and *Siesia.*" *Speculum* 49 (1974): 687–98.

———. "Wace et Geoffrey de Monmouth: Problème de la chronologie des sources." *Romania* 98 (1977): 1–14.

Kellogg, Alfred. "Malory and Color Symbolism: Notes on His Translation of the *Queste del Saint Graal.*" In *Arthur, Langland, Chaucer: Essays in Middle English Literature.* Ed. Alfred Kellogg. New Brunswick, N.J.: Rutgers University Press, 1972, pp. 11–28.

Kelly, Douglas F. *Chrétien de Troyes: An Analytic Bibliography.* London: Grant & Cutler, 1976.

———. *Sens and Conjointure in the Chevalier de la Charette.* The Hague: Mouton, 1966.

———. "The Source and Meaning of Conjointure in Chrétien's *Erec* 14." *Viator* 1 (1970): 179–200.

Kendrick, T. D. *British Antiquity.* London: Methuen, 1950.

Kingsford, Charles L. *English Historical Literature in the Fifteenth Century.* Oxford: Clarendon Press, 1913; repr. New York: Burt Franklin, 1962.

Kipling, Gordon. *The Triumph of Honour: The Burgundian Origins of the Elizabethan Renaissance.* The Hague: Leiden University Press, 1977.

Knowles, James T. *The Story of King Arthur and His Knights of the Round Table.* London: Griffith and Farran, 1862.

Lacroix, Benoit. *L'Historien au Moyen Âge.* Montréal: Institut d'Études Médiévales, 1971.

Lacy, Morris. "The Form of the *Brut's* Arthurian Sequence. In *Jean Misrahi Memorial Volume: Studies in Medieval Literature,* pp. 150–58. Ed. Hans R. Runte, Henri Niedzielski, and William L. Hendrickson. Columbia, S.C.: French Literature Publications, 1977.

Lady Tennyson's Journal. Ed. James O. Hoge. Charlottesville: University Press of Virginia, 1981.

Lagorio, Valerie M. "The Apocalyptic Mode in the Vulgate Cycle of Arthurian Romances." *Philological Quarterly* 57 (1978): 1–22.

Lambert, Mark. *Malory: Style and Vision in Le Morte Darthur.* New Haven, Conn.: Yale University Press, 1975.

Langley, Batty. *Gothic Architecture Improved by Rules and Proportions in many Grand Designs of Columns, Doors, Windows, Chimneypieces, Archades, Colonnades, Porticos, Umbrellos, Temples and Pavillions, & c., with plans, elevations and profiles, geometrically explained.* 1742.

Lanier, Sidney. *The English Novel and the Principle of Its Development.* New York: Charles Scribner's Sons, 1883.

———. *The Boy's King Arthur: Being Sir Thomas Malory's History of King Arthur and His Knights of the Round Table.* New York: Charles Scribner's Sons, 1880.

Lawson, Lewis A. "Walker Percy's Silent Character." *Mississippi Quarterly* 33 (1980): 123–40.

———. "Walker Percy's Indirect Communications." *Texas Studies in Language and Literature* 11 (1969): 867–900.

Layamon. *Brut.* Ed. G. L. Brook and R. F. Leslie. 2 vols. Early English Text Society 250, 277. London: Oxford University Press, 1963–78.

Leckie, R. W., Jr. *The Passage of Dominion: Geoffrey of Monmouth and the Periodization of Insular History in the Twelfth Century.* Toronto: University of Toronto Press, 1981.

Leith, James A. *The Idea of Art as Propaganda in France, 1750–1799: A Study in the History of Ideas.* Toronto: University of Toronto Press, 1965.

Lerner, Robert E. "The Black Death and Western European Eschatological Mentalities." *American Historical Review* 86 (1981): 533–52.

Lewis, C. S. *The Discarded Image: An Introduction to Medieval and*

Renaissance Literature. Cambridge: Cambridge University Press, 1964.

––––––. "The English Prose *Morte*." In *Essays on Malory*, ed. J. A. W. Bennett. Oxford: Clarendon Press, 1963, pp. 7–28.

Life, Page West. *Sir Thomas Malory and the Morte Darthur*. Charlottesville: University Press of Virginia, 1980.

Life and Exploits of King Arthur and His Knights of the Round Table. London: Milner and Company, 1871.

Lindsay, W. M., ed. *Isidori Hispalensis Episcopi Etymologiarum sive Originum*. Oxford: Oxford University Press, 1962.

Lods, Jeanne, ed. "Prologue" to *Les Lais de Marie de France*. Paris: H. Champion, 1959.

Loomis, Roger Sherman, ed. *Arthurian Literature in the Middle Ages: A Collaborative History*. Oxford: Clarendon Press, 1959.

––––––. *The Development of Arthurian Romance*. London: Hutchinson, 1963.

––––––. "Edward I, Arthurian Enthusiast." *Speculum* 28 (1953): 114–27.

––––––. "Verses on the 'Nine Worthies.'" *Modern Philology* 15 (1917–18): 211–19.

Lumiansky, Robert M., ed. *Malory's Originality: A Critical Study of "Le Morte Darthur."* Baltimore: Johns Hopkins University Press, 1964.

Lydgate, John. *Reson and Sensuallyté*. Ed. Ernst Sieper. 2 vols. Early English Text Society, Extra Series 84, 89. London: Kegan Paul, Trench, Trübner, 1901–03.

McAlpine, Monica E. *The Genre of Troilus and Criseyde*. Ithaca: Cornell University Press, 1978.

McKisack, May. "Edward III and the Historians." *History* 45 (1960): 1–15.

Mahoney, John F. "Chaucerian Tragedy and the Christian Tradition." *Annuale Mediaevale* 3 (1962): 81–99.

Mais, Kurt, ed. *Der arthurische Roman*. Darmstadt: Wissenschaftliche Buchges, 1970.

Malory, Thomas. *Le Morte Darthur*. Ed. Oskar H. Sommer. 3 vols. London: David Nutt, 1889–91.

––––––. *La Morte D'Arthur: The History of King Arthur, Compiled by Sir Thomas Mallory*. Abr. and rev. Edward Conybeare. London: Edward Moxon, 1868.

––––––. *The Works of Sir Thomas Malory*. Ed. Eugène Vinaver. 2nd ed., 3 vols. Oxford: Clarendon Press, 1967.

Malory's Originality: A Critical Study of "Le Morte Darthur." Ed. Robert M. Lumiansky. Baltimore: Johns Hopkins University Press, 1964.

Malvezin, Pierre. *Dictionnaire des Racines Celtique.* 2nd ed. Paris: Chez l'auteur, 1923.

Marie de France. *Les Lais de.* Ed. Jeanne Lods. Classiques Français du Moyen Âge, no. 87. Paris: H. Champion, 1959.

Mary, André, ed. François Villon, *Oeuvres.* Paris: Garnier, 1962.

Masterman, Charles F. G. *Tennyson as a Religious Teacher.* First published Methuen, 1900; repr. New York: Octagon, 1977.

Matthews, William. *The Tragedy of Arthur: A Study of the Alliterative "Morte Arthure."* Berkeley: University of California Press, 1960.

Merlin: Roman en prose du XIIIe siècle. Ed. Gaston Paris and Jacob Ulrich. 2 vols. Société des Anciens Textes Français. Paris: Firmin Didot et cie, 1886.

Merriman, James D. *The Flower of Kings: A Study of the Arthurian Legend in England between 1485 and 1835.* Lawrence: University Press of Kansas, 1973.

Michel, Laurence. "The Possibility of a Christian Tragedy." In *Tragedy: Modern Essays in Criticism.* Ed. Laurence Michel and Richard B. Sewall. Englewood Cliffs, N.J.: Prentice-Hall, 1963.

Michell, Edward B. *The Art and Practice of Hawking.* First published 1900; repr. Boston: C. T. Branford, 1960.

Miko, Stephen J. "Malory and the Chivalric Order." *Medium Ævum* 35 (1966): 211–30.

Millican, Charles Bowie. *Spenser and the Table Round: A Study in the Contemporaneous Background for Spenser's Use of the Arthurian Legend.* Cambridge, Mass.: Harvard University Press, 1932.

Minto, William. *Characteristics of English Poets from Chaucer to Shirley.* Edinburgh and London: William Blackwood and Sons, 1874.

Moorman, Charles. *The Book of King Arthur.* Lexington: University Press of Kentucky, 1965.

Morley, Edith J., ed. Richard Hurd, *Letters on Chivalry and Romance* (1762). London: Henry Froude, 1911.

Morris, Celia. "From Malory to Tennyson: Spiritual Triumph to Spiritual Defeat." *Mosaic* 7.3 (1974): 87–98.

Morris, Charles. *King Arthur and the Knights of the Round Table.* 3 vols. London: W. W. Gibbings, 1892.

Muscatine, Charles. *Chaucer and the French Tradition: A Study in Style and Meaning.* Berkeley: University of California Press, 1957.

Newstead, Helaine. "Arthurian Legends." In *A Manual of the Writings in Middle English, 1050–1500: Fascicule 1, Romances.* Ed. J. Burke Severs. New Haven, Conn.: Connecticut Academy of Arts and Sciences, 1967.

Nowald, Inken. *Die Nibelungenfresken von Julius Schorr von Carolsfeld im Königsbau der Münchner Residenz, 1827–1867.* Kiel: Keinsthalle, 1978.

Odgers, William Blake. *King Arthur and the Arthurian Romances.* Paper read before the Bath Literary and Philosophical Association, December 22, 1871. London: Longmans, Green, 1872.

"On the Times, 1388." In *Political Poems and Songs Relating to English History.* Ed. Thomas Wright. 2 vols. London: Longman, Green, Longman & Roberts, 1859–61, 1:270–78.

Orderic Vitalis, The Ecclesiastical History of. Ed. and trans. Marjorie Chibnall. 6 vols. Oxford: Clarendon Press, 1969–80.

Otterbourn, Thomas. *Chronica Regum Angliae.* Vol. 1 of *Duo rerum Anglicarum scriptores veteres.* Ed. Thomas Hearne. Oxford, 1732.

Owen, Douglas D. R., ed. *Arthurian Romance: Seven Essays.* Edinburgh: Scottish Academic, 1970.

Paris, Gaston, and Jacob Ulrich, eds. *Merlin: Roman en prose du XIIIe siècle.* 2 vols. Société des Anciens Textes Français. Paris: Firmin Didot et cie, 1886.

Paston Letters and Papers of the Fifteenth Century. Ed. Norman Davis. 2 vols. Oxford: Clarendon Press, 1971–76.

Patch, Howard R. *The Tradition of Boethius: A Study of His Importance in Medieval Culture.* New York: Oxford University Press, 1935.

———. *The Goddess Fortuna in Medieval Literature.* 1927; repr. New York: Octagon Books, 1967.

Pattison, Robert. *Tennyson and Tradition.* Cambridge, Mass.: Harvard University Press, 1979.

Pauphilet, Albert, ed. *La Queste del Saint Graal.* Paris: E. Champion, 1923.

Payen, Jean-Charles, ed. *La Légende arthurienne et la Normandie.* Condé-Sur-Noireau: Éditions Charles Corlet, 1983.

Payne, F. Anne. *King Alfred and Boethius: An Analysis of the Old English Version of The Consolation of Philosophy.* Madison: University of Wisconsin Press, 1968.

Pearsall, D. A., ed. *The Floure and the Leafe; and, The Assembly of Ladies.* Manchester, England: Manchester University Press, 1980.

Peck, Russell. "Willfulness and Wonders: Boethian Tragedy in the Alliterative *Morte Arthure.*" In *The Alliterative Tradition in the Fourteenth Century.* Ed. Bernard S. Levy and Paul E. Szarmach. Kent, Ohio: Kent State University Press, 1981.

Pelan, Margaret. *L'Influence du "Brut" de Wace sur les romanciers français de son temps.* Paris: E. Droz, 1931.

Percy, Walker. *Lost in the Cosmos: The Last Self-Help Book.* New York: Farrar, Straus & Giroux, 1983.

———. *Lancelot.* New York: Farrar, Straus & Giroux, 1977.

———. *The Moviegoer.* First pub. 1961; repr. New York: Knopf, 1975.

———. "Questions They Never Asked Me." *Esquire* 88 (December 1977): 170–72, 184–94.

———. "The Loss of the Creature." In *The Message in the Bottle.* New York: Farrar, Straus & Giroux, 1975, pp. 46–63.

Perrin, Noel. *Dr. Bowdler's Legacy: A History of Expurgated Books in England and America.* New York: Atheneum, 1969.

Pickens, Rupert T., ed. *The Sower and the Seed: Essays on Chrétien de Troyes.* Lexington, Ky.: French Forum, 1983.

Pochoda, Elizabeth T. *Arthurian Propaganda: Le Morte Darthur as an Historical Ideal of Life.* Chapel Hill: University of North Carolina Press, 1971.

La Queste del Saint Graal: Roman de XIIIe siècle. Ed. Albert Pauphilet. Paris: H. Champion, 1923.

Ramsay, James H. *Lancaster and York: A Century of English History (A.D. 1399–1485).* 2 vols. Oxford: Clarendon Press, 1892.

Ranking, B. Montgomerie. *La Mort D'Arthur: The Story of King Arthur and His Knights of the Round Table.* London: Chatto and Windus, 1871.

Reed, John R. *Perception and Design in Tennyson's "Idylls of the King."* Athens: Ohio University Press, 1970.

Reeves, Marjorie. *The Influence of Prophecy in the Later Middle Ages: A Study in Joachimism.* Oxford: Clarendon Press, 1969.

Reynolds, Joshua. *Discourses on Art.* Ed. Robert R. Wark. New Haven, Conn.: Yale University Press, 1981.

Rhys, Ernest, ed. *Malory's History of King Arthur and the Quest of the Holy Grail.* London: Walter Scott, 1886.

Rickard, Peter. *Britain in Medieval French Literature, 1100–1500.* Cambridge: Cambridge University Press, 1956.

Ricks, Christopher. *Tennyson.* New York: Collier Books, 1972.

———, ed. *The Poems of Tennyson.* London: Longmans, Green, 1969.

Robbins, Rossell Hope, ed. "The Battle of Barnett (1471)." In *Historical Poems of the XIVth and XVth Centuries*. New York: Columbia University Press, 1959.

Robertson, D. W. "Chaucerian Tragedy." *English Literary History* 19 (1952): 1–37.

Robinson, David M. "Honorius and the Wheel of Fortune." *Classical Philology* 41 (1946): 207–16.

Romance of Arthur, The. Ed. James J. Wilhelm and Laila Z. Gross. New York: Garland, 1984.

Rothwell, W. "The Teaching of French in Medieval England." *Modern Language Review* 63 (1968): 37–46.

Royal Historical Society, Transactions of the. 5th Series 22.

Sanford, Eva Matthews. "Honorious and The Wheel of Fortune." *Classical Philology* 42 (1947): 251–52.

Schindler, Herbert. *Nazarener: Romantischer Geist und christliche Kunst im 19. Jahrhunderts*. Regensburg: Friedrich Pustet, 1982.

Schirmer, Walter F., and Ulrich Broich. *Studien zum literarischen Patronat im England des 12. Jahrhunderts*. Wissenchaftliche Abhandlungen der Arbeitsgemeinschaft für Forschung des Landes Nordrhein-Westfalen, no. 23. Köln: Westdeutscher Verlag, 1962.

Schutz, Alexander H., ed. *Dels auzels cassadors*. Columbus: Ohio State University Press, 1945.

Scott, Walter. *Ivanhoe: A Romance*. 2 vols. Boston and New York: Houghton Mifflin, 1913.

Scudder, Vida. *Le Morte Darthur of Sir Thomas Malory and Its Sources*. New York: E. P. Dutton, 1921.

Shatto, Susan. "Tennyson's Library." *The Book Collector* 27 (1978): 494–513.

Short, Ian. "On Bilingualism in Anglo-Norman England." *Romance Philology* 33 (1980): 467–79.

Sieper, Ernst, ed. *Lydgate's Reson and Sensuallyté*. Early English Text Society, Extra Series 84. London: Kegan Paul, Trench, Trübner, 1901.

Solcmon, Stanley J. "Tennyson's Paradoxical King." *Victorian Poetry* 1 (1963): 258–71.

Sommer, H. Oskar, ed. *Malory's Works*. 3 vols. London: David Nutt, 1889–91.

Southern, R. W. "Aspects of the European Tradition of Historical Writing I: The Classical Tradition from Einhard to Geoffrey of Monmouth." *Transactions of the Royal Historical Society*, 5th series, 20 (1972): 173–96.

———. *Medieval Humanism*. New York: Harper & Row, 1970.

Spearing, A. C. *Criticism and Medieval Poetry.* London: E. Arnold, 1964.

Spisak, James W., ed. *Studies in Malory.* Kalamazoo, Mich.: Medieval Institute Publications, 1985.

Staines, David. "King Arthur in Victorian Fiction." In *The Worlds of Victorian Fiction.* Ed. Jerome H. Buckley. Harvard English Studies 6, pp. 267–303. Cambridge, Mass.: Harvard University Press, 1975.

————. *Tennyson's Camelot: The "Idylls of the King" and Its Medieval Sources.* Waterloo, Ontario: Wilfred Laurier University Press, 1982.

Stansby, Richard. "Preface or Advertisement to the Reader." *La Mort d'Arthur: The History of King Arthur.* Repr. Thomas Wright. 3rd ed. 3 vols. London: Reeves and Turner, 1889.

Steinbeck, John. *The Acts of King Arthur and His Noble Knights.* New York: Farrar, Straus & Giroux, 1976.

Stewart, Mary. *The Crystal Cave.* Greenwich, Conn.: Fawcett, 1971.

Strachey, Edward. *Morte Darthur: Sir Thomas Malory's Book of King Arthur and His Noble Knights of the Round Table.* Globe edition. London: Macmillan, 1868.

Strong, Roy. *Recreating the Past: British History and the Victorian Painter.* London: Thames and Hudson, 1978.

Strutt, Joseph. *A Complete View of the Dress and Habits of the People of England.* London: J. Nichols, 1796–99.

————. *Horda Angel-cynnan, or A compleat View of the Manners, Customs, Arms, Habits, etc. of the Inhabitants of England.* London: T. Jones, 1774–76.

————. *The Regal and Ecclesiastical Antiquities of England.* London: Thane, 1773.

Sunderland, John. "Mortimer, Pine and Some Political Aspects of English History Painting." *Burlington Magazine* 116 (June 1974): 317–26.

Sykes, Stephen W. *The Integrity of Anglicanism.* New York: Seabury Press, 1978.

Tatlock, J. S. P. *The Legendary History of Britain: Geoffrey of Monmouth's "Historia Regum Britanniae" and Its Early Vernacular Versions.* Berkeley and Los Angeles: University of California Press, 1950.

Taylor, Henry Osborn. *The Mediaeval Mind.* 2 vols. London: Macmillan, 1914.

Taylor, Lewis J. "Walker Percy and the Self." *Commonweal* 100, no. 10 (May 10, 1974): 233–36.

Tennyson, Alfred Lord. *The Poems of Tennyson.* Ed. Christopher

Ricks. London: Longmans, Green, 1969.

Tennyson, George Clayton. Sermon, February 5 (?), 1824. Tennyson Research Center, Lincoln, England.

Thompson, Edward M., ed. *Chronicon Adae de Usk*. London: J. Murray, 1876.

Thompson, James W. *The Literacy of the Laity in the Middle Ages*. University of California Press Publications 9 (1939); repr. New York: Burt Franklin, 1960.

Thompson, Mary H. L. "'Geoffrey Did Not Invent It': The Roman War in the *Historia Regum Britanniae*." In *Actes du 14e-Congrès International Arthurien*. 2 vols. Rennes: Presses Universitaires, 1985, 2: 627–34.

Thompson, Raymond. "Gawain against Arthur: The Impact of a Mythological Pattern upon Arthurian Tradition in Accounts of the Birth of Gawain." *Folklore* 85 (1974): 113–21.

Thorpe, Lewis. Intro. and trans. *The History of the Kings of Britain, by Geoffrey of Monmouth*. London: Penguin, 1961.

Tilander, Gunnar. *Glanures lexicographiques*. Lund: C. W. K. Gleerup, 1932.

Tillotson, Kathleen. *Novels of the Eighteen-Forties*. Oxford: Clarendon Press, 1954; repr. 1971.

Trevelyan, G. M. *Trinity College: An Historical Sketch*. Cambridge: Cambridge University Press, 1943.

Tyson, Diana B. "King Arthur as a Literary Device in French Vernacular History Writing of the Fourteenth Century." *Bulletin bibliographique de la Société internationale arthurienne* 33 (1981): 237–57.

———. "Patronage of French Vernacular History Writers in the Twelfth and Thirteenth Centuries." *Romania* 100, no. 2 (1979): 180–222.

Usk, Adam of. *Chronicon*. Ed. Edward M. Thompson. London: J. Murray, 1876.

Van der Ven-ten Bensel, Elisa F. W. M. *The Character of King Arthur in English Literature*. 1925; repr. New York: Haskell House, 1966.

van de Vyver, A. "Les traductions du *De Consolatione Philosophiae* de Boèce en littérature comparée." *Humanisme et Rénaissance* 6 (1939): 247–73.

"Varieties." *The Art Union* 3 (December 1, 1844): 360–61.

Varty, Kenneth, ed. *An Arthurian Tapestry: Essays in Memory of Lewis Thorpe*. Glasgow: French Department of the University, 1981.

Villon, François. *Oeuvres*. Ed. André Mary. Paris: Garnier, 1962.

Vinaver, Eugène, ed. *The Works of Sir Thomas Malory.* 3 vols. 2nd ed. Oxford: Clarendon Press, 1967.

Wace. *Le Roman de Brut.* Ed. Ivor Arnold. 2 vols. Société des Anciens Texts Français. Paris: Garnier, 1938.

————. *Le Roman de Rou de Wace.* 3 vols. Société des Anciens Textes Français. Paris: Picard, 1970–73.

————. *The Life of Saint Nicholas.* Ed. Mary S. Crawford. Ph.D. diss., University of Pennsylvania, 1923.

————. *La Vie de Sainte Marguerite.* Ed. E. A. Francis. Classiques Français du Moyen Âge. Paris: Édouard Champion, 1932.

Wais, Kurt, ed. *Der arthurische Roman.* Darmstadt: Wissenschaftliche Buchgesellschaft, 1970.

Warren, Wilfred L. *Henry II.* Berkeley: University of California Press, 1973.

Webb, John. "Translation of a French Metrical History of the Deposition of King Richard the Second." *Archaelogia* 20 (1824): 1–423.

Wertime, Richard A. "The Theme and Structure of the Stanzaic *Morte Arthur. PMLA* 87 (1972): 1075–82.

Weston, Jessie L. *From Ritual to Romance.* 1920; repr. Garden City, N.Y.: Doubleday, 1957.

Whibley, Charles. *Lord John Manners and His Friends.* 2 vols. Edinburgh and London: Blackwood, 1925.

Wiener, Philip P., ed. "Fortune, Fate, and Chance." In *Dictionary of the History of Ideas.* 5 vols. New York: Scribner's, 1973.

Wilhelm, James T. and Laila Z. Gross, eds. *The Romance of Arthur.* New York: Garland, 1984.

Wilson, R. M. "English and French in Ireland: 1100–1300." *History* 28 (1943): 37–60.

Woledge, Brian, and Ian Short. "Liste provisoire de manuscrits du XIIe siècle contenant des textes en langue française." *Romania* 102, no. 1 (1980): 1–16.

Wright, Thomas, ed. *Political Poems and Songs Relating to English History.* 2 vols. Rolls Series 14. London: Longman, Green, Longman, Roberts, 1859–61.

Wright, Thomas, ed. *La Mort d'Arthure: The History of King Arthur and of the Knights of the Round Table.* 3rd ed. 3 vols. London: Reeves and Turner, 1889.

Wright, William Aldis, ed. *English Works of Roger Ascham.* 3 vols. 1904; reissued, Cambridge: Cambridge University Press, 1970.

Zumthor, Paul. *Merlin le prophète: un thème de la littérature polémique de l'historiographie et des romans.* Geneva: Librairie Payot, 1943.

251

CONTRIBUTORS

GEOFFREY ASHE is a historian whose Arthurian books include *The Discovery of King Arthur, Avalonian Quest,* and *A Guidebook to Arthur's Britain.* He has lectured and broadcast widely in Britain and America and has written books in mythological and religious fields as well. He is a contributor to scholarly journals, an associate editor of *The Arthurian Encyclopedia,* and the chairman of Debrett's Arthurian Committee.

STEPHEN C. B. ATKINSON has taught at Missouri Southern State College and Hofstra University and is currently at Rockhurst College in Kansas City, Missouri. He has published on Malory and *Beowulf* and is presently at work on articles dealing with Chaucer, Bunyan, and medieval drama, and on a book exploring the reception history of *Le Morte Darthur.*

JEAN BLACKER-KNIGHT is an Assistant Professor of French at Kenyon College. She has published in *Kentucky Romance Quarterly* and *Romance Philology* and has presented papers on Arthurian and Anglo-Norman topics. She is currently working on a study of twelfth-century Old French literature, chronicles, and saints' lives.

DAVID L. BOYD completed his MA degree in English at the University of Alabama at Birmingham and is a graduate student in the Medieval Studies Program at Yale University. He has presented conference papers on Chaucer and alchemy and on the relationship of the fourteenth-century book trade to *The Canterbury Tales,* as well as publishing book reviews on *Sir Gawain and the Green Knight* and an essay on *The Book of the Duchess.*

MARY FLOWERS BRASWELL is Professor of English at the University of Alabama at Birmingham. She has published on medieval literature, art history, theology, and law in such journals as *The Chaucer Review, Medievalia et Humanistica,* the *Journal of Medieval and Renaissance*

252

Studies, and *Mosaic.* Twice a recipient of a College Teacher's Fellowship from the National Endowment for the Humanities, she is the author of *The Medieval Sinner: Confession and Characterization in the Literature of the English Middle Ages.*

JOHN BUGGE is a member of the Department of English at Emory University. He has published on both medieval and modern writers in such journals as *Mediaeval Studies, Annuale Mediaevale, Papers on Language and Literature,* and *Studies in Medievalism.* He is the author of *Virginitas: An Essay in the History of a Medieval Ideal.*

CAROLINE D. ECKHARDT is Professor of English and Comparative Literature, and Head of the Comparative Literature department, at the Pennsylvania State University. Among her publications are *The Prophetia Merlini of Geoffrey of Monmouth,* a book-length Chaucer bibliography (in press), the edited collection *Essays in the Numerical Criticism of Medieval Literature,* and articles on various aspects of medieval Arthurian texts, including the Merlin prophecies, the English romance *Sir Percyvelle,* and the Provençal romance *Jaufre.* She is presently editing a fourteenth-century English verse chronicle, known as *Thomas Castleford's Chronicle.*

MAUREEN FRIES is Professor of English at the New York State University College at Fredonia. She has published *A Bibliography of Writings by and about British Women Authors* and is currently editing a book on teaching the Arthurian tradition in literature for the Modern Language Association. Her articles have appeared in such journals as *Neuphilologische Mitteilungen, Philosophical Quarterly, Fifteenth-Century Studies,* and *The Journal of Popular Culture.* Professor Fries has held fellowships from NEH, ACLS, The American Philosophical Society, and the Fulbright Commission.

DEBRA N. MANCOFF currently teaches art history in the Department of Art and Art History at Beloit College, in Wisconsin. She was a major contributor on the visual arts to *An Arthurian Encyclopedia* and a contributor to *Victorian Britain: An Encyclopedia*. She has published articles on nineteenth-century Arthurian imagery and Pre-Raphaelite art in such journals as *Avalon to Camelot* and the *Journal of Pre-Raphaelite Studies*. Presently, she is working on an extended study of the theory and commission of history painting in the early Victorian period.

CHARLES MOORMAN is Vice President for Academic Affairs Emeritus and Distinguished Professor of English at the University of Southern Mississippi. He is the author of several books and articles on various phases of medieval literature and currently is engaged in editing the general prologue to the *Canterbury Tales* for the Variorum Chaucer and in studying the relationships among the principal *Canterbury Tales* manuscripts by means of standard statistical procedures.

JAN A. NELSON is Professor of Romance Philology in the Department of Romance Languages and Classics at The University of Alabama. He is co-general editor of *The Old French Crusade Cycle* and editor of the *Beatrix* version of the *Naissance du Chevalier au Cygne* and of the *Chevalier au Cygne* in that series. Professor Nelson has published articles on medieval literature in such scholarly periodicals as *Romania, Neuphilologische Mitteilungen, Olifant,* and *Tenso*. He is presently working on a study of the Swan Knight epics and their place in the Crusade Cycle.

MARYLYN JACKSON PARINS is a member of the English Department at the University of Arkansas at Little Rock. She has published articles in *Studia Monastica* and *Studies in Browning* and has written the essay on modern Arthurian scholarship for the *Arthurian Encyclopedia*. Her most recent work is a volume on Malory for the Critical Heritage series.

MARY L. H. THOMPSON developed her theory of the source for Arthur's campaign in Gaul while teaching Caesar's *De bello Gallico* to high school Latin students at Hastings-on-Hudson, New York. Her earlier research on this topic is

254

included in *Actes du 14e Congrès International Arthurien.* Her current work includes a translation and analysis of Arthurian material in Hector Boece's *Historia Scotorum* and a study of the treatment of Arthur in medieval Latin chronicles.

INDEX